STAKEHOLDER WELLBEING AND VALUE CREATION

Stakeholder Wellbeing and Value Creation

Edited by
Uday Salunkhe
D. N. Murthy
Bharath Rajan
Vaishali Patil

TRANSNATIONAL PRESS LONDON
2022

MANAGEMENT SERIES: 12

Stakeholder Wellbeing and Value Creation

Edited by Uday Salunkhe, D. N. Murthy, Bharath Rajan, Vaishali Patil

First Published in 2022 by Transnational Press London in the United Kingdom, 13 Stamford Place, Sale, M33 3BT, UK.
www.tplondon.com

Transnational Press London® and the logo and its affiliated brands are registered trademarks.

Requests for permission to reproduce material from this work should be sent to: sales@tplondon.com

Paperback
ISBN: 978-1-80135-170-6
Digital
ISBN: 978-1-80135-171-3

Cover Design: Nihal Yazgan
Cover image: Josh Appel on unsplash.com

Transnational Press London Ltd. is a company registered in England and Wales No. 8771684.

CONTENTS

ACKNOWLEDGEMENTS

Many thanks are expressed to all participants of the 3rd International Research Conference organized by the Prin. L. N. Welingkar Institute of Management Development and Research (WeSchool), Mumbai, India on the theme of "Stakeholder wellbeing through value creation". Their participation and valuable contribution by way of research presentations added much value and significance to the shaping of this book.

We are especially grateful to our students, faculty colleagues, and industry experts who stimulated us and brought new ideas and approaches to our attention that helped us broaden our understanding of stakeholder wellbeing and value creation as it is currently practiced.

It has been a continuing pleasure to associate with a class publisher, Transnational Press London, and to produce this significant work. Particularly, we are grateful to Prof. Ibrahim Sirkeci for his continued support and guidance in conceiving and developing this book.

We are also thankful to Dr. Ruchi Singh and Dr. Ragini Jadhav for their valuable support towards the production of this book.

Finally, we wish to express our sincere appreciation to our families and friends for their constant support, and encouragement during the creation of this book.

Uday Salunkhe

D. N. Murthy

Bharath Rajan

Vaishali Patil

CONTRIBUTORS

Prof. Dr. Uday Salunkhe heads S.P. Mandali's Prin. L.N. Welingkar Institute of Management Development and Research (WeSchool) as its Group Director. An 'Edupreneur' and 'turnaround specialist', Dr. Salunkhe's passion for leadership, design thinking and innovation has helped WeSchool carve itself a niche in space of management education. He has distinction of being recipient of the prestigious Eisenhower Fellowship, USA which identifies, empowers and links leaders across the globe. He is actively associated with universities and corporate at national and international level.

Prof. Dr. D.N. Murthy, Professor in Marketing area, has more than 23 years' experience in the Teaching, consulting and research. Post his Ph.D. in Strategic Marketing Management from Bangalore University, he has pursued his Post-Doctoral Research from Fosters Business School, University of Washington, Seattle, USA. With the long years of experience in industry and academia, he has been a consultant for United Nations Industrial Development Organisation (UNIDO) in implementing Business Clusters Project concept in India for machine tool SMEs. He has conducted several MDPs for leading corporates like Apple Inc, Rockwell Automation, Videocon, Emerson engineering among others. He is a regular faculty trainer in the areas of strategic marketing. He has conducted several FDPs in top rated Universities in India and abroad. He was the Dean / Director at IFIM Business School and Kirloskar Institute of Management Studies. He has visited prestigious Universities like Ecole De Grenoble (France), University of Ohio (USA), Howard University (USA), Malardalen University (Sweden) on academic assignments. He has widely traveled to USA, Canada, Germany, France, Finland, Denmark, Sweden, Netherlands, Belgium, France, Switzerland, Thailand, Srilanka, Bangladesh, Nepal and Malaysia. On a faculty exchange program, visited MDU, Sweden and engaged couple of courses.

Prof. Bharath Rajan is the Associate Dean, Research at WeSchool, Mumbai, India. He received his MBA from Georgia State University, Atlanta, USA. He has published in business and marketing journals such as the MIT Sloan Management Review, California Management Review, Journal of the Academy of Marketing Science, Journal of Business Research, Psychology & Marketing, Journal of International Marketing, International Marketing Review, and Industrial Marketing Management, among others. His current research interests include customer engagement, marketing strategy, and new-age technologies.

Dr. Abhinandan N is Assistant Professor who has completed Ph.D in Microfinance on MSEs in Dharwad district Karnataka state, from Kousali Institute of Management Studies, Karnatak University, Dharwad. He has completed his Masters of Commerce (Accounting and Taxation) from Christ University. He has also Qualifies UGC-NET for (Assistant Professor). He has worked as an Assistant Professor in Maharani Lakshmi Ammanni College of Women, Autonomous, Bangalore, Jyoti Nivas College (Autonomous) Bangalore and City college Bangalore also. He has an experienced team player, bringing enthusiasm & energy into group efforts and Capable of working in collaboration with individuals. Articulate & creative, offering innovative & practical solutions. Ha has Lifetime Membership in Indian Commerce Association.

Ms. Manasa K has working as an assistant Professor in PES University specialized in accounting and taxation field. She has completed master's in commerce and secured the highest in the college and to be awarded with gold medal and cleared KSET in the year 2021. She has worked on 12 research papers and successfully presented the papers in National and International Conference and presented paper in International Level Conference at Indian Institute of Management

Dr. Kiran Gangaiah, currently he is Associate Professor in Marketing Area, at Prin L.N. Welingkar Institute of Management Development & Research, Bengalurau. He has nine years of teaching experience handling Marketing papers like Advertising, Sales Promotion, Sales Distribution, Marketing for customer value. He has three years of experience into sales and marketing at Times of India. He is Editorial member and reviewer of international journal of Scientific Research and Education with his Ph.D. in Management from Kuvempu University, Karnataka. His thesis Topic-"A study on responsiveness of customers towards print media and deliverable satisfaction" He has MBA in Marketing from Institute of Management studies, Kuvempu University, Shankaraghatta, Karnataka and his BA in Journalism and Public Administration from Sahyadri Arts & Commerce College, Shimoga Kuvempu University, Karnatak. He has Certification on CRM from IIM-B. He has worked as an Associate Professor at Acharya Bangalore B-School (Dept. of MBA), Lecturer (Guest Faculty) - Sri Adichunchangiri College of business Management, Marketing Officer - Results and Market Department, in Times of India and Marketing Executive - in a Leading Radio Station RED FM 98.3

Dr. Shradha Shivani is a Professor of Marketing and currently the Head of the Department of Management at the Birla Institute of Technology, Mesra. She has more than 27 years of teaching & Research experience. Her special domains are Consumer Behavior, Marketing Communication, Brand Management, and Entrepreneurship. She has worked on various sponsored projects and trained faculty members on adopting OBE effectively. She has also published 35 WoS papers and is a nominated member of UGC & AICTE committees for curriculum design & pedagogy for technical education.

Prof. Evelina Brajesh is a Professor of Marketing in the Marketing Department of the Institute for Technology and Management, Navi Mumbai. She has been involved in Teaching & Research for more than 20 years. She teaches courses in the domain of Marketing Analytics, Consumer Behaviour, Marketing Communication, and Services Marketing. She has significantly contributed to many Research projects sponsored by national and international agencies and has published her work in the areas of Consumer Behaviour, Market Communication, Sustainable practices, and Gender Studies

Dr. Somnath Mukherjee is an Assistant Professor in the Management Department of Birla Institute of Technology (City Centre, Ranchi, India). He is a professional with rich industry and academic experience of more than 22 years. He also has handled Govt. of India-funded Research projects and has mentored Ph.D. scholars. He is an expert in Brand management, Marketing of services, and communication message framing. He is well known as a good professor and has done some remarkable publications in his field.

Miss. Sadiya Fatima is a research scholar in the Department of Management at Birla Institute of Technology, Mesra. She has deep interest in research in marketing domain. She is a Gold medalist in MBA (marketing) from University of Calcutta. She is a dedicated researcher. She has published research papers in Scopus indexed international journals and has presented her work in reputed international conferences. Her current research interests include consumer behaviour, E-commerce, advertising, e-WOM communications and service marketing.

Dr. Deepa Rohit is working as Associate Professor in Marketing (Academics) with Prin. L. N. Welingkar Institute of Management (WeSchool), Mumbai. She has over 17 years of work experience in media, teaching and research. Dr. Deepa has published over 15 research papers in peer reviewed journals, and has presented papers in various international conferences. She is keen in research areas such as cause-related marketing, consumer behavior, advertising and technology adoption. Deepa has taught courses namely, Consumer Behaviour, Integrated Marketing Communication and Technology in Marketing.

Prof. Ravi Vaidee is currently working as Dean Marketing Academics and a core faculty at WeSchool with a teaching experience spanning over 25 years, in the area of Marketing & related subjects. His Industry Exposure spans over 33 years having worked for leading Indian & Global companies with industry experience covering Consumer Durables, Financial Services etc, in the areas of sales, marketing and Internal Audit. He has held very responsible Senior Management positions viz Regional Manager - Financial Services covering the Sub-Continent region and as Senior Manager - Audit, Risk & Compliance - South Asia & Nigeria. Prof. Vaidee has been a corporate trainer for leading Indian Corporates, cutting across sectors and industries - viz Automobile, Crops & Science, Pharma, Capital Goods to name a few. He has taught courses like brand management, marketing strategy, selling & Negotiations and many more.

Dr. Vaishali Patil, Professor and Senior Associate Dean, Research and Publications and IT has more than 21years' experience in teaching and research. Post her MCA, MHRDM and MPhil, she pursued her doctorate in "Risk Management in Software Projects – An Analytical Study" and owns the copyright of her thesis. Approved as a Ph.D. Guide at the University of Mumbai. She has received number of Research grants from Ministry of Earth Science, ICSSR, University of Mumbai, AIMS etc. She has 24 research papers published in National and International Journals. Her research interest area is Management, IT and Social Sciences. She has received Ramaswamy Aiyar Best young teacher award by AIMS. My substantial contribution to towards the concept and design of the research methodology. Wrote Literature review and identified the research gap. Subsequently collected the data and helped in writing the paper.

Mr. Pranav Manjunath Bhat pursued a bachelor's degree in Electronics and Communications Engineering at BMS College of Engineering, Bengaluru. He holds special interest in machine learning, robotics and satellite communications and has pursued several projects related to the same. He was involved in the formulation and conduction of the experiments that validate the study by leveraging his programming skills to help analyse the data collected through surveys and constructing mathematical models of the same. He was also involved in drafting this paper.

Mr. Priyanshu M pursued Bachelor of Engineering (B.E) in Electronics and Communication Engineering from BMS College of Engineering, Bangalore, Karnataka, India. He has several academic interests ranging from VLSI System, Predictive analytics & machine learning. He has several projects regarding the same. He was involved in formulation & validation of behavior modelling which is used in this study. He was responsible for pre-processing data collected from surveys, data analysis and helping in validating mathematical models.

Miss. S Shruti pursued her bachelor's degree in Electronics and communication engineering at BMS College of Engineering, Bangalore, Karnataka, India. She is a diligent engineer who has worked on projects related to machine learning, IoT and hydroponics. Her fields of interest are behavioural economics, marketing and data analytics. She was responsible for collection of data from reliable sources through surveys and was also involved in data analysis and in drafting the manuscript.

Dr. Madhav Murthy is an academician par excellence with a rich background in both technology and management. He obtained his bachelors, masters and PhD degree from Visvesvaraya Technological University, Belgaum. He is currently is serving as a faculty in the Department of Mechanical Engineering at the prestigious B.M.S. College of Engineering, Bengaluru. He is a passionate educator having over 15 years of experience in teaching and mentoring and has taught over 3000 students. He is an active researcher who has published more than 50 research articles in national and international conferences and journals of repute in the domain of Composites, Engineering Education and Management Sciences. Dr. Murthy is a life member of various professional bodies such as IEI, ISTE, ISAMPE, TERA and is the vice chairman of ISAMPE-Bengaluru chapter.

Fathima Raj Kilimas, is passionate about the various interventions in technology, especially in the field of Digital Marketing and Artificial Intelligence. He possesses more than a decade's experience in Consulting, Branding, Digital Marketing, Academics, and the Music Industry. He is currently working as the Senior Manager – Marketing, Branding and OD at Cubera, an AdTech and Big Data Analytics company from Bengaluru, India. He has published case studies, book chapters, multiple international & national journals on Digital Marketing.

Dr. Ashish Chandra is a professor of Healthcare Administration program at University of Houston-Clear Lake and served as faculty chair of the program for ten years. Previously he taught at Marshall University in West Virginia and Xavier University in New Orleans, Louisiana. Dr. Chandra was also a healthcare and management consultant. He is published in Hospital Topics, Journal of Medical Marketing, Clinical Research and Regulatory Affairs, Journal of Healthcare Management, among others. He has served as vice president of MBAA International, president of the Association of Collegiate Marketing Educators, and on the Board of Directors of both the Federation of Business Disciplines and the Marketing Management Association.

Prof. Narendra K. Rustagi is Director of the Center for Global Business Studies in the School of Business at Howard University. Until June 2010, he served as the Chair of the Department of Information Systems and Decision Sciences in the School of Business, Howard University. He is also a tenured Professor and has been teaching in the Department since 1987. Prof. Rustagi is really passionate about the role of education, especially about the role of education on pluralism in peaceful growth in societies. With that as a mission, he actively supported and took initiatives for developing forums through conferences starting with the conference of the International Digital Business Academy in 2005. He is active in holding of the conferences, especially in building a cluster of colleagues interested in efficiency in the delivery of education, especially regarding education on the issue pluralism and peaceful growth.

Dr. Vijaya Kumar Bhima Rao has over 30 years of corporate experience of which 15+ years in product development spanning phones, tablets, wearables, embedded systems. He has vast leadership experience ranging from starting and leading companies, evaluating, and proposing new technologies for emerging markets. He is a member of the board of studies at Visveswaraya Technological University's Smart Manufacturing program. He holds a bachelor's degree in mechanical engineers, MS degrees in Industrial engineering & Information systems, MBA, and Ph.D.

Dr. R A Dakshina Murthy is presently working as Sr. Associate Dean – Operations at Prin. L.N. Welingkar Institute of Management Development & Research, and he worked for over 22 years in industry as General Manager- Operations. He established the Quality Control and Manufacturing facility for composite products for Aerospace and Defence applications. He has variety of experience in the areas of Purchase and Supply Chain Management, Product Development and Manufacturing, Quality Control and Quality Management System. His specialized teaching area include Lean Production Planning & Control, World Class Manufacturing, Project Management, TQM, ERP and

Supply Chain Management & Logistics. He has to his account five publications in the International Journal and have presented research paper in National & International conference in India.

Dr. Madhumita Guha Majumder is a Teacher-Scholar-Administrator as she is involved in knowledge creation through research, knowledge dissemination through teaching and training, administration through institution building and through designing effective academic programs. Currently, she is working as a Professor & Program Head, Research & Business Analytics at Prin. L.N. Welingkar Institute of Management Development and Research, Bangalore. She is involved in high quality research which has two key dimensions including application of Analytics in business decision making and policy related research. Her current research is based on diversified areas including knowledge management, financial management, employee engagement & consumer analytics. She has published many research papers in national & international refereed journals of high repute and has also contributed chapters to several books. She offers outstanding organizational & cross functional leadership with a strong track record of creating business models for the organization.

M. Khurrum S. Bhutta is a Professor of Operations at Ohio University. He has a Ph.D. in Production and Operations Management from The University of Texas at Arlington. He has published in several reputed journals, books and conference proceedings. He has been awarded several excellence awards and certificates for his professional activities. He is currently a member of the Decision Sciences Institute and Production Operations Management Society & Academy of Management.

Dr. Vandana Panwar, Associate Professor of Finance at the Prin. L. N. Welingkar Institute of Management Development and Research in Mumbai- India. She has 20 years of teaching, 22 years of research experience, authored book titled-"Venture Capita Funding- Indian and International experiences" and worked on Pre & Post funding evaluation of projects assisted by Council for Advancement of People's Action in Rural Technology and Asia Region-World Association for Christian Communication. Area of interest: Venture Capital, Project Management and Entrepreneurship Development.

Prof Christopher Erickson is the Garrey E. and Katherine T. Carruthers Chair for Economic Development at New Mexico State University where he has been on the faculty since 1987. He has been funded by the Environmental Protection Agency, the Department of Energy and the NSF. He is currently serving as interim department head for Economics, Applied Statistics, and International Business. In 2021, Chris became the founding director of the Center for Border Economic Development.

Alan Tupicoff, President – Australia & New Zealand Institute of Sustainable Management and Fellow – Australian Institute of Project Management. He has been a Consultant and Trainer specialising in Sustainable Management, presenting at a number of international universities and conferences. He has over 35 years' experience in regard to management and has authored a series of book relating to "Simplified Sustainability" and has an interest in assisting individuals and organisation to achieve create and deliver their goals to real "Value / Benefit".

Vikram Kanodia is a technology leader who focuses on developing innovative ways in which technology can drive value through enterprise and society. He has deep experience in technology operations, M&A and strategy. Vikram has worked with global firms like EY to help manage digital transformation and corporate transaction projects in multi-billion-dollar firms across industries.

Vikram is passionate about driving social impact through education and upskilling. He currently serves on the CSR committee at Datamatics, as part of his role in the CEO's office at Datmatics. Vikram holds a degree in Finance and Analytics from Carnegie Mellon University.

Dr Rima Ghose Chowdhury is a seasoned HR leader and practitioner with over two decades of experience in Corporate and Academia, Dr Rima Ghose Chowdhury has been instrumental in building Technology and Leadership capabilities and championed Change management, in reputed enterprises like IBM, Sony Pictures Networks India, Quinnox Consultancy Services, Haldia Petrochemicals. Deeply passionate about developing Leaders, Dr Rima has been an International Mentor for HR students of Middlesex University Business School, UK, trained Trainer by Sony Pictures Entertainment, UK on 'Energy Project' and actively practises a People-first philosophy in the geographies (India, US, UK, Philippines) she manages as CHRO of Datamatics Global.

CHAPTER 1

PERSPECTIVES ON STAKEHOLDER WELLBEING AND VALUE CREATION

Bharath Rajan[1], Uday Salunkhe[2], D. N. Murthy[3]

Introduction

In the current ecosystem framework of operations, multiple entities are necessary for the effective functioning of the framework. In such a system, the relationship of a company with the other entities, formally referred to as stakeholders, is typically a symbiotic one, wherein the mutual interest and expectations of all stakeholders are satisfied. While commonly known stakeholders of a company include customers, employees, investors, suppliers, distribution partners, the community, and the government; the complexity of modern business models will likely include several other entities, in addition to the common stakeholders.

In this regard, stakeholder wellbeing is a concept that has received global attention. Particularly, recent academic studies have investigated stakeholder wellbeing on various topics such as employee performance (Marques, 2019), firm growth (Kumar & Ramachandran, 2021), employee wellbeing (Kobayashi et al., 2018), sustainability (Clifton & Amran, 2011), and health outcomes (Kindermann et al., 2021), among others. With specific reference to value creation, recent academic studies have investigated topics on stakeholder capabilities (Garriga, 2014), customer value (Kilroy & Schneider, 2017), and leadership (Kujala et al., 2019), among others. The continued growth in the academic research in stakeholder wellbeing and value-creation space indicates a growing and vibrant body of knowledge that has much to uncover on these topics.

While the efforts in better understanding and executing stakeholder wellbeing are ongoing in the academic and policy circles, as a recent development, companies, and practitioners are beginning to enter this important discussion. In doing so, the importance and significance of companies featuring in this discourse are unmistakable. Further, the centrality of companies in driving wellbeing among stakeholders is, therefore, evident. That is, through a commercial exchange, value can be created and/or destroyed for the companies and the stakeholders through their respective actions (Kumar & Rajan, 2017). And therefore, the process of value creation can serve as a medium for companies to ensure stakeholder wellbeing.

This book is the outcome of the conference that was organized by the Prin. L. N. Welingkar Institute of Management Development and Research (WeSchool), Mumbai, India between January 27-28, 2022, on the theme of "Stakeholder wellbeing through value creation". It is the express purpose of this book to present impactful and meaningful studies that uncover various facets of value creation and stakeholder wellbeing from an academic research perspective. The nine articles contained in this

[1] Bharath Rajan is the Associate Dean, Research at the Prin. L. N. Welingkar Institute of Management Development and Research (WeSchool), Mumbai, India. E-mail: bharath.rajan@welingkar.org.
[2] Uday Salunkhe is the Group Director at the Prin. L. N. Welingkar Institute of Management Development and Research (WeSchool), Mumbai, India. E-mail: director@welingkar.org.
[3] D. N. Murthy is the Dean, Research and Dean, Marketing at the Prin. L. N. Welingkar Institute of Management Development and Research (WeSchool), Bengaluru, India. E-mail: narasimha.murthy@welingkar.org.
Acknowledgement: The authors thank several of their colleagues and the participants of the 3rd International Research Conference on "Stakeholder Wellbeing Through Value Creation" held at Prin. L. N. Welingkar Institute of Management Development and Research (WeSchool), Mumbai, India on January 27-28, 2022, for their valuable participation.

book, altogether, cover a wide array of customer, firm, and societal perspectives on the topic of value creation. Each article either explicitly addresses the value management process or investigates a phenomenon that has implications on value management. Collectively, these articles underscore the need to devote more research and attention to organizational concerns regarding stakeholder wellbeing and value creation. Considering this, the observation emerging from this book indicates the need to develop new conceptual approaches and undertake deeper investigations for value management such that the stakeholder wellbeing is ensured. In effect, these papers point toward the need for a more organized understanding of management strategies that can be considered by organizations.

Conceptual Overview of this Book

The following integrative framework (see Figure 1) organizes the nine articles contained in this book based on conceptual understanding on the perspectives of value creation. Specifically, the proposed integrative framework identifies that the articles contained here investigates value perspectives that can be viewed as customer-focused, firm-focused, and community-focused. The key motivation for this book is – how can value be managed such that the stakeholder wellbeing is ensured. Accordingly, the articles contained in this book collectively consider varied study contexts, research approaches, data sources, and conceptual points-of-view to explore the above-mentioned motivation.

Figure 1 – Integrative framework for this book

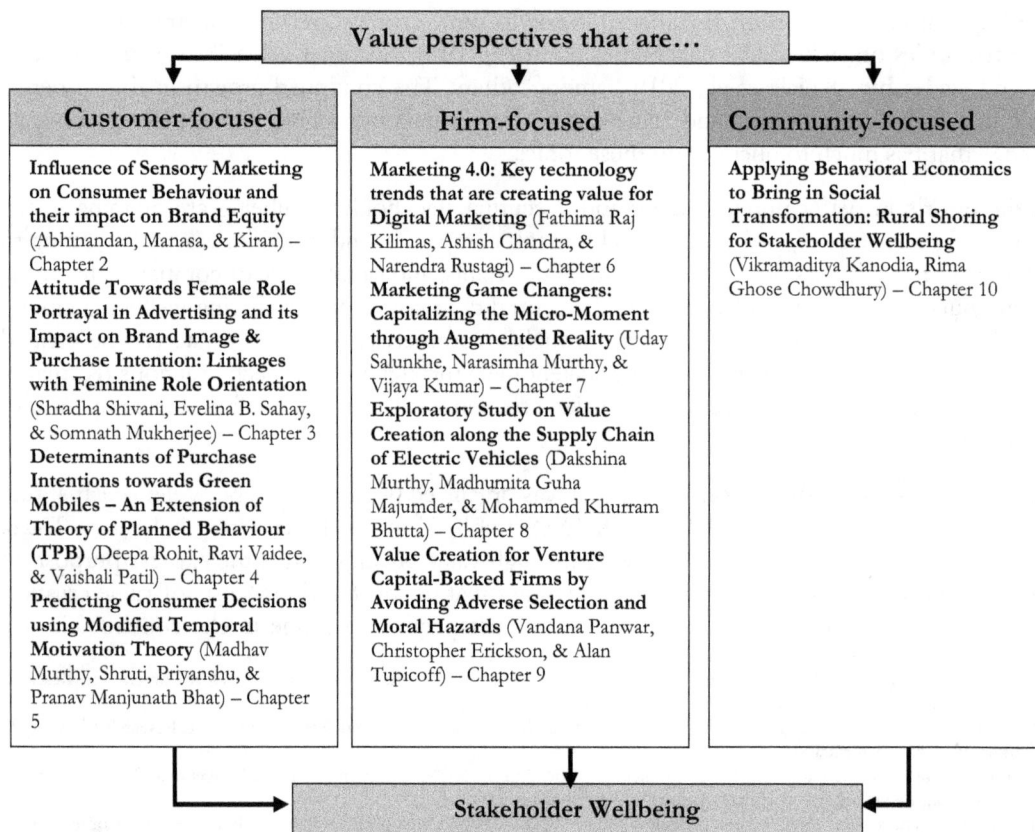

Value perspectives that are...		
Customer-focused	**Firm-focused**	**Community-focused**
Influence of Sensory Marketing on Consumer Behaviour and their impact on Brand Equity (Abhinandan, Manasa, & Kiran) – Chapter 2 **Attitude Towards Female Role Portrayal in Advertising and its Impact on Brand Image & Purchase Intention: Linkages with Feminine Role Orientation** (Shradha Shivani, Evelina B. Sahay, & Somnath Mukherjee) – Chapter 3 **Determinants of Purchase Intentions towards Green Mobiles – An Extension of Theory of Planned Behaviour (TPB)** (Deepa Rohit, Ravi Vaidee, & Vaishali Patil) – Chapter 4 **Predicting Consumer Decisions using Modified Temporal Motivation Theory** (Madhav Murthy, Shruti, Priyanshu, & Pranav Manjunath Bhat) – Chapter 5	**Marketing 4.0: Key technology trends that are creating value for Digital Marketing** (Fathima Raj Kilimas, Ashish Chandra, & Narendra Rustagi) – Chapter 6 **Marketing Game Changers: Capitalizing the Micro-Moment through Augmented Reality** (Uday Salunkhe, Narasimha Murthy, & Vijaya Kumar) – Chapter 7 **Exploratory Study on Value Creation along the Supply Chain of Electric Vehicles** (Dakshina Murthy, Madhumita Guha Majumder, & Mohammed Khurram Bhutta) – Chapter 8 **Value Creation for Venture Capital-Backed Firms by Avoiding Adverse Selection and Moral Hazards** (Vandana Panwar, Christopher Erickson, & Alan Tupicoff) – Chapter 9	**Applying Behavioral Economics to Bring in Social Transformation: Rural Shoring for Stakeholder Wellbeing** (Vikramaditya Kanodia, Rima Ghose Chowdhury) – Chapter 10

Stakeholder Wellbeing

Source: Authors' classification

The proposed framework in Figure 1 illustrates this point and serves as a guide to understanding this book. Under the proposed classification, the articles collectively discuss business approaches impacting value creation and stakeholder wellbeing.

In short, the proposed framework corresponds to recognizing the direction of value flows (i.e., customers, firms, or community) and the subsequent creation of stakeholder wellbeing. While all the articles focus on the creation of value from either of the three perspectives, the resulting stakeholder wellbeing is either explicitly addressed or implicitly understood. The following sections provide a detailed discussion on these categories as they relate to the chapters in this book.

Customer-focused Value Perspective

As a stakeholder group, customers share a particularly close relationship with firms from a value standpoint. On one hand, firms deliver value to customers through firm offerings that are intended to satisfy customers (Anderson & Narus, 1998; Oliver, 1980). In return, customers provide value to the firm through their loyalty (Dick & Basu, 1994; Dowling & Uncles, 1997; Oliver, 1999), their contribution to firm profits (Reinartz & Kumar, 2000, 2003), and indirect engagement (Kumar et al., 2010, 2019). The following four chapters provide a customer-focused perspective wherein, value is generated and delivered to the customers by the firm.

For instance, Chapter 2 titled "Influence of Sensory Marketing on Consumer Behaviour and their impact on Brand Equity" by Abhinandan and colleagues investigates the influence of sensory marketing practices on consumer behaviour. They refer to sensory marketing as marketing practices that leverages all five senses to influence perceptions, memories, and learning processes, with the aim of manipulating consumers' motivations, desires, and behaviour. The idea behind using sensory marketing as a value-creating tool is that it can allow marketers to understand the customer needs and requirements that can aid in the development of related offerings which can ultimately lead to stakeholder wellbeing-related outcomes such as the establishment of customer loyalty and improvements in brand image. Using restaurants as the study setting, the authors survey the methods adopted by restaurants in using sensory marketing practices and how consumers respond to such practices. They find that sensory marketing practices have a positive influence on consumer behaviour by providing a unique experience. Moreover, the authors found that consumers are willing to pay more for the unique experience, arising out of the sensory marketing practices, thereby potentially leading to the creation of stakeholder wellbeing (i.e., the firm).

Next, Chapter 3 titled "Attitude Towards Female Role Portrayal in Advertising and its Impact on Brand Image & Purchase Intention: Linkages with Feminine Role Orientation" by Shivani and colleagues investigates the offensiveness of female role representation in advertising, as well as its influence on brand image, purchase intention, and the likeability of the advertisements. Using a 2-phase study approach, the authors find that the perceived offensiveness of female representation does not change across those who have diverse opinions on women's roles in society. Further, it was found that respondents have a higher favorable reaction in terms of brand image and ad liking for non-stereotyped representation. However, they do not observe any significant difference between male and female respondents' responses in this regard. They also find the communicative influence of depiction type on actual customer purchasing decisions to be negligible. The authors present this study as additional proof for not relying too much on stereotyped female representation in advertising. Subsequently, the implication is that the offensive representation of women in advertising can lead to value depletion and thereby a negative influence on stakeholder wellbeing (in this case the consumers).

Further, Chapter 4 titled "Determinants of Purchase Intentions towards Green Mobiles – An Extension of Theory of Planned Behaviour (TPB)" by Rohit and colleagues investigates the purchase behaviour of Indian consumers towards green mobile phones. Using the theory of planned behaviour framework, the authors also include two additional determinants such as environmental awareness and environmental concern, to conduct this study. Through structural equation modeling, the authors find that that environmental awareness and environmental concern positively influence consumer attitudes towards green mobile phones, which in turn positively impacts purchase intentions. Likewise, subjective norm and perceived behavior control have been found to be significantly influencing purchase intentions. While the study objective and findings directly relate to stakeholder wellbeing through the consumer perspective, extended implications regarding wellbeing are also drawn relating to other stakeholders such as government, industry, and society.

Chapter 5 titled "Predicting Consumer Decisions using Modified Temporal Motivation Theory" by Murthy and colleagues aims to model consumer behaviour using the temporal motivation theory (TMT). Specifically, the authors are interested to study how consumers make decisions when multiple choices are involved. To conduct this study, the authors apply this theory in two different settings – predicting customer retention in online food delivery services, and consumer buying decisions involving smartphones. Both these applications are characterized by the availability of two or more choices to the consumer. Through these investigations, these authors show that the TMT can produce valuable results in cases involving multiple choices. Specifically, they establish how firms can benefit from the use of TMT in such instances. Moreover, they show that such a usage of TMT can add value not only to the firms (through efficient use of resources and capabilities), but also deliver value to customers through the development of useful offerings.

Firm-focused Value Perspective

As mentioned earlier, value creation in a commercial exchange occurs via (a) firms creating value for their stakeholders, and (b) stakeholders creating value for the firm (Kumar & Rajan, 2017). In this two-way flow, regardless of the direction, stakeholder wellbeing can occur following the creation of value. The following four chapters explore the topic of value creation by firms to their stakeholders (e.g., consumers). In doing so, these chapters cover various domains such as marketing, supply chain, and finance to demonstrate how value can be created in each of these areas to the stakeholders.

For instance, Chapter 6 titled "Marketing 4.0: Key technology trends that are creating value for Digital Marketing" by Kilimas and colleagues review the major emerging technologies (e.g., artificial intelligence, machine learning, Internet of Things, blockchain, etc.) to determine their usefulness in digital marketing initiatives. To do this, the authors use a mix of in-depth interviews and literature review to first understand what each of the emerging technologies can offer. Based on this, they identify six emerging technologies (i.e., artificial intelligence, voice assistants, immersive experience, Internet of Things, blockchain, and big data) that are most ideally suited to be used in firms' digital marketing initiatives. This is determined based on the technologies' ability to assist to create, communicate, deliver, and exchange value as deemed important by the consumers. Following the identification of the six technologies, the authors discuss them in the context of digital marketing, along with their business applications and managerial implications. They conclude the study by how all these technologies can converge and be used cohesively in digital marketing initiatives.

Similarly, Chapter 7 titled "Marketing Game Changers: Capitalizing the Micro-Moment through Augmented Reality" by Salunkhe and colleagues reviews how companies should use augmented reality to capitalize on the "micro-moments" of customer purchasing behavior. Popularized by Google, micro-moments are reflexive, yet intent-driven interactions of the consumers that can be capitalized by the brands to influence consumers' decisions (Ramaswamy, 2015). By reviewing literature in this area, the authors describe the importance of using augmented reality in marketing to influence consumers during their micro-moments. Based on this, the authors advance a micro-moment framework focused on consumer purchases (i.e., I-want-to-buy moment). Further, the authors provide industry examples and practices to showcase how this might be possible. The study concludes by providing actionable items that firms can consider capitalizing on the micro-moments that can create value for consumers.

Further, Chapter 8 titled "Exploratory Study on Value Creation along the Supply Chain of Electric Vehicles" by Dakshina Murthy and colleagues investigate the issues and challenges faced by the electric vehicles industry with reference to their supply chain. Using an opinion mining approach, the authors attempt to enumerate the various actions required for a smoother transition leading to new ways of usage, handling, and servicing of motor vehicles. The authors find that stakeholders have a balanced approach while expressing their sentiments about the upcoming EV industry. Moreover, they find that automakers are looking for favourable policies from the government to facilitate the transition to electric vehicles. From a consumer point of view, the authors offer that the facilities for charging batteries at convenient locations, and their easy and affordable replenishment are the major concerns. The study concludes with the identification of areas that need attention from the industry members so that value creation can occur.

Next, Chapter 9 titled "Value Creation for Venture Capital Backed Firms by Avoiding Adverse Selection and Moral Hazards" by Panwar and colleagues investigate the factors that determine the possibility of avoiding any moral hazard by venture capitalists (VCs) in developing countries like India. Using literature review and prior VC frameworks, the authors advance an organizing framework to understand the value creation process for VCs by investigating the likelihood of avoiding moral hazards. Specifically, they identify four entrepreneur-related factors that determine the likelihood to avoid moral hazards, which ultimately is linked to value creation for VCs. They also identify a moderator that influences the relationship between the likelihood to avoid moral hazards and entrepreneurial profits. Following the development of the framework, the authors discuss the managerial implications of the framework and identify future research directions.

Community-focused Value Perspective

Communities form a part of the fabric that firms operate in. At any given time, a firm can function amidst multiple communities. Communities are typically formed around causes (e.g., environment, diversity), consumer emotions (e.g., love, anger), company offerings (e.g., feedback on products, technical help groups), corporate governance (e.g., privacy, human rights), or a combination of the above. It is also important to note that not all communities are formed around the local geographic region of the firm. With internet acting as a galvanizing force, communities typically grow in strength based on the positive network effects offered by the online medium. Moreover, while communities do not typically take part in the normal course of the firm's economic exchange, their existence has a definite impact on the creation of value.

Regardless of how a community is formed, their potential for value creation and stakeholder wellbeing is best understood through the information they provide. Any interaction with the community stakeholders will provide the firm with information on a particular aspect that can in turn be converted to value creating activities. That is, the information obtained via the interaction between the firm and the community can be productively used to create overall value for all stakeholders.

In this regard, Chapter 10 titled "Applying Behavioral Economics to Bring in Social Transformation: Rural Shoring for Stakeholder Wellbeing" by Kanodia and Chowdhury investigate the concept of rural shoring regarding business process outsourcing operations in India. Rural shoring refers to moving business processes from traditional urban centres to non-traditional rural areas. Through the real-world case of DataHalli (a BPO) in Bellary district of Karnataka, the authors focus on applying behavioural economics in rural shoring for overall stakeholder wellbeing. They find ample evidence for transformations in multiple areas, including education, health, family income and personal growth, thereby establishing the potential of behavioural economics in driving social change. Based on the changes witnessed in the rural area involved in the DataHalli business, the authors managerial and societal implications of the rural shoring model that can create value for the society.

A Roadmap for Future Research

While the chapters in this book conclude with the identification of areas for future research, we also identify specific lines of research for researchers to consider in the future. Considering the studies covered in this issue and related evolving topics (not covered in this book), we propose the following research areas for future research:

- The studies appearing in this book relate to only one country (i.e., India). Considering the applicability of the topic of value creation and stakeholder wellbeing to be universal, more insights can be generated by considering other the experience of other countries. Further, considering the varied ways in which value creation manifests, it would be interesting to investigate the country-level experiences or differences in value creation and how that can impact stakeholder wellbeing. Therefore,

  RQ1: Are there value creation processes and approaches that can be generalized across developed and emerging countries?

  RQ2: Can generalized insights and findings be developed for emerging countries and developed countries, respectively, that account for country-specific characteristics?

- Value creating actions among firms is an ongoing process. This can be seen at all levels of businesses (i.e., global, regional, national, local, etc.). Businesses continue to develop innovative ways of delivering and seeking value, particularly at the consumer level (e.g., product decisions, package sizes, alternative delivery modes, flexible payment options, etc.). While these efforts continue to uncover value, the performance of such efforts are unclear. Therefore,

  RQ3: What outcome measures can be used to determine stakeholder wellbeing when value creation is being attempted? Specifically, what type(s) of value creating activities are (not) likely to result in stakeholder wellbeing?

- From a firm perspective, an ongoing challenge regarding value creation pertains to the formation, deployment, and movement of teams. In many cases, employees (i.e., frontline employees) are often the final touchpoint where value is exchanged. With recent changes in business models (e.g., work from anywhere, hybrid nature of work, etc.), regular business operations are undergoing significant value transformation. For instance, the work-from-anywhere format has found acceptance in many industries and countries as an accepted way of functioning, while also creating value for the firm through cost savings. However, the management of teams and work output when employees are spread out remains a challenge. Therefore,

RQ4: What resource optimization rules can be developed that can be used to maximize output, while ensuring value creation? Additionally, what management skills (e.g., technical, managerial, operational, etc.) should companies develop to maximize their value creation?

- Data and analytics continue to power organizations in all areas of operation. While harnessing the power of data, companies undertake efforts to make sure that value is created. In doing so, the generation of timely *and* relevant insights are key to sustaining value. Whereas data was primarily aggregated using technology thus far, we are in an era where technology plays a more central role in data collection and analyses. New-age technologies such as artificial intelligence, machine learning, and the Internet of Things, among others, are being used by companies across all domains and functions. Further, data-driven insights are being generated in real-time that are providing companies with the most updated information that is relevant to the business context. Therefore,

RQ5: What data rules (i.e., types of data, sources of data, frequency of data collection, unit of data collection, etc.) can companies adopt to ensure consistency in the creation and delivery of value to all stakeholders to ensure their wellbeing?

The future research directions highlighted here represent only suggested directions and not an exhaustive list. A focused analysis of an organization's performance and challenges will likely reveal areas where more research efforts are necessary. Further, value creation and stakeholder wellbeing are areas that can benefit immensely from interdisciplinary research by integrating knowledge from various functional domains such as marketing, finance, operations, media and communications, human resources, and strategy development, among others. We hope the research roadmap presented here contributes to a start in this direction.

Conclusion

Firms and their stakeholders exist in a perpetual cycle of value creation. For without value creation, the respective entities would likely not continue a business relationship. While firms concern themselves with the creation of valuable offerings for their stakeholders, they are also conscious of how much value they receive in return. By giving and getting value, a business relationship establishes a case for its existence and in the process, leads to the creation of stakeholder wellbeing. In this rapidly changing world, and looking ahead, companies need guidance and solutions in their pursuit of value creation and value excellence. From such guidance will emerge stakeholder wellbeing.

All the chapters contained in this book aim to generate novel insights and new directions for companies to consider as they explore ways to create value and stakeholder wellbeing. The authors of the studies in this book have done a commendable job of investigating these timely and relevant topics. The results and insights provided by the studies in this book will equip firms with the required knowledge in their pursuit to create value.

In conclusion, we are extremely privileged to have presided over the editorial process for this book. In this regard, we extend our gratitude to the *Transnational Press London* for making this book possible. We now eagerly look forward to future research that will follow this book.

References

Anderson, J. C., & Narus, J. A. (1998). Business marketing: Understand what customers value. *Harvard Business Review, 76*, 53–67.

Clifton, D., & Amran, A. (2011). The stakeholder approach: A sustainability perspective. *Journal of Business Ethics, 98*(1), 121–136.

Dick, A. S., & Basu, K. (1994). Customer loyalty: Toward an integrated conceptual framework. *Journal of the Academy of Marketing Science, 22*(2), 99–113.

Dowling, G. R., & Uncles, M. (1997). Do customer loyalty programs really work? *Sloan Management Review, 38*, 71–82.

Garriga, E. (2014). Beyond stakeholder utility function: Stakeholder capability in the value creation process. *Journal of Business Ethics, 120*(4), 489–507.

Kilroy, D., & Schneider, M. (2017). Customer value, shareholder wealth and stakeholder wellbeing. In *Customer value, shareholder wealth, community wellbeing* (pp. 179–192). Springer.

Kindermann, G., Domegan, C., Britton, E., Carlin, C., Isazad Mashinchi, M., & Ojo, A. (2021). Understanding the dynamics of green and blue spaces for health and wellbeing outcomes in Ireland: A systemic stakeholder perspective. *Sustainability, 13*(17), 9553.

Kobayashi, K., Eweje, G., & Tappin, D. (2018). Employee wellbeing and human sustainability: Perspectives of managers in large Japanese corporations. *Business Strategy and the Environment, 27*(7), 801–810.

Kujala, J., Lehtimäki, H., & Freeman, E. R. (2019). A stakeholder approach to value creation and leadership. *Leading Change in a Complex World: Transdisciplinary Perspectives*.

Kumar, V., Aksoy, L., Donkers, B., Venkatesan, R., Wiesel, T., & Tillmanns, S. (2010). Undervalued or overvalued customers: Capturing total customer engagement value. *Journal of Service Research, 13*(3), 297–310.

Kumar, V., & Rajan, B. (2017). What's in it for me? The creation and destruction of value for firms from stakeholders. *Journal of Creating Value, 3*(2), 142–156.

Kumar, V., Rajan, B., Gupta, S., & Pozza, I. D. (2019). Customer engagement in service. *Journal of the Academy of Marketing Science, 47*(1), 138–160.

Kumar, V., & Ramachandran, D. (2021). Developing firms' growth approaches as a multidimensional decision to enhance key stakeholders' wellbeing. *International Journal of Research in Marketing, 38*(2), 402–424.

Marques, J. F. (2019). Attributes Leaders Need to Enhance Wellbeing and Performance in Their Workplace. *Organization Development Journal, 37*(4).

Oliver, R. L. (1980). A cognitive model of the antecedents and consequences of satisfaction decisions. *Journal of Marketing Research, 17*(4), 460–469.

Oliver, R. L. (1999). Whence consumer loyalty? *Journal of Marketing, 63*(4_suppl1), 33–44.

Ramaswamy, S. (2015). How micro-moments are changing the rules. *Think with Google*.

Reinartz, W. J., & Kumar, V. (2000). On the profitability of long-life customers in a noncontractual setting: An empirical investigation and implications for marketing. *Journal of Marketing, 64*(4), 17–35.

Reinartz, W. J., & Kumar, V. (2003). The impact of customer relationship characteristics on profitable lifetime duration. *Journal of Marketing, 67*(1), 77–99.

CHAPTER 2

INFLUENCE OF SENSORY MARKETING ON CONSUMER BEHAVIOUR AND THEIR IMPACT ON BRAND EQUITY

Abhinandan N[1], Manasa K[2], Kiran G[3]

Introduction

"A memorable experience can forge a stronger connection to the product or service, increase satisfaction, and influence the consumer's behaviour and attitude" The senses play a key role in consumer perceptions and exert a powerful influence over buying decisions. Marketers have long sought to integrate the senses into brand communications, even though generally in a limited and partial way. Today, sensory marketing is recognized as an essential tool for strengthening the connection between brand and consumer by stimulating all the senses and generating emotions. As part of the marketer's quest to connect with and adapt to today's constantly evolving and increasingly demanding consumers, sensory marketing is now considered to be a top-priority activity. Sensory marketing leverages all five senses to influence perceptions, memories, and learning processes, with the aim of manipulating consumers' motivations, desires, and behaviour. The goal is to create a sensory experience that strengthens the connection with users through a process that involves both the rational and the emotional parts of the brain, although to varying degrees.

Consumer behaviour can be influenced by sensory marketing to generate experiences at every stage of the buying process: activation of desire, awareness of the product or service, assessment of the product or service in relation to other options, purchase, and post-purchase evaluation of use or consumption. This sort of 360° sensory marketing serves to define the points of contact between the consumer and the brand at every behavioural stage: before the purchase, during the purchase, and during final use. The main strategic objective of sensory marketing is to communicate a brand image—in other words, sensory branding. The goal is to use the senses to reinforce the product's attributes, functional or emotional benefits, values, and personality, conveying its relevance to the consumer and helping to communicate its brand identity, while at the same time—and most importantly—communicating the product's differential value for a specific segment of customers in an increasingly competitive market. Thus sensory branding is developed through a sensory strategy, which determines which senses will be used in the communication of the image and connects each sense with the consumer, while also defining the messages and experiences to be developed by each sense.

Sensory Marketing is a type of marketing practice that appeals to all the senses in relation to the brand. The businesses use the five senses of human beings i.e, smell, touch, taste , sound and sight as a strategy to build customer awareness, loyalty and satisfaction. These practices can forge emotional associations in the customer's mind by appealing to their senses. A multi sensory brand experience

[1] Dr. Abhinandan N, Assistant Professor, Department of Commerce, Maharani Lakshmi Ammanni College for Women, Autonomous, India. E-mail: drabhinandan.n@gmail.com
[2] Manasa K, Research Student, Maharani Lakshmi Ammanni College for Women, Autonomous, India. E-mail: manasakopplu@gmail.com
[3] Dr. Kiran G, Associate professor, Welingkar Institute of Management Development and Research Bangalore, India. E-mail: kirangowda0810@gmail.com

generates certain beliefs, feelings, thoughts and opinions to create a brand image in the mind of customers.

Consumer Behaviour is one of the most sensitive aspect according to the marketers. And gaining consumer loyalty where the consumers prefer to purchase a specific product/service over others in the present competitive environment is one of the most challenging and difficult task for the marketers. One of the way to retain the existing and to gain new customers is through attaching emotional contact with the product/service, this is possible through using the sensory marketing practices . There are various types under which the brands can use sensory marketing :

➢ **Visual Sensory Marketing (Sight):**

Sight has been the most used and the most prominent senses of all because eyes contain two third of senses cells in the body. Firms or brands utilize this senses in order to establish its identity and ultimately create a sight experience for an individual. Design is one of the most important aspects of a product or a service, it through the design that firms and brands can express personality which an individual identifies with. On the other hand Packaging is another important aspect that affect the sense of sight and tactics used to market this sense.

➢ **Aural Sensory Marketing (Sound):**

Sound along with sight accounts for a major part of the brand communication. Since many years, sound has been applied in the mass marketing to create awareness about a firm and its products/service mainly in television and radio. Another way of using sound as marketing practice is through playing the music in the showrooms, restaurants etc which creates a different experience for the customers and the consumers who are attracted to such practice may develop a brand loyalty toward such products/service Many restaurants at present use music as its marketing strategy where customers having a like towards listening to music is often attracted to such restaurants. The marketer ensures that the music being used is soothing and not too loud so that it is not disturbing or irritating the consumers.

➢ **Gustative Sensory Marketing (Taste):**

The sense of taste is considered to be the most distinct emotional sense. But the taste experienced and liked by the one customer may not be the same to other, hence this factor is independent to each individual. Because the taste of food liked by one person may not be like by another person due to various reasons. Hence attracting customers through the varied taste can also help the form in creating a brand image. This strategy drive more efforts on the form as each customer has their own taste and preferences. A restaurant providing varied kind of dishes with variety of taste can attract more customers, similarly a restaurant producing unique types of food apart from the competitor can create a separate brand image in the minds of consumers.

➢ **Tactile Sensory Marketing (Touch):**

Touch is very important in sensory branding because it strengthens the experience an individual has when interacting with a product. Tactile marketing can be used by the brands which can be facilitated by different sense expressions such as material and surfaces, temperature and form and steadiness. Many people have a positive responses to touch which can be a positive response to services.

> ➢ **Olfactory Sensory Marketing (Smell):**

Of all the five senses, smell is believed to be linked the most to the emotion. As a part of promotional strategy, many brands now sell scents and aromas to different brands and firms in order to enhance their marketing and brand identity. The distinctive aromas used in the restaurants drive the customers towards it which creates an impression and emotional link between the customers and the food being served in the restaurant , finally leading to creation of image of the brand in the minds of customers

Thus these are the various types of practices which keep the senses as its basis in driving the customers towards its product/service.

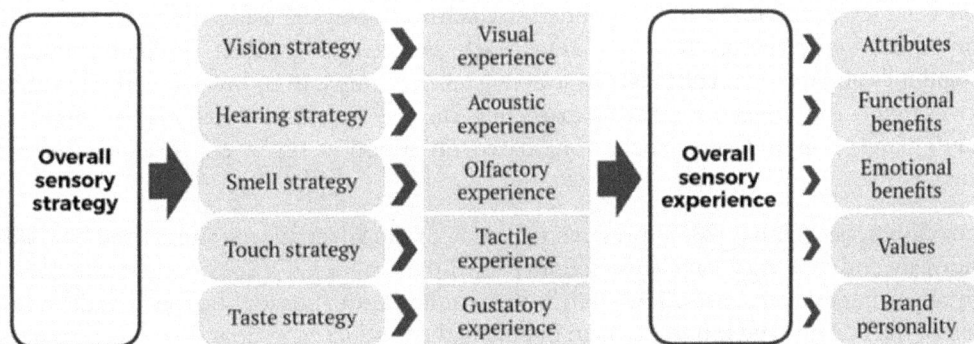

Source: IE Insights

The present study is undertaken in order to identify the awareness of the consumers about the sensory marketing practices used by restaurants such as good ambience, soothing music, cleanliness etc which influence their purchasing behaviour and to check whether these practices help the restaurants to influence the consumer purchasing behaviour and helps in building brand image in the minds of consumer.

Review of Literature

Dr Rupa Rathee and Ms Pallavi Rajain (2017) has undertaken research on sensory marketing-investigating the use of five senses. The main objective of the research article is to study the use of five senses in marketing the products and services. From the findings of the study it is being concluded that the senses affect an individual emotionally and help in creating a bond between the consumer and the products or services which is long lasting and thus leads to repurchase and spending more time a particular retail setting. In the times to come companies using the senses to appeal the customers will go beyond relationship marketing and thus carve a niche for themselves and become profitable but however there is an ethical aspect to be considered as to what levels the use of the senses allows the free will of customers to function.

Anıl Değermen Erenkol & Merve AK (2015) aim to discuss sensory marketing practices of business and the influence of consumers on such practice as well as examining the response to such practice. A casual research methodology was adopted for the purpose of study and a total of 206 responses were being analysed. From the findings obtained the researcher suggests that as sensory marketing is a relatively new tool which is expected to influence purchasing decisions of consumers and encourage consumers to pay more and repurchase through perception. If these two issues are discussed on future details, sensory marketing will achieve a wider conceptual framework and marketing professionals will have more useful results. Finally it is being concluded that due to intensifying competition in globalizing markets with increased product and service diversity on one hand and rapidly advancing technology on the other, it becomes increasingly more challenging for the business to influence and attract consumers who are able to reach more information faster, and traditional marketing methods prove to be insufficient to influence the purchasing decisions of the consumers.

EL-Hussein M. Ali & Mohamed O. Ahmed (2019) has conducted the research on 'Sensory Marketing and its Effect on Hotel Market-Share: Perception of Hotel Customers'. The purpose/objective of the study is to investigate the effect of sensory marketing on Egyptian hotel market share among customer's perception and actual behaviour based on implementing seven elements of sensory marketing within five-star hotels in Cairo. A quantitative approach was use to achieve its aim and data was being collected from 400 respondents which was analysed using the SPSS software. The findings of the study reveals few limitations such as need to conduct qualitative research to understand fully about SM and difficulty in selecting proper sample to be investigated. Thus the study tries to examine the effect of sensory marketing on the Egyptian hotel market share among customer's perception and actual behaviour based on adoption seven core elements of sensory marketing.

Sudeshna Mukherjee (Sinha) (2015) presents the study of the advertising strategy used by Cadbury's over the years and how they have successfully forged the emotional associations in the consumers mind by appealing to their senses. The study bring out the various sensory factors that directly affect the brain of the humans and influence them in buying the products and how such sensory factors are being used as marketing strategy by Cadbury's. From the detailed study the author concludes that it is the brand association that influence the people to buy the product and build brand loyalty over the product which delivers a quality service.

Dr. Gaurav Kumar Joshi, Dr. Rakesh Shirase Prof. Sangeeta Rajput (2019) studied the impact of sensory marketing on purchase behavior. The objectives of the study is to know the level of awareness among the sensory marketing in Pune, to identify and describe sensory strengths and potentials of sensory marketing in Pune and to know the impact of sensory branding strategy. The study collected the data from the primary sources and the findings of the study from the data being collected showed that most of the customers were aware that stores take many steps to attract them through sensory marketing practices but the customers were not aware of the term sensory branding and hence there exist a significant relationship between the variables of the study.

Anand Y. Bhatt and Dr. Ira Bapna (2018) looked into the perception of youth towards sensory marketing. The objectives of the study were to explain the concept of sensory marketing and to understand the perception of youth towards sensory marketing. The study was an explorative investigation where the data was being collected from 100 youngsters. The author from the data being collected and analysed finds and concludes that there is a need to understand and explore the basics of sensory marketing and a better understanding has to be developed among the youngsters.

Alex Fahrur Riza , Dwi Marlina Wijayanti (2018) discuss the triangle of sensory marketing model. The purpose of the study was to examine the framework of brand experience associating with customer loyalty. The study has used primary sources to collect the data with s sample size 185 respondents. From the data being collected and analysed the researcher suggests that using application of sensory marketing make customers satisfied and loyal to the brand which will make the customers difficult to switch to another brand.

Margareta Nadanyiova, Jana Kliestikova, Juraj Kolencik (2018) studied about the sensory marketing as a supporting tool for building brand value. The aim of the study is to provide literature review on the issue from several foreign and domestic authors. The article discusses the essence of a brand, brand value, sensory marketing and also analyses it to use as a support tool for building brand value in practice through secondary research data which was obtained from companies reports, statistical reports. published reports etc. The study thus brings out the sensory marketing practices of various brands like Starbucks, Netflix etc as a part of the study and finally concludes that use of sensory marketing as a tool for strengthening brand value perceived by customers has many benefits to the brands like customer loyalty, increasing customers and many more.

Problem Statement

In the present competitive environment most of the companies and brands aims to survive in the market by advertising, sample marketing and various others forms to attract customers. But most of the companies are not concentrating on the factor of sensory marketing which emotionally attaches the customer to the product which in turn build brand loyalty among the customers. Now the customers no longer buy the product in order to satisfy the functional needs rather they associate the emotional experience around it Experience marketing has established a significant position in the market and nowadays play a significant role in the consumer markets. Hence there is a high scope for the companies and service providers to create brand for themselves by improving the quality of product/service and associating their products or services to the emotional senses and thus creating a loyalty among the customers. Along with this, the practice of sensory marketing is much more beneficial for the service providers like restaurants where the customers build a loyalty on the basis of the unique food taste, visual appeals, aroma and many more. As food is considered as one of the easiest way of attracting the attracting a person, the food caterers, hotels and restaurants can use such ways in attracting the customers by using the human senses as a means to develop their business which is beneficial to the business as well as to the customer satisfaction. Hence, lack of awareness of such sensory marketing practices among the customers and service providers is identified as the problem and the research gap of the study. Hence the objective of this study is to identify the sensory factor that mostly influence the consumer behaviour.

The limitations of the study needs to be pointed as the study is limited to consumers visiting restaurants either often or rarely. It is confined to a specific industry i.e, food service industry.

Hence we developed the following hypotheses:

H1 There is a significant relationship between Aural Senses and Consumer Satisfaction

H2: There is a significant relationship between Visual Senses and Consumer Satisfaction

H3: There is a significant relationship between Olfactory Senses and Consumer Satisfaction

H4: There is a significant relationship between Tactile Sense and Consumer Satisfaction

H5: There is a significant relationship between Gustative Sense and Consumer Satisfaction

Research Methodology

The present study has collected the data from both primary as well as secondary sources. The primary data was being collected through mailed questionnaire method, of which total of 194 respondents took part in the research. And the secondary data was being collected through online magazines, online websites, journals and newspapers. The mailed questionnaire consisted of questions that collected the responses from the customers who visit restaurants and how are they influenced by the sensory marketing practices and strategies used by those restaurants. The present study aims at identifying the consumer behaviour with respect to the sensory marketing practices used by the business and whether such practices helps the business in building customer loyalty and brand image.

Data Analysis

The table 01 represents responses of consumers towards the use of music as mode of sensory marketing practice. From the tables 01 and 02, we can observe that majority of the consumers who visit the restaurants regularly i.e, 47.9% and 60.3% respondents have agreed that the music played in the restaurant makes them more relaxed and creates a pleasant environment which in turn helps to have a good experience in the restaurant. As majority of the respondents enjoy the music being played, it could be used as a sensory marketing strategy by the restaurants in order to create a unique experience and build brand awareness among the consumers.

01. Analysis of data collected with respect to Aural Senses i.e, 'Sound' used as basis in Sensory Marketing:

Table 01: Music played in restaurants makes me more relaxed and enjoyable

Sl no	Responses	No of respondents	Percentage of respondents
01	Strongly Disagree	06	3.1
02	Disagree	05	2.6
03	Neutral	62	32
04	Agree	93	47.9
05	Strongly Agree	28	14.4
Total		194	100

Table 02 : Music creates a pleasant environment in restaurants

Sl no	Responses	No of respondents	Percentage of respondents
01	Strongly Disagree	01	0.5
02	Disagree	07	3.6
03	Neutral	33	17
04	Agree	117	60.3
05	Strongly Agree	36	18.6
Total		194	100

Correlations

		MUSIC	CONSUMER SATISFACTION
MUSIC	Pearson Correlation	1	.118
	Sig. (2-tailed)		.100
	N	194	194
CONSUMER SATISFACTION	Pearson Correlation	.118	1
	Sig. (2-tailed)	.100	
	N	194	194

It is observed from the above analysis that there is a significant relationship between the sensory marketing practice related to music and consumer satisfaction. It means that when the music is being played in the restaurant it helps in impacting the consumers behaviour and leads to consumer satisfaction and hence null hypothesis is being rejected on the basis of the results.

02. Analysis of data collected with respect to Visual Senses i.e, 'Sight' used as basis in Sensory Marketing:

Table 03: The colour and lighting of restaurant needs to be visually appealing for me			
Sl no	Responses	No of respondents	Percentage of respondents
01	Strongly Disagree	03	1.5
02	Disagree	08	4.1
03	Neutral	34	17.5
04	Agree	117	60.3
05	Strongly Agree	32	16.5
Total		194	100

Table 04: If the food is presented in visually appealing manner, I will want to try it			
Sl no	Responses	No of respondents	Percentage of respondents
01	Strongly Disagree	03	1.6
02	Disagree	09	4.7
03	Neutral	24	12.5
04	Agree	118	61.5
05	Strongly Agree	38	19.8
Total		194	100

From the responses shown in Table 04, it is evident that majority of the respondents consider visual appeal of the restaurant and food as an important factor as it influences their decisions in visiting the decision. Hence, having a good and attractive visual could be more beneficial for the business in attracting the customers towards it. Accordingly, a hypothesis has been framed and analysed. Statistical tests are summarised below.

Correlations			
		CONSUMER SATISFACTION	SIGHT
CONSUMER SATISFACTION	Pearson Correlation	1	.346**
	Sig. (2-tailed)		.000
	N	194	194
SIGHT	Pearson Correlation	.346**	1
	Sig. (2-tailed)	.000	
	N	194	194

**. Correlation is significant at the 0.01 level (2-tailed).

The analysis shows a significant relationship between consumer satisfaction and the sensory marketing practice related to sight, as the significant value (2 tailed) is 0.01. It means that a restaurant having a attractive visual appeal would be more likely to satisfy the customers than the other customers.

03. Analysis of data collected with respect to Olfactory Senses i.e, 'Smell' used as basis in Sensory Marketing:

Tables 5 and 6 represent the use of Sensory marketing related to the Olfactory senses and the responses of the consumers relating to it. From the responses being collected it is observed that the 58.8% of the consumers judge the quality of the food being served on the basis of the aroma of the food and 57.75 of the respondents agree that the aroma and the unique fragrance of the food can make them to revisit the restaurant. Hence it can be said that a restaurant can create a brand image by using this factor as marketing strategy to attract the customers towards their services.

Sl no	Responses	No of respondents	Percentage of respondents
01	Strongly Disagree	01	0.5
02	Disagree	17	8.8
03	Neutral	33	17
04	Agree	114	58.8
05	Strongly Agree	29	14.9
Total		194	100

Table 05: The quality of food can sometimes be judged based on the aroma

Sl no	Responses	No of respondents	Percentage of respondents
01	Strongly Disagree	02	01
02	Disagree	10	5.2
03	Neutral	27	13.9
04	Agree	112	57.7
05	Strongly Agree	43	22.2
Total		194	100

Table 06: The aroma of some dishes can make me revisit the restaurant

Accordingly, the hypothesis was being tested and the results are shown below. It is observed that from the below correlation analysis there is a significant relationship between the sensory marketing practice related to olfactory sense and the consumer satisfaction. It means when the aroma of the food is good the consumer is satisfied with the quality of service and revisits the restaurants.

Correlations			CONSUMER SATISFACTION	SMELL
CONSUMER SATISFACTION		Pearson Correlation	1	.258**
		Sig. (2-tailed)		.000
		N	194	194
SMELL		Pearson Correlation	.258**	1
		Sig. (2-tailed)	.000	
		N	194	194

**. Correlation is significant at the 0.01 level (2-tailed)

04. Analysis of data collected with respect to Tactile Sense i.e, 'Touch' used as basis in Sensory Marketing

Sl no	Responses	No of respondents	Percentage of respondents
01	Strongly Disagree	04	2.1
02	Disagree	23	11.9
03	Neutral	61	31.4
04	Agree	89	45.9
05	Strongly Agree	17	8.8
Total		194	100

Table 07: I would like to touch or feel the cutlery which is artistically crafted or designed

Table 8 represents about the sensory marketing practices relating to the tactile senses i.e, touch. According to most of the respondents the artistic crafts in the restaurants used as decor is being considered as attractive and drives their attention and helps them to better the restaurants which is considered as beneficial to the marketers and around 39.2% of the respondents have agreed that touch as a sense helps in building social attachment during the dining. The hypothesis being framed relating to the particular sense is being analysed and the results of the study is presented below.

Table 08: Touch as sense bring feeling of social attachment during the dining

Sl no	Responses	No of respondents	Percentage of respondents
01	Strongly Disagree	03	1.5
02	Disagree	33	17
03	Neutral	65	33.5
04	Agree	76	39.2
05	Strongly Agree	17	8.8
Total		194	100

Correlations

		CONSUMER SATISFACTION	TOUCH
CONSUMER SATISFACTION	Pearson Correlation	1	.395**
	Sig. (2-tailed)		.000
	N	194	194
TOUCH	Pearson Correlation	.395**	1
	Sig. (2-tailed)	.000	
	N	194	194

**. Correlation is significant at the 0.01 level (2-tailed).

It is observed that there exist a significant relationship between the two variables of the study i.e, touch as sensory marketing practice and consumer satisfaction. It means when the restaurants use the sensory marketing strategies relating to tactile sense then the consumers are more likely to get satisfied.

05. Analysis of data collected with respect to Gustative Senses i.e, 'Taste' used as basis in Sensory Marketing:

Table 09: I remember the restaurants for the unique taste of food and/or drinks.

Sl no	Responses	No of respondents	Percentage of respondents
01	Strongly Disagree	01	0.5
02	Disagree	03	1.5
03	Neutral	10	5.2
04	Agree	118	60.8
05	Strongly Agree	62	32
Total		194	100

Table 10: The quality of food and service inspires me to revisit the restaurant

Sl no	Responses	No of respondents	Percentage of respondents
01	Strongly Disagree	01	0.5
02	Disagree	00	00
03	Neutral	07	3.6
04	Agree	99	51
05	Strongly Agree	87	44.8
Total		194	100

The above table represents the use of Gustative sense as means for sensory marketing and the consumers responses towards it. From the data being collected it is observed that majority of the respondents have agreed that the unique taste of food makes them to remember the restaurant and around 44.8% of the respondents have stated they the quality of food and service strongly inspires them to revisit the restaurant again Hence from the above responses it could be noted that the restaurants can build a brand loyalty among the consumers by providing unique taste of food with quality service. The hypothesis being framed for the above factor of sensory marketing is being analysed using the appropriate statistical tools and the results are as follows:

Correlations			
		CONSUMER SATISFACTION	TASTE
CONSUMER SATISFACTION	Pearson Correlation	1	.353**
	Sig. (2-tailed)		0.000
	N	194	194
TASTE	Pearson Correlation	.353**	1
	Sig. (2-tailed)	.000	
	N	194	194

**. Correlation is significant at the 0.01 level (2-tailed).

It is observed that there exist a significant relationship between the consumer satisfaction and taste as means of sensory marketing. It means when the taste of food is unique then the consumers are likely to better remember the restaurants better due to the unique experience which enables in the creation of consumer loyalty.

The below table shows the results of the data being collected from a total of 194 respondents regarding the quality of service provided by the restaurants that used sensory marketing promotional strategies. From the data being collected it was observed that majority of the respondents counting to 117 agreed that the restaurants involved in sensory marketing strategies focused on quality of service along with the promotional activities. From the above data it could be observed that the restaurants involved in sensory marketing strategies also focused on quality of service along with the promotional activities which is an important factor for driving the consumer loyalty towards their product/service.

Table 11: Restaurants which had adopted sensory marketing strategies not only focused in promotional strategy but also provide quality service

Sl no	Responses	No of respondents	Percentage of respondents
01	Strongly Disagree	02	01
02	Disagree	04	2.1
03	Neutral	45	23.2
04	Agree	117	60.2
05	Strongly Agree	26	13.4
Total		194	100

Table 12: Are you aware of Sensory Marketing

Sl no	Responses	No of respondents	Percentage of respondents
01	Yes	83	42.8
02	No	39	20.1
03	Maybe	72	37.1
Total		194	100

The above table represents the level of awareness about the concept of sensory marketing among the consumers. Among the total responses 42.8% respondents were aware of the concept of term of sensory marketing and its practices where as 20.1% were not and the remaining of the respondents were not aware of the term of sensory marketing instead were familiar to such promotional strategies.

Findings and Suggestions

Sensory marketing strategies used by the restaurants could influence the consumer behaviour and make them revisit the restaurant due to the unique experience and the emotional senses associated with the services being provided leading to brand loyalty.

There is awareness about the sensory marketing strategies used by the restaurants among the consumers but a certain percentage of the consumers are not aware of the term sensory marketing and sensory branding instead are having the awareness about its existence and practice in the market.

The consumers don't mind in spending extra money on the unique experience which the restaurant offers them.

It is suggested that the restaurants could use this emerging technique in building a brand image in the minds of the consumers which could lead them to having a stable position in the competitive market.

Conclusion

In order to fend competition the retailers have to focus their attention towards the sensory aspects like sight, smell, taste, touch and sound. These practices provide a unique ambience to the customers. The study shows that sensory marketing could influence positively on the consumer experience on brands and has a positive impact on the consumer loyalty. The present study shows that the human sensory cues like sight, smell, taste, touch and sound can affect our preferences, choices and memories. However certain limitations do exist in the study but from the study it was being found that there is a great scope for the marketers to use these strategies to create a brand image in the minds of the consumers by making the consumer satisfied with their need along with the unique experience.

References

IE Insights: https://www.ie.edu/insights/articles/sensory-marketing-straight-to-the-emotions/

Dr Rupa Rathee and Ms Pallavi Rajain - 'Sensory Marketing-Investigating The Use Of Five Senses , Vol. 7 Issue 5, May – 2017, pp. 124~133 ISSN(o): 2231-5985

Anıl Değermen Erenkol & Merve AK- 'Sensory Marketing' , Vol. 3, No. 1, pp. 1-26 ISSN: 2372-5109, URL: http://dx.doi.org/10.15640/jasps.v3n1a1

EL-Hussein M. Ali & Mohamed O. Ahmed - Sensory Marketing and its Effect on Hotel Market-Share: Perception of Hotel Customers, Vol. 7, No. 1, pp. 116-126 ISSN: 2372-5125, URL : https://doi.org/10.15640/jthm.v7n1a12

EL-Hussein M. Ali & Mohamed O. Ahmed, Journal of Tourism and Hospitality Management June 2019, Vol. 7, No. 1, pp. 116-126 ISSN: 2372-5125 (Print), 2372-5133 (Online) URL: https://doi.org/10.15640/jthm.v7n1a12

Sudeshna Mukherjee (Sinha), Advances in Economics and Business Management (AEBM) p-ISSN: 2394-1545; e-ISSN: 2394-1553; Volume 2, Issue 13; July-September, 2015 pp. 1291-1295 https://potravinarstvo.com/journal1/index.php/potravinarstvo/article/view/1465

Dr. Gaurav Kumar Joshi, Dr. Rakesh Shirase, Prof. Sangeeta Rajput, SaiBalaji International Journal of Management Sciences, ISSN.2349-6568 Volume II, Issue IV, August 2019

Anand Y. Bhatt and Dr. Ira Bapna- Perception of Youth towards Sensory Marketing, E ISSN 2320 – 0871, International Research Journal of Indian languages, 17 January 2018, http://shabd-braham.com/ShabdB/archive/v6i3/sbd-v6-i3-sn25.pdf

Riza, Alex & Wijayanti, Dwi. (2018). The Triangle of Sensory Marketing Model: Does it Stimulate Brand Experience and Loyalty?. Esensi: Jurnal Bisnis dan Manajemen. 8. 10.15408/ess.v8i1.6058.

Nadanyiova, Margareta & Majerova, Jana & Kolencik, Juraj. (2018). Sensory Marketing from the Perspective of a Support Tool for Building Brand Value. Economics and Culture. 15. 96-104. 10.2478/jec-2018-0011.

CHAPTER 3

ATTITUDE TOWARDS FEMALE ROLE PORTRAYAL IN ADVERTISING AND ITS IMPACT ON BRAND IMAGE & PURCHASE INTENTION: LINKAGES WITH FEMININE ROLE ORIENTATION

Shraddha Shivani[1], Evelina Sahay[2], Somnath Mukherjee[3], Sadiya Fatima[4]

Introduction

Advertising has become a vital element of society's cultural and economic fabric, and a fundamental technique of marketing communications (Lane et al., 2005; Lauer, 2007; Pellicer, 2017). Messages communicated through advertisements work to sell through persuasion and imagination (Baack et al., 2016; Dahlén et al., 2008; Hartnett et al., 2016; West et al., 2019). As a result, modern marketing techniques rely primarily on innovative advertising to attract customers and influence their purchasing decisions (Ahmed, 2016; Fatima, 2015; Kumar, 2013; Muhammad Awan et al., 2016; Rai, 2013). Individuals' attention to and elaboration of advertising stimuli is controlled chiefly by three types of elements. First, qualities of the stimuli, such as the impression of the product's femininity or masculinity. Second, qualities of the individual, such as gender-role orientation, that can be traditional or non-traditional. Third, there's a chance that situational considerations play a role such as the subject's surroundings at the moment of exposure.

A thorough exploration of contemporary commercials in India demonstrates that advertisers resort to using gender stereotyping as one of the simplest methods of connecting with consumers (Anand, 2013; Sandhu, 2019). It has been discovered that portraying women in gender roles has a direct impact on the efficacy of advertising since women are more conscious of gender stereotypes in advertising (Drake, 2017; Grau & Zotos, 2016). Not only does this create a stereotype but also sets up unrealistic expectations from a gender and conveys ideal behavior of men and women (Grau & Zotos, 2016; Sharma & Bumb, 2021). The consensus regarding the research on gender role portrayal in advertising over the past four decades have depicted women in advertisements as if they (1) need the protection of men (2) are dependent on men (3) are not making important decisions, (4) mainly represented in home-settings (5) homemakers and (4) sex objects (Matthes et al., 2016; Paek et al., 2011; Verhellen et al., 2016). For a long time, the traditional roles that women assume in commercials have been a source of popular outrage. To establish favorable and strong association between the brand and consumers, firms often use gender imagery in the advertisement. For example detergent ads (like Surf excel- Unilever) in India are targeted at kids and mothers who are expected to do the laundry. Also health drinks (Bournvita- Cadbury) show women as the caretakers and responsible for child's heath. Though men of different skin tone and size appear in advertisements, but mainly female who are thin and fair appear in Indian advertisements to denote a symbol of beauty. According to Kang (1997)

[1] Dr Shraddha Shivani, Professor and Head, Department of Management, Birla Institute of Technology, Mesra, Ranchi.
E-mail: shraddhashivani@bitmesra.ac.in
[2] Evelina Sahay, Assistant Professor, Marketing Department, Institute for Technology and Management, Kharghar, Navi Mumbai.
E-mail: evelinasahay@gmail.com
[3] Dr Somnath Mukherjee, Assistant Professor, Department of Management, Birla Institute of Technology, City Centre, Ranchi.
E-mail: smukherjeebit@bitmesra.ac.in
[4] Sadiya Fatima, Research Scholar, Department of Management, Birla Institute of Technology, Mesra, Ranchi.
E-mail: sadiya.fatima4@gmail.com

advertising images help in the interpretation of the present world and consequently influence the public opinion of ideal gender role (Gilly, 1988). Portrayal of gender in advertising plays a pivotal role and continues to be the focal point of marketing practitioners, social scientists and researchers since it influences the consumer perceptions and buying decisions. According to Zhou and Chen, (1997) 'Stereotypes are often used in advertising to convey images with which potential buyers may identify so as to increase advertising effectiveness'. Advertisers frequently use gender stereotyping to persuade and have a strong connect between the brand and the consumer. The formation and reinforcement of sexist attitudes, beliefs, and behaviours, such as distorted body image, sexual harassment, and violence against women, is often linked to repeated exposure to stereotyped portrayals of women's roles in advertising (Gulas & McKeage, 2000).

During the last few years, the socio-economic status of women in India has changed significantly. Furthermore, India being one of the world's greatest economies with diverse population characteristics, it is very difficult to make inferences with the help of a few previous pieces of research. Subsequently, most of the researches involves content analysisfor examining the female role portrayal in advertisements (Mallika Das, 2011; Kumari & Shivani, 2015a). And, very few studies have investigated the impact of such portrayals on marketing communication effectiveness and have studied female responses only. Moreover, much research has examined the role of stereotypes as cognitive shortcuts, far less research has specifically investigated the offensiveness of stereotypes per se. In recent years there has been no significant work to find out the impact of such communication, especially on the young population, in India. Empirical evidence of a relationship between Gender Role Identity (GRI) and the communication effectiveness of female portrayal is also very limited. Therefore, this work was undertaken to investigate the impact of communication usingstereotyped female portrayal on youngsters especially in determining the effectiveness of the communication in terms of Ad Liking, Brand Image, and Purchase Intention and correlating the impact with the GRI of the respondents. Since the main purpose of advertisement is to attract consumers to buy a product (Sharma & Bumb, 2021), it is also their responsibility to do it ethically without promoting offensive images. For advertisers who largely continue to portray women in a Stereotypical manner it is pertinent to question this strategy with respect to its impact on Advertising Effectiveness as well as from Ethical standpoint. The central idea of this research therefore has Social, Ethical and Business dimensions. The current work is expected to provide a more contemporary assessment of the portrayal of women in advertising in the backdrop of their improved socio-economic status in society. Moreover, it can also help marketers drive gender equality through advertising in Indian market. Since advertising is aimed at increasing sales and educating the consumers, this medium can be well utilized to change how gender stereotypes have been pre-positioned in the society. This will lead to creation of a new and unbiased environment where advertising is free of gender stereotypes and is solely targeted at sales and sustainability of the product. People thereby could compare products and services based on its attributes and build an environment that is free of gender biases related to products.

Literature Review and Hypothesis

The field of social psychology has extensively investigated stereotyping throughout the years and has consequently provided social scientists with an enriched knowledge base. As per Kahnemann and Tversky, stereotyping is a phenomenon or mental shortcut of the human brain which essentially stems from our ability to classify things and beings (Galli, 2011), and these heuristics over time become biases and are difficult to change. Defined in basic terms, astereotype is a "cognitive belief about the personal attributes of a group of people". Offense evidently occurs when such beliefs are over-generalized, derogatory in nature, and/or simply erroneous. Often juxtaposed with prejudice (an affective phenomenon) and discrimination (a behavioral phenomenon), research has indicated that stereotypes are often automatic responses to stimuli, are manipulated by both personal and social influences, and are socially practical. Although coverage of the offensive nature of stereotypes is seemingly scant in the literature, acknowledgment of stereotyping in a study of offensive advertising is important and directly relevant.

With the movement toward market segmentation during the last century, marketers and advertisers have relied more and more on the benefits of stereotypes. The ability of stereotypeusage to expedite communication has been demonstrated (Herz & Diamantopoulos, 2013). In addition, several researchers have verified that the use of stereotypes is often automatic for people (Dijksterhuis et al., 2001; Kawakami et al., 2002). Hence, through the incorporation ofstereotypic messages, advertisers can communicate more rapidly through both lower levels ofneeded cognition and the automatic generation of stereotypes. Although such use may assist mass communicators disseminate their messages, it may also lead to offending certain individuals due to erroneous generalizations similar to those mentioned above.

This cannot be ignored that gender portrayals through advertising can have societal effects (Eisend, 2019; Middleton & Turnbull, 2021). In addition to flawed generalizations, offense surrounding stereotypes may also be associated with incorrect attributions of behavior. Specifically, individuals often attribute the poor qualities of another to that person's internal dispositions or some other outwardly noticeable trait and subsequently discount the influence of situational factors external to another (Ross, 1977).

Prior studies on Gender stereotypes in advertisements

Gender portrayal in advertising has been studied for a long in many countries. This section examines a number of research studies on gender depictions in print and television advertising in various nations including China (Cheng, 1997), Australia (Browne, 1998) and France (Furnham et al., 2000). Research on gender portrayal started in the 1970s. Observers at the time believed that advertising depicted men and women in more current and non- traditional roles. However, research done in the 1980s disproved this prediction, since both male and female characters in advertising messages continued to be depicted in stereotyped positions. Furthermore, with a few exceptions, the outcomes of study conducted in the 1990s and 2000 were shown to be consistent with past studies.

Most of the researches evaluating female portrayal in advertising have reported stereotyped portrayal of females on parameters like age of the central female character, her occupation, her credibility, location setting of the message, gender of voice overused in the message, and product category in which female characters are used (Lysonski, 1985). A study by Gilly, (1988) indicated that amongst Australia, Mexico, and the U.S television commercials, when compared to American television advertising, Mexican commercials showed significant variations in gender depiction. Furnham & Voli, (1989) studied stereotypical gender roles in Italian television advertising and found consistent findings with prior investigations. Mazzella et al., (1992) found a substantial gap in the role portrayal of men and women in another study on gender representation in Australian television ads. Mwangi, (1996) revealed gender stereotyping in the television commercials of Kenya.

In compared to ads in the Netherlands, Odekerken-Schröder et al., (2002) observed that magazine advertisements in the United Kingdom presented female characters less in a working posture and more as sex objects. Whereas, on the flip side, women were seen to be unhappy with portrayal disparities such as "the woman belonging in the home," "women not being in a position to make important decisions," "women being seen by men as "sex objects," and "women being viewed as dependent upon men." Milner & Higgs, (2004) found that the way women are portrayed in ads differs from their actual experience of their place in society. Investigations published in Spanish periodicals during the latter three half of the twentieth century by Royo-Vela et al., (2007) revealed that, while gender stereotypes exist, male and female depictions have changed significantly. The study done to assess the perception of young girls regarding gender roles and gender identities in Hong Kong by Chan et al., (2011) investigated the kind of media pictures that female teenagers in the nation find appealing, as well as what such images represent to them.

On the other hand, according to Ali & Shahwar, (2011), the representation of women in advertising has an impact on their buying patterns as well as their self-image (body image) and sexuality. Chan et al., (2012) looked at how adolescent girls used commercial images to negotiate their gender roles. The findings reveal that pictures about dieting, body image, and physical appearance are highly valued by adolescent girls. Women's role depiction in Chinese advertising has moved from that of an equal partner to that of a more westernized image of women as objects of beauty and desire, according to Ye et al., (2012). A multi-country investigation by Prieler et al., (2015) found stereotypical representations of both genders with respect to age, work, authority, and beauty in television commercials from Hong Kong, Japan, and South Korea. As per Mckenzie et al., (2018), the continuous use of gender stereotypes in ads, as well as a growing dependence on imagery that sexualizes and objectifies women, hinders attempts to promote gender equality in Australia. In contrast, Houston, (2019) discovered that advertising depicts women with mobility limitations as a type of 'safe quirkiness.'

Gender Portrayal in Indian advertisements

The advent of 'New Indian Women,' women in many avatars as homemakers, and how advertising discourses in India have led to their creation. The findings clearly show that the old patriarchy has not changed. In reality, the new woman has 'planned' and 'negotiated' her place inside the prevailing social order. As a matter of fact, advertising has been criticized for using gender stereotypes for more than a decade (Eisend, 2019). Although gender role stereotypes are reducing in western countries but the status has not change in Asia as well as Africa (Furnham & Farrager, 2001 ; Sharma & Bumb, 2021) However, Das, (2000) foundthat conventional role depictions of men and women in Indian magazine advertising decreased little over time, but that most commercials remained to portray gender in a stereotyped or traditional position. Women in Indian magazine advertising are typically represented in conventional positions such as preoccupied with physical appearance, housewives, and sex objects, according to Dwivedy et al., (2009). In contrast to women, males were favored by advertisers to represent central individuals, and their voice-over was found to dominate in most ads, according to Das, (2011), whilst women were mostly shownin relationship roles to others. While research in India determined that the female depiction inIndian advertising is mostly stereotyped another study concluded that the female portrayal in Indian advertising remains mainly stereotypical (Kumari & Shivani, 2013). Males and females have diverse perceptions of women in Indian television ads, according to Das & Sharma, (2016). Most of the previous studies are focused on western countries with respect to role portrayal. Researches being scanty in Indian origin paves a way for researchers to investigate this important topic. Moreover, earlier studies have included female samples (Orth & Holancova, 2004) or industry professionals (Tuncay Zayer & Coleman, 2015) which is not sufficient for the interpretation of the results.

To summarize it can be said that few studies have looked at the influence of gender representation on the performance of advertising tactics that focused primarily on corporate image and buy intent throughout the previous few decades. Cognitive reactions were used as parameters in certain studies to assess the impact of communication. The consequences of gender stereotyping in advertising were studied by Lavine et al., (1999). The study discovered that when female and male respondents were exposed to sexist commercials, they developed unfavorable opinions about their body type, as opposed to non-sexist advertisements or a no ad control condition. Furthermore, Morrison & Shaffer, (2003) discovered that individuals with conventional gender-role orientations had a higher buy intention for items advertised in traditional ads than for brands of the same products shown in non-traditional advertisements. Prejudices showed mild impacts of gender role incongruity on the emotional dimensions (in terms of approval and disapproval), according to Orth & Holancova, (2004), however surprise, the third dimension of emotion, was directly influenced by role incongruity. On the other hand, Harker et al., (2005) discovered that conventional Feminist 'pessimists' found stereotyping insulting, however the 'Optimist' feminist group did not. Advertisers, on the other hand, continue to fall short of employing accurate role depictions, and women were seen to be unsatisfied with their existing role portrayal. Theodoridis et al., (2013) discovered that between respondents of the same gender but different age brackets, there are disparities in overall opinions regarding stereotypes in advertising and in sentiments toward specific stereotypical commercials. Female representation in advertising is connected with an Ad like, the believability of Ad, brand liking, brand recognition, brand recall, and brand image, according to Kumari & Shivani, (2015b), but has a weaker influence on intention to purchase.

Based on the above literature the following hypotheses were formulated for phase 1 and phase 2 respectively.

For phase 1

H1: Strength of gender role identity (GRI) will significantly affect the "Perceived portrayal importance" (PPI) and "perceived portrayal offensiveness" (PPO) of female portrayal in advertising.

H2: Stereotyped portrayal of females in ads will negatively affect brand image

H3: Stereotyped portrayal of females in ads will negatively affect purchase intention.

H4: Stereotyped portrayal of females in ads will negatively affect ad liking

H5: The response of female and male consumers will be significantly different for GRI, PPI and PPO

For phase 2

H1: Strength of gender role identity (GRI) will significantly affect the "Perceived portrayal importance" (PPI) of female portrayal in advertising.

H2: Stereotyped portrayal of females in ads will negatively affect brand image (BI)

H3: Non-stereotyped portrayal of females in ads will positively affect Brand Image (BI)

H4: Stereotyped portrayal of females in ads will negatively affect purchase intention (PI)

H5: Non-Stereotyped portrayal of females in ads will positively affect purchase intention (PI)

H6: Stereotyped portrayal of females in ads will negatively affect ad liking (Ad Like)

H7: Non-Stereotyped portrayal of females in ads will positively affect ad liking (Ad Like) **H8:** The response of female and male consumers will be significantly different for GRI

H9: The response of female and male consumers will be significantly different for PPI

H10: The response of female and male consumers will be significantly different for Ad Like

H11: The response of female and male consumers will be significantly different for Brand Image (BI)

H12: The response of female and male consumers will be significantly different for Purchase Intention (PI)

Methodology

The study was conducted in two phases. In the first phase, the research hypothesis was tested empirically. In the second phase, a quasi-experiment was conducted to measure the cause effect relationships included in the hypothesis.

Study population

The survey was conducted at Mumbai, Tier 1 city, and Ranchi, Tier 2 city of India to make the sample representative of the population of young urban Indian consumers. 245 respondents including males and females were selected for the study in the first phase and250 respondents in the second phase. The respondents were in the age group of 17-27 years having completed high school education and exposure to advertisements. Using Convenience sampling, respondents were selected while trying to maintain randomness of the selections.To maintain the randomness, we selected every 5th student from the available roll-list of various colleges.

The sample size was derived using the formula,

Sample Size (n) $= \pi(1 - \pi) z^2 / D^2$

where, D = 95% confidence level i.e., +/- 0.05; Z Score = 1.96; and $\pi=$ Population proportion. The sample size was decided by taking a cue from similar studies where people have usually worked with 200-300 samples and the study has given true and insightful results.

Study design

The data for this study was collected using a survey approach. In all rounds of the study, a structured self-administered questionnaire was employed as a tool. The questionnaire was created in order to meet the study's goal of assessing customer answers and testing research hypothesis. A five-point Likert-type scale was used in the survey, with 1 indicating strong disagreement and 5 indicating strong agreement. Initially, we considered Arnott's Female Autonomy Inventory but the respondents were not comfortable answering such questions. So,looking at the mindset of the youngsters and ease of applicability we administered the scale of Gender Role Identity (GRI) on all respondents; even though some changes were brought inthe questionnaire by rewording questions without changing the meaning. The questionnaire was divided into seven parts.

Phase 1: All of the measures were created with the research objectives in mind, as well as past studies on gender depictions. Four statements related to PPI (Perceived Portrayal importance) and four statements related to PPO (Perceived Portrayal Offensiveness) were included to find if all the respondents consider the portrayal of women important and if so, dothey find it offensive as well and to what extent. Then, a 12-question scale to measure GenderRole identity inventory (Shaw & Wright, 1967) was used to find the role identity of respondents. To investigate the communication impact, three factors were identified: Ad liking, brand image (BI), and purchase intention (PI).

To determine the influence of female stereotypes in advertising on marketing communication a total of twelve statements were given to know the effect on BI, PI, and Ad Liking. Thus, a total of thirty-two statements were selected after the face validity and alpha reliability test. The demographic information of the respondents included gender, age group, education, occupation, income group, and category.

Phase 2: The GRI Scale was the same as the instrument used in phase I of the study. The scales for the effect of advertising messages on AD Liking, BI, and PI were also based on the items in the scales used in Phase I with slight modifications in the statements to include the reference of the advertising message that they were exposed to while the questionnaire was being administered on them.

For treatment design six different print advertising messages (posters) for a dummy brand ofa gender-neutral product (Coconut water) with 3 stereotypical and 3 non-stereotypical imageswere developed. Initially, 40 different images were selected and a panel of 6 members including academicians, advertisers, and reputed civil society members were requested to categorize the images as Stereotyped or Non-Stereotyped. Care was taken to ensure that all the images used to develop the message copy were Open-source content. Based on the majority view 6 images were selected to represent the following categories of the depiction offemales as per classification used in previous research, mainly by Das, (2000).

- Stereotyped: Housewife, Dependent and Decorative (for STT)

- Non-Stereotyped: Professional, Bossy, and Sporty (for NSTT)

The message copy was designed using basic message design principles. Each respondent was shown any one of these messages. An attempt was made to get nearly the same number of responses for each of the 6 message versions while picking messages for respondents as randomly as possible.

Method Validation

Although these instruments were already tested in previous work. However, we re-tested the instruments for validity by their Cronbach's alpha score and found that the instrument passed the test with a score value of 0.80.

Measures of Marketing Communication Impact

All of the factors were discovered after a thorough research of the marketing communication literature. (Please see Table 1)

Statistical Analysis

All of the statements were put to the test to see if they were reliable and genuine. The datawas analyzed with SPSS 28.0. Based on the research hypothesis, bivariate regression, independent sample Chi-square test and ANOVA were used in the study. We also used descriptive statistical analysis to get an overview of data and to infer new findings.

Results

Phase 1

In Phase 1, PPI and PPO was investigated to find the role of female portrayal in ads, based on gender, age group, education, occupation, income group and category of the respondents. Additionally, GRI was explored to see its impact on Ad liking, Brand Image and Purchase Intent based on the demographic profile of the respondents.

Socio-demographic profile

The key demographic and socioeconomic characteristics of respondents who were includedin the study are shown in Figure 1. Females constituted 57.85% of the population, while men constituted 42.15%. Among them, a maximum number of respondents were 18 years old, followed by 19 years old and 17 years old individuals. The majority of the female and male participants were found to have completed their secondary school. The distribution of demographic variables indicates that the respondents include males and females both with mostly secondary school with moderate income levels. (Please see Figure 1)

Perceived Portrayal Offensiveness

It was found that the majority of respondents, irrespective of gender (58%) are less offensive towards the stereotypical role portrayal of a woman in Ads (measured by PPO). However, among them, female respondent seems to have higher intolerance for such ads (23%) compared to men (18%). Furthermore, we discovered that a considerable number of female respondents (58%) find such depictions less offensive. While on the other side, all male SC category respondents (100%) find stereotyped depictions of women in advertisements insulting. Results are shown in Table 2 and Figure 2 (a) and (b). Furthermore, Table 3 and Figure 2 (c) represent that about 58% of respondents irrespective of income level are largely less concerned with offensive female role portrayal and the females in the income group of 25000-50000 may have some concerns. (Please see Table 2, Table 3 and Figure 2)

Gender Role Identity (GRI) of respondents

We have found that all categories have high Gender Role Identity but the level of GRI is remarkable for SC which is 100% (Table 4 and Figure 3 (a)). We sliced the data to represent the GRI based on income group and gender and found that the income group most affirmativeof gender freedom is Rs. 25000 – Rs. 50000 (Table 5 and Figure 3 (b)). However, females in a lower-income group show lower GRI; somewhat showed their oppressed state of mind. (Please see Table 4, Table 5 and Figure 3)

Mean score of constructs

To understand how people who support gender equality react to advertising that depicts women in (offensive) stereotyped ways, the framework PPI (Perceived Portrayal Importance) and PPO (Perceived Portrayal Offensiveness) were considered. The mean score of males and females for most of the constructs show uniformity except for the Purchase intention where females score on the higher side (3.15) as compared to males (2.8) and for Ad liking also where females score high (3.2) as compared to a neutral male score (3.005), as shown inTable 6 and Figure 4.

The mean score of GRI which is 3.5 shows that the majority of the people agree that female freedom is important for them (Table 6 and Figure 4). However, it is alarming to find that there are a little more than 10% of the respondents who were found to have low GRI which means 1 in every 10 young members of the society still doesn't carry a progressive view on the role of women in society. Consistent with the GRI results the mean score of PPI (Perceived Portrayal Importance) is also on the higher side which is 3.7 (Table 6 and Figure 4). This indicates that not only do the majority of the youngsters agree with the idea of femalefreedom but also the portrayal of females in Ads is an important issue for them. The linear relationship postulates that the strength of GRI significantly affects the PPI (Table 7). This indicates that the positive feminine role orientation indicated by GRI is positively related to the perceived importance of female portrayal in advertising.

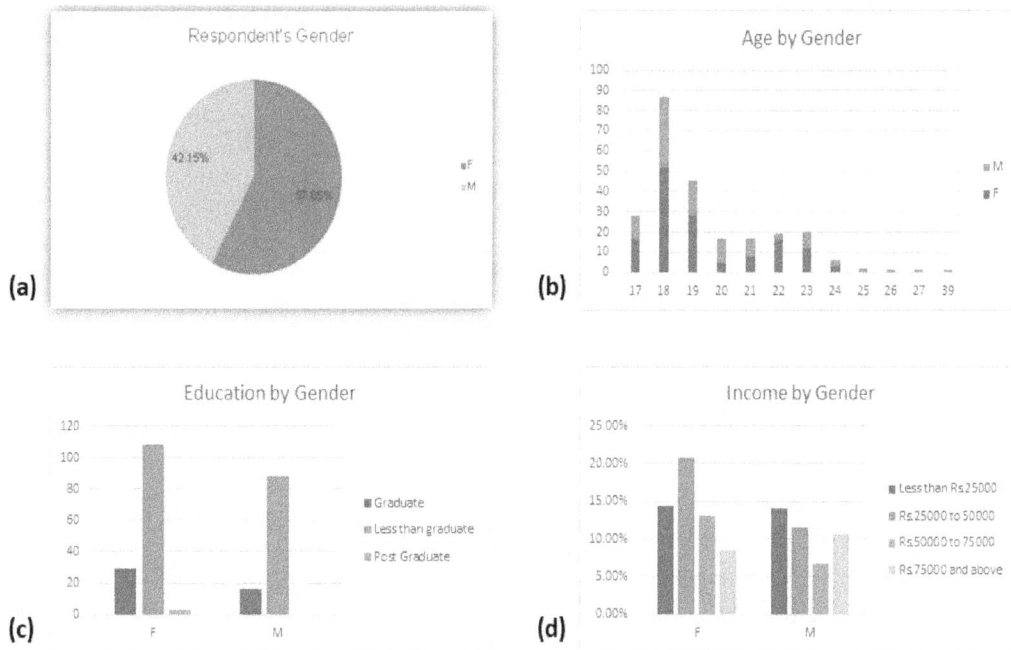

Figure 1: Socio-demographic profile of respondents based on (a) gender, (b) age, (c)education, and (d) income

The mean score for Perceived Portrayal Offensiveness (PPO) is found to be low at 2.7 on a 5-point scale (Table 6 and Figure 4). It may therefore be observed that the positive beliefs of young consumers towards female freedom and female portrayal in ads is not reflected in the PPO measurement (Table 7). Data suggests that youngsters by and large agree that female portrayal in ads is important for them but due to their inherent biases they probably fail to recognize the offensiveness

37

of such advertisements. It is pertinent to mention here that, as concluded from a review of literature earlier in this report, almost all the content analysis based evaluations of female portrayal in advertising in India have concluded that the portrayal is largely stereotyped in an offensive manner. However, the empirical findings from the group of young respondents of this research do not corroborate the findings of those studies.

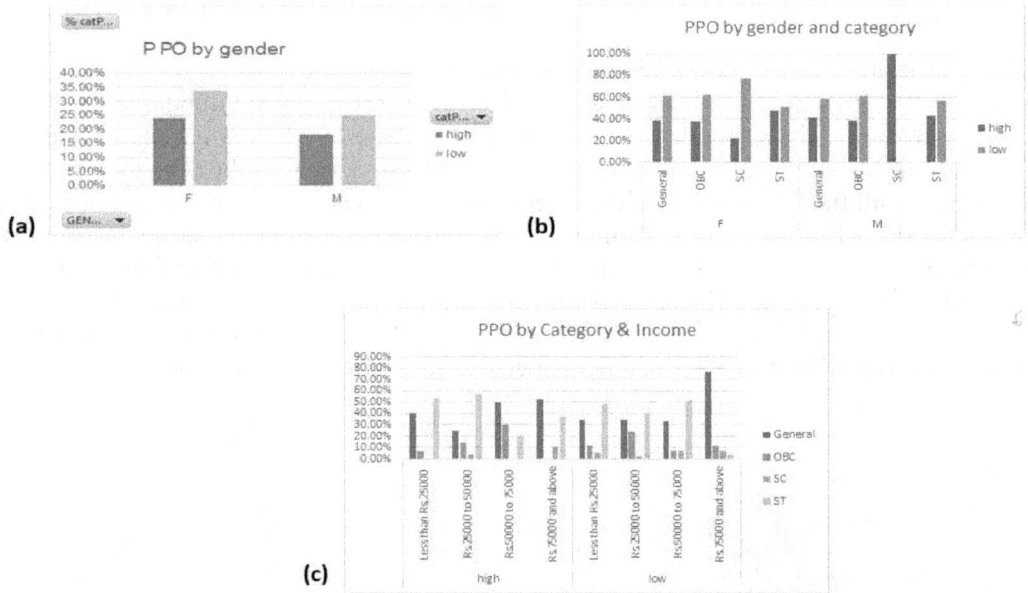

Figure 2: Representation of Perceived Portrayal Offensiveness based on respondents' (a) gender, (b) category, and (c) income

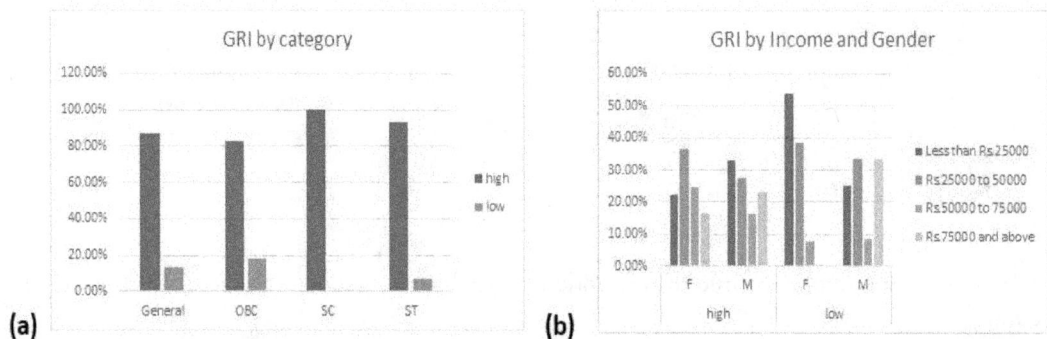

Figure 3: Representation of Gender Role Identity based on respondents' (a) category and (b) income

38

(a)   **(b)**

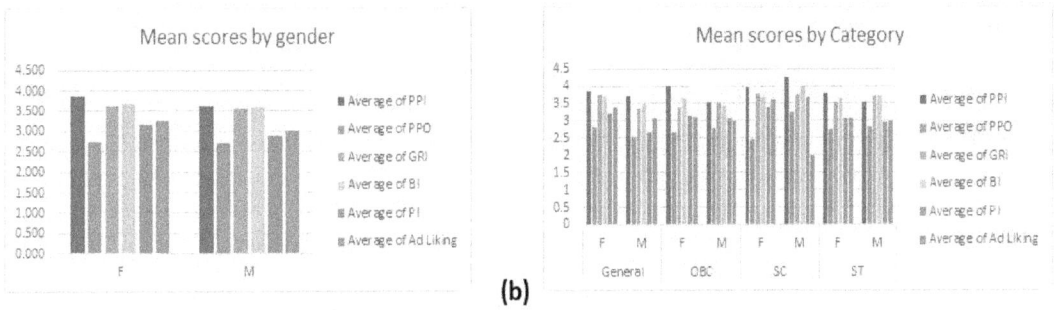

Figure 4: Representation of Mean scores based on respondents' gender and category

Figure 5: Socio-demographic profile of respondents based on (a) gender, (b) category, (c) education,

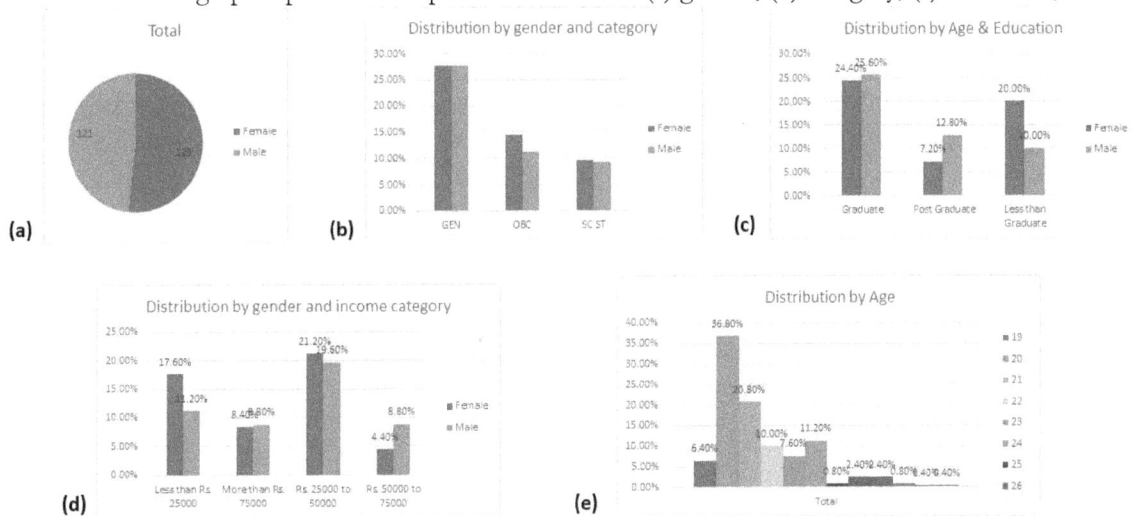

(a)   **(b)**   **(c)**

(d)   **(e)**

(d) income and (e) age

The mean score for the impact of portrayal on Brand Image (BI) is 3.65 which tells that youngster agree to the fact that such stereotypical portrayal of females affects their brand image of product/services (Table 6 and Figure 4). But when it comes to Purchase Intent (PI) people are neutral as per the mean score of the impact of portrayal on PI which is just 3.05 (Table 6 and Figure 4). It appears that young consumers are not mindful of the portrayal of females in the advertising messages of the brands while making their brand choices. Similarly, based on the mean ad-liking score of 3.14 we conclude that young consumers' ad- liking for such ads with stereotyped portrayal is close to neutral. It can be inferred that even though young audiences believe that female portrayal is an important issue they are neutral towards their actual portrayal in advertising that they are exposed to.(Please see Table6,Table 7, Figure 4 and Figure 5)

Phase 2

In Phase 2, quasi experiment was conducted keeping the scales of GRI to be same but the scales used to study the effect of advertising on Ad liking, Brand Image and Purchase Intent were slightly

39

modified. Three stereotypical and three non-stereotypical Ad posters were made and were presented to the respondents.

Socio-demographic profile

The key demographic and socioeconomic characteristics of respondents who were includedin the study are shown in Figure 5. Females constituted 51.60% of the population, while men constituted 48.40%. 36.80% of the respondents were 20 years old, followed by 20.80% 21 years old respondents constituting both male and female. Among them, both male and femalerespondents were from general category, followed by OBC and SC. The 24.40% female and 25.60% were found to have completed their graduation. The income of 21.20 % females and 19.60 % males had an interquartile range of Rs 25,000 to 50,000. (Please see Figure 5)

Gender Role Identity

Figure 6 establishes the homogeneity of the population for STT and NSTT groups, as there is no huge difference in response towards GRI by both the groups. Results suggest no significant difference between the GRI of Male and Female respondents as vindicated by the Chi-Square Test of Independence (Please see Table 8). The GRI measure for males and females does not differ significantly, emphasizing the changing mentality of the young male Indian population. (Please see Figure 6)

Perceived Portrayal Importance

Figure 7 establishes the homogeneity of the population for STT and NSTT groups, as there is very little difference in response towards PPI by both the groups. Results suggest no significant difference between the Male and Female respondents with respect to their PPI. This is further vindicated by the Chi-Square Test of Independence. (Please see Figure 7)

Ad Liking

Very little difference between the overall measure of Ad Liking between the male and female respondents was seen (Please see Figure 8). This finding is also supported by the Chi-Square test of Independence. The observed data vindicates and establishes that Ad Liking is considerably higher for non-stereotyped messages as compared to the stereotyped messages. The same gets established by the Chi-Square test of Independence also.

Brand Image (BI)

No significant difference in the measure of the overall impact on Brand Image for Male and Female consumers was observed (Please see Figure 9). The acquired data suggests that STT portrayal affects BI negatively while the NSTT portrayal has a positive impact on BI as is evident from the no. of 'High' category data in STT and NSTT treatment results. It is significant to note that among Male respondents the NSTT ad treatment has shown a positive impact on BI with 45.7% of respondents having a "high" BI score. The same gets established by the Chi-Square test of Independence also (Please see Table 8).

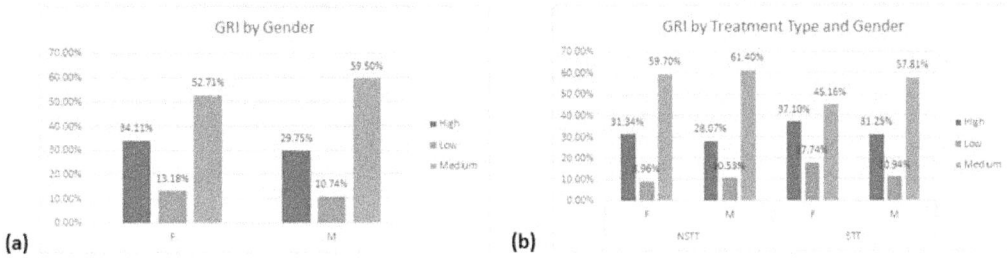

Figure 6: Graphical representation of GRI by treatment type and gender

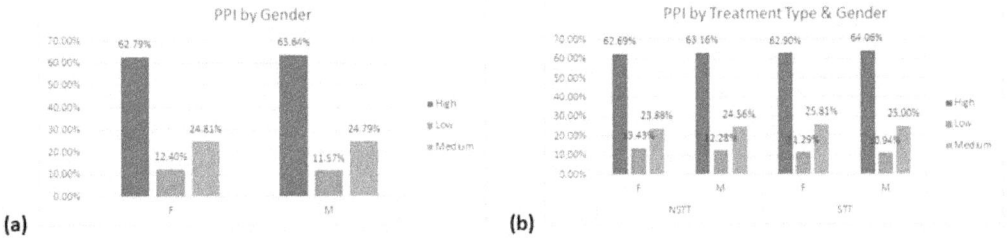

Figure 7: Graphical representation of PPI by treatment type and gende

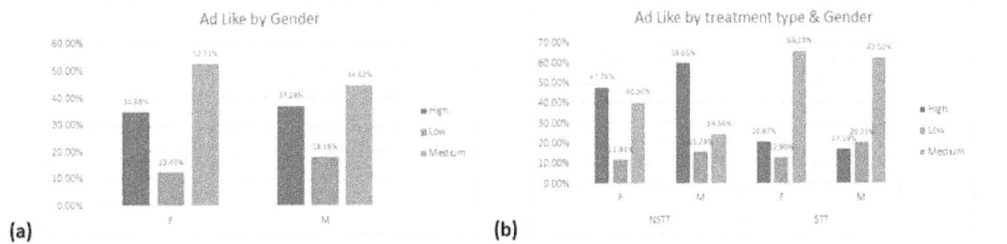

Figure 8: Graphical representation of Ad Liking by treatment type and gender

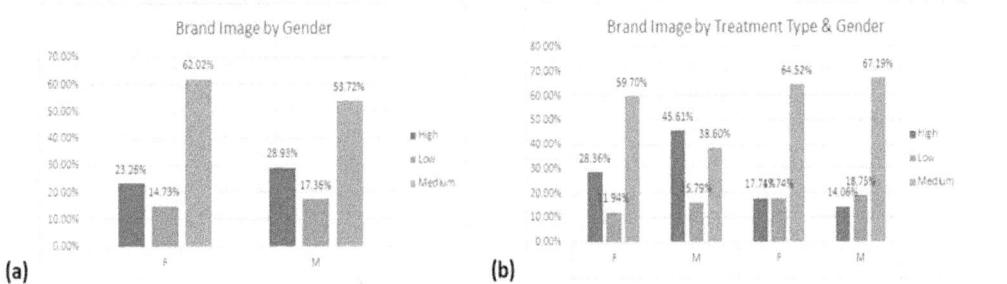

Figure 9: Graphical representation of Brand Image by treatment type and gender

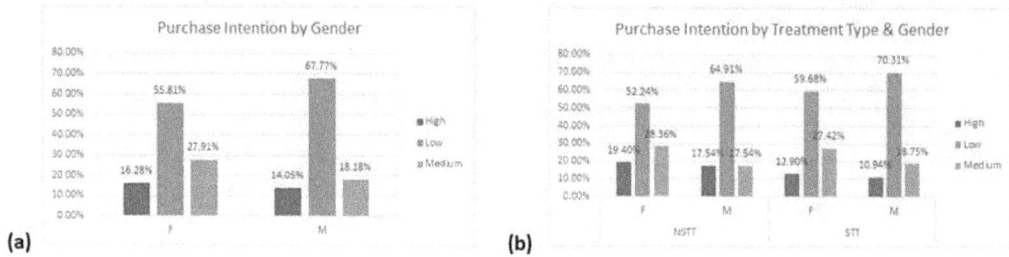

Figure 10: Graphical representation of Purchase Intention by treatment type andgender

Purchase Intention

Results indicate that there is a difference in male-female response for the 'Low' PI category-as the no. of 'lows' is considerably more for the male respondents (Please see Figure 10). Though for the 'High' and 'medium' categories, the difference doesn't seem to be significant. The observed results direct that the no. of 'lows' is maximum for both NSTT and STT treatment. The same gets vindicated by the Chi-Square test of independence. This piece of information is very important as it shows that the Stereotypical portrayal is not appreciated highly as it is not increasing the PI of youngsters. The data rather suggest a comparatively better response for NSTT treatment, even though not huge (Please see Table 8).

Interpretation of the ANOVA Results

Table 9 shows that there is a substantial variation in the results when different treatmentkinds are considered. From the cut-off value of 0.05, the F-value is significantly greater than F-Crit, and the P-value is quite low (due to negative exponential value). The column data shows that there is no significant difference in the outcomes for BI and Ad Liking between the two genders. However, the treatment kinds and their link to the gender wise response datafor BI and Ad Liking, as revealed by the interaction data, show a considerable difference. TheF-value is also higher than the F-Crit, and the P-value is quite low. This implies that respondents had higher favorable replies for non-stereotyped depiction in terms of Brand Image and Ad Liking, but there is no significant difference between male and female respondents. Furthermore, it is obvious that the influence of communication on the type of representation on the actual purchase choice of customers is negligible. (Please see Table 9)

Discussion

In the phase 1, it was found that the majority of respondents, irrespective of gender are less offensive towards the stereotypical role portrayal of a woman in Ads (measured by PPO).

Also, female respondent showed higher intolerance for such ads as compared to men. Furthermore, we discovered that a considerable number of female respondents find such depictions less offensive. While on the other side, all male SC category respondents found stereotyped depictions of women in advertisements insulting. It was interesting to find that all categories have high Gender Role Identity but the level of GRI is remarkable for SC which is 100%. However, females in a lower-income group show lower GRI; somewhat showed their oppressed state of mind.

Results also showed that majority of the youngsters agree with the idea of female freedom but they consider portrayal of females in Ads as crucial, but is not reflected in the PPO measurement. It was

42

also found that the positive feminine role orientation indicated by GRI is positively related to the perceived importance of female portrayal in advertising. Past studies done in India on female portrayal in advertising have concluded that the portrayal is largely stereotyped in an offensive manner, but this empirical study do not corroborate the findings of those studies. This research shows that youngsters agree stereotypical portrayal of females affects their brand image of product/services but Purchase Intent (PI) has no impact on it. Therefore, young consumers though agree but are not mindful with respect to ad liking or brand choices.

In phase 2, it was seen that the GRI measure for males and females does not differ significantly, emphasizing the changing mentality of the young male Indian population. Moreover, there was no significant difference between the Male and Female respondents with respect to their PPI. Also, very little difference was seen between male and female with respect to Ad Liking. But Ad Liking was found considerably higher for non-stereotyped messages with respect to the stereotyped messages. However, no significant difference in the measure of the overall impact on Brand Image for Male and Female consumers. Results also indicate that the Stereotypical portrayal is not appreciated highly as it is not increasing the PI of youngsters. This implies that respondents show liking for non-stereotyped advertisements and associate with them for Brand Image and Ad Liking, but there is no significant difference between male and female respondents.

Moving away from the contributions of this study, results of this research are in accordance with the past studies done by Mayer et al. (2019), Paliwoda et al. (2009) and Sharma and Bumb (2021). Although with changing scenarios, female role portrayals have started to change in advertisements (Teng et al., 2020), the same is still in very nascent stage in India.

Implications

Theoretical implications

Findings of this study have significant theoretical implications. It shows that the perceived offensiveness of female representation does not change across those who have diverse opinions on women's roles in society. The PPI score demonstrates that not only do the majority of young people agree with the concept of female liberty but that the representation of women in advertisements is also a crucial concern for them. According to the data, young people generally agree that female depiction in marketing is important to them, but they are likely to miss the offensiveness of such adverts owing to their inherent prejudices. According to the study, stereotyped portrayals of women have an influence on their brand image of products/services and have a lower impact on purchase intent and ad likeliness. It may be deduced that, while young people agree that female depiction is an essential problem, they are unconcerned about how women are portrayed in advertising. The obtained results reveal that respondents have a higher favorable reaction in terms of Brand Image and Ad Liking for Non-Stereotyped representation, however, there is no significant difference between Male and Female respondents' responses. However, the communicative influence of depiction type on actual customer purchasing decisions is negligible. The representation of women in the advertising of the brands they contemplate or buy has been found to have no effect on the purchase intention of young customers, or in other words, their brand choice.

Managerial Implications

This study brings forward significant managerial implications for marketers and businesses. As the results highlight, when it comes to brand selections, it appears that young customers are unconcerned with how females are portrayed in brand advertising messaging. Hence, advertisers should not rely too much on stereotyped female representation in advertising since it does not assist young consumers to develop favorable brand preferences for the marketed products. Instead, businesses should create commercials that affirm and stimulate women's progressive roles, reflecting the evolving condition of women in Indian society. The societal influence of such statements in the media might offer independent and working women a voice in making decisions. This can help marketers gain significant long-term rewards by establishing their brand as a trustworthy and socially responsible one. This highlights the necessity for a social marketing strategy to alter people's values throughout their lives, beginning in elementary school.

Limitations and Future Research

There are significant limitations to the current study that must be acknowledged and addressed. Firstly, this study is limited to only two cities Mumbai and Ranchi. Moreover, only young individuals of age group 17 to 27 were included for the study using convenience sampling method. Therefore, deeper research is required using a more representative sample to generalize the findings. Secondly, the authors have tried their best to conduct literature review through various sources. Still there is a possibility of inclusion of more research papers which could build a broader dimension of the variables of interest for this study. Thirdly, data collection was done in two phases but there was no control of the participant's mood at the time of survey. Future researches can apply other statistical tools and more creative ways of data collection. Also, the scales reported in this study met the bare minimum of reliability requirements, they might be enhanced and adjusted for greater reliability by including different geographical regions and a larger sample size. Similarstudies of the other study regions would add breadth and depth to our research findings, since the Indian market is not only large but also geographically spread, with a wide range of geographies, religions, languages, economies, and cultures. This study in particular investigated the impact of female role portrayal in advertising upon brand image, purchase intention and ad liking. Future studies can also cater to the other aspects of consumer behavior like repurchase intentions and brand loyalty to gain a deeper knowledge. Also, it would be interesting to compare the role of male and female role portrayal in advertisements. Advertising agencies should also be included in the survey to gain more insights (Redij, 2021).

Declaration of Conflicting Interests

In line with the research objectives, authorship, and/or dissemination of this work, the author reported no potential conflicts of interest.

Funding

For the research, authorship, and/or publishing of this paper, the author received financial assistance from Indian Council of Social Science Research.

References

Ahmed, S. (2016). Impact of Advertising on Consumers' buying behavior through Persuasiveness, Brand Image, and Celebrity endorsement. *Global Media Journal, 6*(2), 149.

Ali, S., & Shahwar, D. (2011). The representation of men and women in the advertisementsof Pakistani electronic media. *Journal of Media and Communication Studies, 3*(4), 151– 159. https://doi.org/10.5897/JMCS.9000048

Anand, R. (2013). Gender stereotyping in Indian recruitment advertisements: A contentanalysis. *International Journal of Business Governance and Ethics, 8*(4), 306–322.https://doi.org/10.1504/IJBGE.2013.059161

Baack, D. W., Wilson, R. T., van Dessel, M. M., & Patti, C. H. (2016). Advertising to businesses: Does creativity matter? *Industrial Marketing Management, 55*, 169–177. https://doi.org/10.1016/j.indmarman.2015.10.001

Browne, B. A. (1998). Gender stereotypes in advertising on children's television in the 1990s:A cross-national analysis. *Journal of advertising, 27*(1), 83-96.

Chan, K., Leung ng, Y., & Williams, R. B. (2012). What do adolescent girls learn about gender roles from advertising images? *Young Consumers, 13*(4), 357–366. https://doi.org/10.1108/17473611211282608

Chan, K., Tufte, B., Cappello, G., & Williams, R. B. (2011). Tween girls' perception of gender roles and gender identities: A qualitative study. *Young Consumers, 12*(1), 66–81. https://doi.org/10.1108/17473611111114795

Chan, T. Y., Wu, C., & Xie, Y. (2011). Measuring the lifetime value of customers acquired from google search advertising. *Marketing Science, 30*(5), 837-850.

Cheng, H. (1997). 'Holding up half of the sky'? A sociocultural comparison of gender-roleportrayals in Chinese and US advertising. *International Journal of Advertising, 16*(4), 295-319.

Courtney, A. E., & Lockeretz, S. W. (1971). A Woman's Place: An Analysis of the Roles Portrayed by Women in Magazine Advertisements. *Journal of Marketing Research,8*(1), 92–95. https://doi.org/10.1177/002224377100800114

Dahlén, M., Rosengren, S., & Törn, F. (2008). Advertising creativity matters. *Journal of Advertising Research, 48*(3), 392–403. https://doi.org/10.2501/S002184990808046X

Das, Madhusmita, & Sharma, S. (2016). Portrayal of Women in Indian TV Advertisements: A Study of Audience Perception. *IUP Journal of Marketing Management, 15*(3), 57–94.

Das, Mallika. (2000). Men and women in Indian magazine advertisements: A preliminary report. *Sex Roles, 43*(9–10), 699– 717. https://doi.org/10.1023/a:1007108725661

Das, Mallika. (2011). Gender Role Portrayals in Indian Television Ads. *Sex Roles, 64*(3), 208–222. https://doi.org/10.1007/s11199-010-9750-1

Dijksterhuis, A., Spears, R., & Lépinasse, V. (2001). Reflecting and Deflecting Stereotypes: Assimilation and Contrast in Impression Formation and Automatic Behavior. *Journal of Experimental Social Psychology, 37*(4), 286–299. https://doi.org/10.1006/jesp.2000.1449

Drake, V. E. (2017). The Impact of Female Empowerment in Advertising (Femvertising).Journal of Research in Marketing, 7(3), 593–599.

Dwivedy, A. K., Patnaik, P., & Suar, D. (2009). Role portrayals of men and women in print ads. *Psychological Studies, 54*(3), 171–183. https://doi.org/10.1007/s12646-009-0024-3

Eisend, M. (2019) Gender Roles. *Journal of Advertising* 48(1): 72–80.

Fatima, S. (2015). Impact of Advertisement on Buying Behaviours of the consumers : Study of Cosmetic Industry in Karachi City . *International Journal of Management Sciences and Business Research, 4*(10), 125–137.

Furnham, A., & Farragher, E. (2000). A cross-cultural content analysis of sex-role stereotyping in television advertisements: A comparison between Great Britain and New Zealand. *Journal of Broadcasting & Electronic Media, 44*(3), 415-436.

Furnham, A., & Voli, V. (1989). Gender Stereotypes in Italian Television Advertisements. *Journal of Broadcasting & Electronic Media, 33*(2), 175–185.https://doi.org/10.1080/08838158909364071

Furnham, A., Babitzkow, M., & Uguccioni, S. (2000). Gender stereotyping in television advertisements: A study of French and Danish television. *Genetic, social, and general psychology monographs, 126*(1), 79.

Galli, E. (2011). Kahneman, D., Thinking, Fast and Slow. *Journal of Public Finance and Public.*

Gilly, M. C. (1988). Sex Roles in Advertising: A Comparison of Television Advertisementsin Australia, Mexico, and the United States. *Journal of Marketing, 52*(2), 75–85. https://doi.org/10.1177/002224298805200206

Grau, S. L., & Zotos, Y. C. (2016). Gender stereotypes in advertising: A review of current research. *International Journal of Advertising, 35*(5), 761–770. https://doi.org/10.1080/02650487.2016.1203556

Gulas, C. S., & McKeage, K. (2000). Extending social comparison: An examination of the unintended consequences of idealized advertising imagery. *Journal ofadvertising, 29*(2), 17-28.

Harker, M., Harker, D., & Svensen, S. (2005). Attitudes Towards Gender Portrayal in Advertising: An Australian Perspective. *Journal of Marketing Management, 21*(1–2), 251–264. https://doi.org/10.1362/0267257053166820

Hartnett, N., Kennedy, R., Sharp, B., & Greenacre, L. (2016). Creative that sells: How advertising execution affects sales. *Journal of Advertising, 45*(1), 102–112.https://doi.org/10.1080/00913367.2015.1077491

Herz, M. F., & Diamantopoulos, A. (2013). Activation of country stereotypes: Automaticity, consonance, and impact. *Journal of the Academy of Marketing Science, 41*(4), 400–417. https://doi.org/10.1007/s11747-012-0318-1

Houston, E. (2019). 'Risky' representation: the portrayal of women with mobility impairmentin twenty-first-century advertising. *Disability and Society, 34*(5), 704–725. https://doi.org/10.1080/09687599.2019.1576505

Kang, M. E. (1997). The portrayal of women's images in magazine advertisements:Goffman's gender analysis revisited. *Sex roles*, *37*(11), 979-996.

Kawakami, K., Young, H., & Dovidio, J. F. (2002). Automatic stereotyping: Category, trait, and behavioral activations. *Personality and Social Psychology Bulletin*, *28*(1), 3–15. https://doi.org/10.1177/0146167202281001

Kumar, D. D. P. (2013). The Role of Advertising in Consumer Decision Making. *IOSR Journal of Business and Management*, *14*(4), 37–45. https://doi.org/10.9790/487x- 1443745

Kumari, S., & Shivani, S. (2013). A Content Analysis of Female Portrayals in Indian Magazine Advertisements. *3rd Biennial Conference of the Indian Academy ofManagement (IAM)*, 1–30.

Kumari, S., & Shivani, S. (2015a). Mapping the portrayal of females in contemporary indian advertisements. *MediaWatch*, *6*(2), 173–187.https://doi.org/10.15655/mw/2015/v6i2/65660

Kumari, S., & Shivani, S. (2015b). Female Portrayals in Advertising and Its Impact on Marketing Communication—Pieces of Evidence from India: *Management and Labour Studies*, *39*(4), 438–448. https://doi.org/10.1177/0258042X15578022

Lane, W. R., King, K. W., & Russell, J. T. (2005). *Kleppner's Advertising Procedure: International Edition*. Pearson Prentice Hall.

Lauer, L. D. (2007). Advertising can be an effective integrated marketing tool. *Journal of Marketing for Higher Education*, *17*(1), 13–15. https://doi.org/10.1300/J050v17n01_03

Lavine, H., Sweeney, D., & Wagner, S. H. (1999). Depicting Women as Sex Objects in Television Advertising: Effects on Body Dissatisfaction. *Personality and Social Psychology Bulletin*, *25*(8), 1049–1058. https://doi.org/10.1177/01461672992511012

Lysonski, S. (1985). Role Portrayals in British Magazine Advertisements. *European Journal of Marketing*, *19*(7), 37–55. https://doi.org/10.1108/EUM0000000004724

Matthes, J., Prieler, M., & Adam, K. (2016). Gender-Role Portrayals in Television Advertising Across the Globe. *Sex Roles*, *75*(7–8), 314–327. https://doi.org/10.1007/s11199-016-0617-y

Mayer, J. M., Kumar, P., & Yoon, H. J. (2019). Does sexual humor work on mars, but not on Venus? An exploration of consumer acceptance of sexually humorous advertising. *International Journal of Advertising*, *38*(7), 1000-1024.

Mazzella, C., Durkin, K., Cerini, E., & Buralli, P. (1992). Sex role stereotyping in Australian television advertisements. *Sex Roles*, *26*(7–8), 243–259.https://doi.org/10.1007/BF00289910

McArthur, L. Z., & Resko, B. G. (1975). The portrayal of men and women in american television commercials. *Journal of Social Psychology*, *97*(2), 209–220.https://doi.org/10.1080/00224545.1975.9923340

McCulloch, C. (1981). Sex-role stereotyping in British television advertisements. *British Journal of Social Psychology*, *20*(3), 171–180. https://doi.org/10.1111/j.2044- 8309.1981.tb00529.x

Mckenzie, M., Webster, A., & Bugden, M. (2018). Advertising (in)equality: the impacts of sexist advertising on women's health and wellbeing. *Women's Health Issues Paper*, *14*, 1–40.

Middleton, K., & Turnbull, S. (2021). How advertising got 'woke': The institutional role ofadvertising in the emergence of gender progressive market logics and practices. *Marketing Theory*, *21*(4), 561-578.

Milner, L. M., & Higgs, B. (2004). Gender sex-role portrayals in international television advertising over time: The australian experience. *Journal of Current Issues and Research in Advertising*, *26*(2), 81–95. https://doi.org/10.1080/10641734.2004.10505166

Morrison, M. M., & Shaffer, D. R. (2003). Gender-role congruence and self-referencing as determinants of advertising effectiveness. In *Sex Roles* (Vol. 49, Issues 5–6, pp. 265– 275). Springer. https://doi.org/10.1023/A:1024604424224

MuhammadAwan, A. G., Ismail, Majeed, F., & Ghazal, F. (2016). Effects of Advertisement on Consumer's Buying Behaviour with References to FMCGs in Southern Punjab-Pakistan. *Journal of Marketing and Consumer Research Journal*, *19*(2015), 22–30.

Mwangi, M. W. (1996). Gender roles portrayed in Kenyan television commercials. *Sex Roles*, *34*(3–4), 205–214. https://doi.org/10.1007/BF01544296

Odekerken-Schröder, G., De Wulf, K., & Hofstee, N. (2002). Is gender stereotyping inadvertising more prevalent in masculine countries? A cross-national analysis. *International MarketingReview*, *19*(4), 408–419.https://doi.org/ 10.1108/ 02651330210435690

Orth, U. R., & Holancova, D. (2004). Men's and women's responses to sex role portrayals in advertisements. *International Journal of Research in Marketing*, *21*(1), 77–88. https://doi.org/10.1016/j.ijresmar.2003.05.003

Paek, H. J., Nelson, M. R., & Vilela, A. M. (2011). Examination of Gender-role Portrayals in Television Advertising across Seven Countries. *Sex Roles*, *64*(3), 192–207. https://doi.org/10.1007/s11199-010-9850-y

Paliwoda, S. J., Slater, S., Liu, F., Cheng, H., & Li, J. (2009). Consumer responses to sex appeal advertising: a cross-cultural study. *International marketing review*.

Pellicer, M. (2017). Advertising and its Social Responsability. *Revested Comunicacion Vivat Academia*, *19*(139), 43–51.

Prieler, M., Ivanov, A., & Hagiwara, S. (2015). Gender representations in East Asian advertising: Hong Kong, Japan, and South Korea. In Communication and Society (Vol. 28, Issue 1, pp. 27–42). Universidad de Navarra. https://doi.org/10.15581/003.28.1.27-41

Rai, N. (2013). Impact of advertising on consumer behaviour and attitude with reference to consumer durables. *International Journal of Management Research and Business Marketing*, 58–65.

Redij, A. (2021, April). Evolution Of Gender Stereotypes In Advertising. In Multi-Disciplinary Inter-Collegiate Online Student Resea Rch Convention 2021 Changing dynamics of Covid er a: new nor ma l in society and industry (Vol. 9, No. 2, p. 221).

Ross, S. A. (1977). The Determination of Financial Structure: The Incentive-Signalling Approach. *The Bell Journal of Economics*, *8*(1), 23. https://doi.org/10.2307/3003485

Royo-Vela, M., Aldás-Manzano, J., & Küster-Boluda, I. (2007). Gender role portrayals and sexism in Spanish magazines. *Equal Opportunities International*, *26*(7), 633–652. https://doi.org/10.1108/02610150710822285

Sandhu, N. (2019). Fueling Gender Stereotypes: A Content Analysis of Automobile Advertisements. *Business Perspectives and Research*, *7*(2), 163–178. https://doi.org/10.1177/2278533719833815

Sharma, S., & Bumb, A. (2021). Role Portrayal of Women in Advertising: An Empirical Study. *Journal of International Women's Studies*, *22*(9), 236-255.

Shaw, M. E., & Wright, J. M. (1967). *Scales for the measurement of attitudes*. McGraw-Hill.

Theodoridis, P. K., Kyrousi, A. G., Zotou, A. Y., & Panigyrakis, G. G. (2013). Male and female attitudes towards stereotypical advertisements: A paired country investigation. *Corporate Communications*, *18*(1), 135–160. https://doi.org/10.1108/13563281311294173

Tuncay Zayer, L., & Coleman, C. A. (2015). Advertising professionals' perceptions of the impact of gender portrayals on men and women: a question of ethics?. *Journal of Advertising*, *44*(3), 1-12.

Verhellen, Y., Dens, N., & de Pelsmacker, P. (2016). A longitudinal content analysis of gender role portrayal in Belgian television advertising. *Journal of Marketing Communications*, *22*(2), 170–188. https://doi.org/10.1080/13527266.2013.871321

West, D., Koslow, S., & Kilgour, M. (2019). Future Directions for Advertising Creativity Research. *Journal of Advertising*, *48*(1), 102–114. https://doi.org/10.1080/00913367.2019.1585307

Ye, L., Ashley-Cotleur, C., & Gaumer, C. (2012). Do Women Still Hold Up Half the Sky? Portrayal of Women in Chinese Advertising: 1980-2001. *Journal of Marketing Development and Competitiveness*, *6*(3), 67–82.

Zhou, N., & Chen, M. Y. (1997). A content analysis of men and women in Canadian consumer magazine advertising: Today's portrayal, yesterday's image?. *Journal of Business Ethics*, 485-495.

List of Tables and figures

Table 1: Source of variables selected to measure marketing communication

Variable	Definition	Sources
Gender RoleIdentity	It is a twelve-statement scale to measurethe role identity of people.	Shaw, M.E. and Wright, J.M. Scales for the Measurement of Attitudes. New York:Mcgraw-Hill,1967
Perceived Role Offensiveness	It is a four-statement scale to measure the sensitiveness of respondents towards the stereotypical female role portrayal.	Ford et al (1991), Ford andLaTour (1996), Harker (2005) and Lundstrom et al (1999).
Perceived Portrayal Importance	It is a self-developed four statement scale to find out if at all stereotypical female role portrayal is important forrespondents.	Self —constructed and testedfor validity
Ad Liking	Liking is assessed in terms of how much you like the Ad and how much you like the brand. According to theAdvertising Research Foundation (ARF), one of the best indicators of customer action is liking for the brand or Ad. As a result, Ad liking and brand liking are chosen as marketing communication measuring scales.	Kanungo & Johar (1975),Stafford (1998), Reichert (2002), Wells et. al., (2008)
Brand Image	It is described as a consumer's mental impression of a product or brand. It's the image that customers have of a certain brand.	Severn et. al, (1990), Low & Lamb Jr (2000), Harker et.al., (2005), Zimmeiman & Dahlberg (2008), Wells et. al, (2008), Lee (2012)
Intention tobuy	It is the probability that a buyer will purchase a specific product or brand.	Kanungo & Johar (1975),Severn et. al., (1990), Stafford (1998), Orth & Holancova (2004), Harker et. al., (2005), Zimmerman & Dahlberg (2008), Wells et. al., (2008), Lee (2012)

Table 2: Results of Perceived Portrayal Offensiveness based on respondents' genderand category

% PPO	PPO Category		
Gender	High (%)	Low (%)	Grand Total (%)
Female	23.77	33.61	57.38
Male	18.03	24.59	42.62
	41.80	58.20	100.00
Category			
Female	41.43	58.57	100.00
General	38.98	61.02	100.00
OBC	37.50	62.50	100.00
SC	22.22	77.78	100.00
ST	48.21	51.79	100.00
Male	42.31	57.69	100.00
General	41.46	58.54	100.00
OBC	38.89	61.11	100.00
SC	100.00	0.00	100.00
ST	43.18	56.82	100.00
	41.80	58.20	100.00

Table 3: Results of Perceived Portrayal Offensiveness based on respondents' income

% PPO	Category				
Income	General (%)	OBC (%)	SC (%)	ST (%)	Total (%)
High	40.40	12.12	3.03	44.44	100.00
Less than Rs.25000	40.63	6.25	0.00	53.13	100.00
Rs.25000 to 50000	25.00	14.29	3.57	57.14	100.00
Rs.50000 to 75000	50.00	30.00	0.00	20.00	100.00
Rs.75000 and above	52.63	0.00	10.53	36.84	100.00
Low	42.03	15.22	5.07	37.68	100.00
Less than Rs.25000	34.29	11.43	5.71	48.57	100.00
Rs.25000 to 50000	34.00	24.00	2.00	40.00	100.00
Rs.50000 to 75000	33.33	7.41	7.41	51.85	100.00
Rs.75000 and above	76.92	11.54	7.69	3.85	100.00
	41.35	13.92	4.22	40.51	100.00

Table 4: Results of Gender Role Identity based on respondents' category

% GRI	GRI Category		
	High (%)	Low (%)	Total (%)
General	87.00	13.00	100.00
OBC	82.35	17.65	100.00
SC	100.00	0.00	100.00
ST	93.00	7.00	100.00
	89.34	10.66	100.00

Table 5: Results of Gender Role Identity based on respondents' category

% GRI	Income				
	Less than Rs.25000 (%)	Rs.25000 to 50000 (%)	Rs.50000 to 75000 (%)	Rs.75000 and above (%)	Total (%)
High	26.89	32.55	21.23	19.34	100.00
Female	22.31	36.36	24.79	16.53	100.00
Male	32.97	27.47	16.48	23.08	100.00
Low	40.00	36.00	8.00	16.00	100.00
Female	53.85	38.46	7.69	0.00	100.00
Male	25.00	33.33	8.33	33.33	100.00
	28.27	32.91	19.83	18.99	100.00

Table 6: Results of Mean scores based on respondents' gender and category

	Average of PPI	Average of PPO	Average of GRI	Average of BI	Average of PI	Average of Ad Liking
Gender						
Female	3.858	2.743	3.613	3.671	3.157	3.245
Male	3.622	2.709	3.543	3.573	2.872	3.005
	3.758	2.728	3.583	3.629	3.036	3.142
Category						
General	3.809	2.695	3.582	3.612	2.993	3.264
OBC	3.765	2.735	3.470	3.524	3.108	3.044
SC	4.000	2.550	3.767	3.700	3.433	3.450
ST	3.679	2.778	3.605	3.676	3.013	3.023
	3.758	2.728	3.583	3.629	3.036	3.142

Table 7: Hypothesis testing results

S.No.	Hypothesis	R^2	Std. Error of estimate	Durban-Watson	Coefficients		Supported
1	GRI PPI	0.046	0.542	1.74	Beta	0.150	Yes.
					t	3.830	Predictive and linear
					Sig	0.001	relationship is established.
2	GRI PPO	0.002	0.738	1.98	Beta	0.039	No
					t	0.603	
					Sig	0.547	

Table 8: Independent Samples Test: Differences between Males and Females

		Female (Observed)	Male (Observed)	Total	FemaleExpected	O-E	(O-E)²	(O-E)²/E	Male Expected	O-E	(O-E)²	(O-E)²/E	Chi stat	df	Crit Value
Genderwise GRI	High	44	36	80	41.28	2.7	7.4	0.2	38.7	-2.72	7.4	0.2	1	2	6
	Medium	68	72	140	72.24	-4	17.98	0.3	67.8	4.24	17.9	0.3			
	Low	17	13	30	15.48	1.5	2.31	0.2	14.5	-1.52	2.31	0.2			
	Total	129	121	250				0.6				0.6			
GenderwisePPI	High	81	77	158	81.53	-1	0.28	0	76.5	0.53	0.28	0	0	2	6
	Medium	32	30	62	31.99	0	0	0	30	-0.01	0	0			
	Low	16	14	30	15.48	0.5	0.27	0	14.5	-0.52	0.27	0			
	Total	129	121	250				0				0			
Genderwise Ad Like Observed values(STT)	High	13	11	24	11.81	1.2	1.42	0.1	12.2	-1.19	1.42	0.1	1	2	6
	Medium	41	40	81	39.86	1.1	1.31	0	41.1	-1.14	1.31	0			
	Low	8	13	21	10.33	-2	5.44	0.5	10.7	2.33	5.44	0.5			
	Total	62	64	126				0.7				0.7			
Genderwise Ad Like Observed values(NSTT)	High	32	34	66	35.66	-4	13.41	0.4	30.3	3.6	13.41	0.4	3	2	6
	Medium	27	14	41	22.15	4.9	23.49	1.1	18.9	-4.85	23.49	1.3			
	Low	8	9	17	9.19	-1	1.41	0.2	7.81	1.19	1.41	0.2			
	Total	67	57	124				1.6				1.9			
Genderwise Brand Image – BI Observed values(STT)	High	11	9	20	9.84	1.2	1.34	0.1	10.2	-1.6	1.34	0.1	0	2	6
	Medium	40	43	83	40.84	-1	0.71	0	42.2	0.84	0.71	0			
	Low	11	12	23	11.32	-0	0.1	0	11.7	0.32	0.1	0			
	Total	62	64	126				0.2				0.2			
Genderwise Brand Image – BI Observed values (NSTT)	High	19	26	45	24.31	-5	28.24	1.2	20.7	5.31	28.24	1.4	6	2	6
	Medium	40	22	62	33.5	6.5	2.25	1.3	28.5	-6.5	42.25	1.5			
	Low	8	9	17	9.19	-1	1.41	0.2	7.81	1.19	1.41	0.2			
	Total	67	57	124				2.6				3			
Genderwise Purchase Intention-PI Observed values(STT)	High	8	7	15	7.38	0.6	0.38	0.1	7.62	-0.62	0.38	0.1	2	2	6
	Medium	17	12	29	14.27	2.7	7.45	0.5	14.7	-2.73	7.45	0.5			
	Low	37	45	82	40.35	-3	11.22	0.3	41.7	3.35	11.22	0.3			
	Total	62	64	126				0.9				0.8			
Genderwise Purchase Intention-PI Observed values(NSTT)	High	13	10	23	12.43	0.6	0.33	0	10.6	-0.57	0.33	0	2	2	6
	Medium	19	10	29	15.67	3.3	11.09	0.7	13.3	-3.33	11.09	0.8			
	Low	35	37	72	38.9	-4	15.24	0.4	33.1	3.9	15.24	0.5			
	Total	67	57	124				1.1				1.3			

Table 9: Results of ANOVA

Treatment Type	BI(Males)	BI(Females)	Ad Like (Males)	Ad like (Females)	Total	
Housewife						
Count	20.00	20.00	20.00	20.00	80.00	
Sum	54.83	62.67	54.00	62.83	234.33	
Average	2.74	3.13	2.70	3.14	2.93	
Variance	0.37	0.43	0.46	0.34	0.43	
Dependent						
Count	20.00	20.00	20.00	20.00	80.00	
Sum	56.50	56.00	56.67	56.83	226.00	
Average	2.83	2.80	2.83	2.84	2.83	
Variance	0.23	0.33	0.21	0.27	0.25	
Decorative						
Count	20.00	20.00	20.00	20.00	80.00	
Sum	51.33	53.50	47.50	54.50	206.83	
Average	2.57	2.68	2.38	2.73	2.59	
Variance	0.61	0.24	0.68	0.50	0.51	
Bossy						
Count	20.00	20.00	20.00	20.00	80.00	
Sum	64.00	61.83	65.67	63.00	254.50	
Average	3.20	3.09	3.28	3.15	3.18	
Variance	0.48	0.50	0.71	0.09	0.43	
Professional						
Count	20.00	20.00	20.00	20.00	80.00	
Sum	73.50	66.33	88.67	72.83	301.33	
Average	3.68	3.32	4.43	3.64	3.77	
Variance	0.77	0.34	0.04	0.32	0.52	
Sporty						
Count	20.00	20.00	20.00	20.00	80.00	
Sum	79.33	79.83	76.97	88.50	324.63	
Average	3.97	3.99	3.85	4.43	4.06	
Variance	0.40	0.10	0.76	0.03	0.36	
Total						
Count	120.00	120.00	120.00	120.00		
Sum	379.50	380.17	389.47	398.49		
Average	3.16	3.17	3.25	3.32		
Variance	0.72	0.49	0.96	0.58		

ANOVA Source of Variation	SS	df	MS	F	P-value	F crit
Sample	131.65	5	26.33	68.60	2.14E-53	2.23
Columns	2.01	3	0.67	1.74	0.16	2.62
Interaction	20.58	15	1.37	3.58	7.04E-06	1.69
Within	175.01	456	0.38			
Total	329.25	479				

CHAPTER 4

DETERMINANTS OF PURCHASE INTENTIONS TOWARDS GREEN MOBILES – AN EXTENSION OF THE THEORY OF PLANNED BEHAVIOUR (TPB)

Deepa Rohit[1], Ravi Vaidee[2], Vaishali Patil[3]

Introduction

The Indian economy consistently experienced an upward growth and is now the world's 3rd largest economy, with only the United States of America (USA)and China ahead; and third largest in terms of Purchasing Power Parity (PPP) (IBEF, 2021). India's GDP is pegged at $ 2.9 trillion, estimated to reach a whopping $ 5 trillion by 2024 and $ 10 trillion by 2030 or 2031 (investindia.gov.in, 2019). According to the World Economic Forum (2019), India's market size is pegged to grow at a thriving $ 6 trillion in the coming years (Future of Consumption in Fast-Growth Consumer Market – India, 2019). However, such a prodigious growth has also been at the cost of cultural changes, mass consumption of nature and natural resources giving way to developing infrastructure and urbanization, changing consumer trends and consumption patterns, demanding consumers', leading to a new wave consumerism.Furthermore, the rise in consumer demand has led to a higher and greater consumption causing a virtuous and vicious cycle of demand, manufacture, consumption; leaving behind a huge amount of waste arising out of unusable, non-recyclable products (Booi Chen & Teck Chai, 2010; Joshi & Rahman, 2015). While, such wastes can be attributed to all industries and sectors, the packaging & electronic industries, in particular the computer, computer component segment and the telecommunication sector – specifically mobile handsets appearto be major contributors of e-waste, currently in India.

Mobile phones are necessity in the current connected and virtual world. Currently, 2200 billion mobile handsets are manufactured only in India (India: Value of Mobile Phone Production, 2021). Indian telecom industry is the world's 2nd largest market with a subscriber base of 1.16billion out of a 1.3 billion population base with the mobile economy growing and contributingsubstantially to India's Gross Domestic Product (GDP) according to a report prepared by GSM Association (GSMA) in collaboration with Boston Consulting Group (BCG) (www.ibef.com; 2021). The necessity for this study is reinforced all the more necessary by the telecom industry's PAN India penetration rate of over 95% and its role as a significant producer of electronic trash by way of outdated, useless phones. The study gets enormous relevance from a business or industry perspective because it is a company or industry that manufactures and markets such phones. Therefore, contacting the generator's source will aid in resolving this major challenge.

---

[1] Dr. Deepa Rohit, Associate Professor, S. P. Mandali's, Prin. L.N. Welingkar Institute of Management Development & Research, L N Road, Matunga (CR), Mumbai- 400019, India. E-mail: deepa.rohit@welingkar.org
[2] Prof. Ravi Vaidee, Deputy Dean (Marketing- Academics), S. P. Mandali's, Prin. L.N. Welingkar Institute of Management Development & Research, L N Road, Matunga (CR), Mumbai- 400019, India. E-mail: ravi.vaidee@welingkar.org
[3] Dr. Vaishali Patil, Senior Associate Dean- Research & Publications & Information Technology, S. P. Mandali's, Prin. L.N. Welingkar Institute of Management Development & Research, L N Road, Matunga (CR), Mumbai- 400019, India. E-mail: vaishali.patil@welingkar.org

Even while the above scenario of e-waste was growing, eco-system was experiencing a new wave thinking arising out of a global awareness and sensitization movement towards sustainability. Recognizing the growing need for sustainable developments, marketers are focusing on eco-innovation and green products, thus enabling green consumption. Green consumption relates to consumer disposition towards purchasing, using and disposing off environmentally responsible products (Moisander, 2007). Production and consumption of eco-friendly products, support to eco-innovation and green consumption, usage of renewable energy sources and reduction of plastic are some of the ways towards sustainable development (Veleva & Ellenbecker, 2001; Wijekoon & Sabri, 2021). Such initiatives towards sustainable development was further strengthened with the United Nations' Sustainability Development Goals (SDGs) set for 2030 which encouraged matured industries/marketers to quickly adopt sustainability as their goal, and thematically calling the same as Green Marketing. According to American Marketing Association; green marketing is the marketing of products that are presumed to be environmentally safe. Any marketing activity of the firm that is intended to create a positive impact or to lessen the negative impact of a product on the environment, in order to capitalize on the consumer's concern about environmental issues is known as Green Marketing (Soonthonsmai; 2007). In India, Nokia launched a campaign 'Recycle Mobile' for a short tenure, which helped a brand to gain consumer confidence and thereby create value for the brand. Likewise, these set of marketing initiatives help the organization to create value for the company and project a better image to its stakeholders.

A green product refers to products that embed environmental friendly product components in the making of such products and strategies such as recycling or with recycled content, reduced packagingor using less toxic materials post consumption of the same (Chen & Teck Chai, 2010). Prior studies have examined and proposed positive consumer behavior intentions towards green products (Nam, Dong & Lee, 2017; Vazifehdoust et al, 2013; Dilotsotlhe, 2021). Much of the studies have been based on the theoretical framework of the theory of reasoned action (TRA) and the theory of planned behavior (TPB) proposed by Ajzen (1985). Likewise, the present study is based on the TPB with an extension contextually around green mobile handsets focusing on two determinants namely, environmental awareness and environmental concern. It also seen that where individuals are concerned about environmental issues and ownresponsibility towards sustainability by his virtue or his awareness of green products, he/ sheis more likely to have a positive bend towards green products leading to a favourable behavior intention such as purchase intentions (Amel et al. 2009; De Moura et al., 2012; Mitomo & Otsuka, 2012). Many individuals view marketing as a tool to promote consumption since it places a strong emphasis on meeting customer needs.

Green marketing has developed gradually over time, and customers worldwide are becoming more concerned and interested in environmental conservation. This demonstrates unequivocally that environmental concerns are now being taken seriously by people all across the world, and as a result, their consumption and purchase habits are changing. Consumer preferences not only reflect price and quality preferences, but also social, ethical, and moral principles. As a result, people are buying and using more green and environmentally friendly items due to their growing concern for society and sense of duty. Since consumers themselves are major contributors to environmental degradation and pollution, any environmentally responsible behaviour on their part can go a long way in reducing the issue of resource depletion and bringing down pollution levels that have reached alarming heights in the nation. As a consequence of their growing environmental awareness and the resulting demand for green products, corporate organisations may feel pressure to go green and begin promoting green goods. Thus, green marketing and products enable value creation for the companies and its stakeholders.

Green consumption and consumerism as grown rapidly in the developed nations, although, ata nascent stage in developing nations like India, thus, necessitating in-depth studies in such markets (Raghavan & Vahanti, 2009; Khare, 2015; Paul et al., 2016). Consequently, the present study aims to fill the gaps by developing statistically validated model to understand the determinants of purchase intentions of Indian consumers towards green mobile handsets. The study will provide insights into consumer behavior towards green mobile handsets and will beuseful to the industry, policy makers, marketers, consumers and society at large.

The paper has been well-thought through commencing with the introduction– explaining the need and significance of the study, literature review and theoretical framework to develop research hypotheses, research methodology to justify the methods, sampling and research instrument design, the results of the data and discussion and finally implications, conclusion, limitations and scope for further study.

Literature Review

Defining green marketing & green product

Green marketing has become a mainstream strategy in current business world (Kassaye, 2001). It refers to several activities undertaken by firms that are concerned about the environment problems such as producing eco-friendly products, change in packaging, productmodification or environmental marketing (Johri, & Sahasakmontri, 1998). These environmentfriendly products that are less harmful toward nature, recyclable, biodegradable, energy efficient and renewable can be termed as green products (Makdoomi & Nazir, 2016). Chen & Chai (2010) defined green product as a product which has reduced packaging, uses less toxic raw-materials, recycled components and can be recycled. Prior studies have revealed that consumers have positive attitude towards green products and purchase intentions (Liu et al, 2012; Schmeltz, 2012; Chan & Lau, 2002; Vazifehdoust et al, 2013).

Theory of Planned Behaviour (TPB)

The theory of planned behaviour (TPB) is an extension of the theory of reasoned action (TRA) as proposed by Ajzen (1985). The TPB model posits that an individual's behaviour is dependent on one's intention to behave in a particular way, thus, behaviour intentions is a determinant to the actual behaviour (Ajzen, 1985). Moreover, the TPB suggests that the behavioural intention (BI) comprises of three determinants namely, attitude towards the behaviour, subjective norm, and the perceived behavioural control. An attitude towards behaviour (Att) denotes the overall evaluation of an individual towards the intended behaviour typically measured in the evaluation of the outcomes and importance of the outcomes. Subjective norm (SN) represents an individual's perception of the behaviour in context of the social pressure exerted by one's reference group. Additionally, the perceived behaviour control (PBC) refers to an individual's perception of the level of control he/she has while performing the behaviour (Ajzen, 2005). The TPB framework has been widely used to explain simple behaviours to complex decision making (Ajzen, 2012). Therefore, it is considered as one of the significant theoretical frameworks to predict human behaviour including purchase behaviour (Chen & Tung, 2014). Likewise, the TPB theory has been deployed in examining green purchase intentions (Kalafatiset al., 1999; Kim and Chung, 2011;Chen and Peng, 2012; Jebarajakirthy & Lobo, 2014; Kabadayi et al, 2015; Dilotsotlhe, 2021), recycling behaviour (Davis et al., 2009; Khan et al, 2019), towards green hotels (Chen & Tung, 2014), and towards green sportswear (Nam, Dong

& Lee, 2017). Therefore, the present study has used the theory of TPB as a theoretical framework to develop hypotheses and conjectured model.

Table 1. Literature Review

Author & Title	Finding
Angela Paladino & Serena Ng (2013)	This study explores subjective norms, attitudes, perceived control, environmental concern, altruism, risk aversion, price consciousness, engagement, branding, environmental knowledge, and their connection to purchase intentions utilising the theories of reasoned action and planned behaviour intention.
Von Mohrenfels H.W. & Klapper D (2012)	This paper addresses how extended packaging influences brand perception and willingness to pay. The study shows that for green products that were produced organically and sustainably, this technology can be used to heighten the brand perception.
Hsiang Te Liu & Ruey-Chyn Tsaur (2020)	The theory of reasoned action (TRA) is used in this study to examine consumers' purchase intentions and determine how brand equity, green marketing, as well as consumers' understanding of and attitudes toward the environment, affect these intentions along with the influence of government subsidies on consumers' willingness to buy environmentally friendly smartphones. In this study, environmental protection awareness is viewed as the subjective norm in the theory of reasoned action, and to some extent, it functions as a societal norm. As an extension of the theory of reasoned action and another research benefit of this study, this article also views green marketing as a consumer incentive.
Ghorai and Sengupta (2021)	The paper outlines the difficulties and knowledge around green marketing's role in mitigating environmental damage along with its needs and importance.
Sujith T S (2017)	The purpose of this study is to determine consumer attitudes, levels of awareness, and purchasing patterns toward environmentally friendly products.
Pradeep M.D., Suresh & A Kuckian (2016)	The article analyses the ramifications of green marketing in the Indian business environment.
Abdul Ghafoor Awan & Sammar Wamiq (2016)	This paper's determined the connection between environmental consciousness and green marketing
Bhavana & Thiruchanuru (2018)	The study offered a brief overview of how environmentally conscious generation Y and generation Z react to various factors, including consumer traits, marketing strategy, effects of price and quality, advertisements, and the most crucial elements influencing consumers' decisions to buy green products. For the purpose of examining green consumer behaviour during decision making process.
Tiwari (2014)	The discusses the difficulties that green marketing faces while describing the Indian market's current situation.
Gurmeet Singh H (2013)	The study examined how ethics have changed over the past few years. Marketing must have a larger viewpoint to serve society and the environment and is being carried out by many businesses by

	embracing the new concept of "Green Marketing" in order to deal with issues of values, ethics, and moral dilemmas.
Shwu-Ing Wu & Jia-Yi Chen (2014)	Green consumption is not the outcome of governmental regulation; rather, it results from consumer ideals. Concern for the environment and behavioural objectives are substantially correlated with green consumption behaviour. The study put forward a framework to create a relationship model of green consumption behaviour that would explain the connections between the perceived advantages of green consumption behaviour, the perceived risks, moral responsibility, normative beliefs, control strength, control beliefs, attitude, subjective norms, behaviour control, behaviour intention, and actual behaviour.
Bhatia, M., & Jain, A (2013)	This study provided factors that influence customer decision-making on whether or not to purchase a green product.

Theoretical framework and hypotheses

Concept	DEFINITION
Green Marketing	The terms "green marketing," "environmental marketing," and "sustainable marketing" all relate to a company's efforts to create, advertise, charge for, and distribute products and services that are environmentally friendly. "Green marketing is the promotion of items that are thought to be safe for the environment. It includes a wide variety of actions, such as product modification and alteration, adjustments to the current production process, modifications to the package design, and adaptation of marketing to reflect contemporary psychology.
Green Consumer	A green customer is one who is aware of their responsibilities and environmental responsibilities and who supports environmental concerns to the point where they will transfer allegiance from one product or provider to another, even if it means paying more. A person who buys only things that are eco-friendly or ecologically friendly is considered to be a green customer since they care deeply about the environment. Consumers who are ambivalent about important environmental concerns but don't act or think in an ecologically conscientious manner. True Browns: Consumers who don't care about the environment may even have animosity against media with a strong environmental focus.
Green Products	Green products are those that are safe for the environment, recyclable, made of recyclable parts, and energy efficient. They also have lower emissions of gas and harmful compounds. A green product is one that is environmentally friendly and made to have as little of an impact as possible during its entire life cycle and even after it has served its purpose. Typically, green products may be distinguished by their focus on minimising waste and boosting resource efficiency. They are produced utilising non-toxic materials and eco-friendly processes, and they have received certification from reputable agencies like Energy Star, Forest Stewardship Council, etc.

Environmental Awareness (EA)

EA can be defined as an individual's knowledge and beliefs concerning environment and sustainable consumption (Kaufmann et al, 2012). It refers to what people know about environment protection, how their behaviours can support sustainability and their understanding of overall eco-friendly products. Thus, if an individual has a higher EA, he/she would be more prone to have a positive attitude towards behaving responsibly and thereby demonstrating higher positive behavior intentions (De Moura et al, 2012; Young & Hwang, 2008; Vazifehdoust et al, 2013; Kaufmann et at., 2012). Thus,

H1: Environmental awareness (EA) will have an impact on attitude towards green mobiles (Att)

Environmental Concern (EC)

Environmental concern (EC) refers to concern towards environmental problems including pollution, population and nature protection (Van Liere & Dunlap, 1980; 1981). An individual's concern towards environmental problems has a strong impact on one's attitude towards protecting environment (Kaufmann et al, 2012; Hu et al, 2010; Paul, Modi & Patel, 2016). EC is also a predictor of environmental behaviours which are mediated via attitude towards those specific behaviors (Weigel, 1983; Rehman & Dost, 2013). Thus,

H2: Environmental concern (EC) will have an impact on attitude towardsgreen mobiles (Att)

Attitude towards green mobiles (Att)

Attitude can be defined as an individual's favourable/ unfavourable, positive/ negative evaluation towards an object (Ajzen & Fishbein, 1980). Referring TRA & TPB, an attitude towards a specific behavior is measured as an individual's assessment of outcomes of the specific behaviour and evaluation of those outcomes (Ajzen, 2012). Attitude is enduring disposition towards a behavior intention; hence it is a determinant of the intentions (Fishbein & Ajzen, 1975). Prior studies have examined the relationship between attitude-behaviour intention with a specific environmentally friendly behaviours such as recycling, ecological intentions (chan, 2001) and purchase intentions of green products (Mostafa, 2007; Yadhav & Pathak, 2017; Vazifehdoust et al; 2013). Thus,

H3: Attitude towards green mobiles (Att) will have an impact on purchaseintentions towards green mobiles (PI)

Subjective Norm (SN)

Subjective norm (SN) refers to a normative influence exerted on an individual by one's reference group (Ajzen & Fishbein, 1980). SN is a social pressure and comprise of one's normative beliefs towards the behavior intentions and an individual's motivation to comply with such pressure. Numerous studies have revealed that such social pressure influences consumers' behavior intentions namely, purchase intentions towards green products (Biswas& Roy, 2015; Zhoa et al, 2014; Wahid et al, 2011; Han et al, 2010; Paul, Modi & Patel,2016). Thus,

H4: Subjective norm (SN) will have an impact on purchase intentions towards green mobiles (PI)

Perceived Behaviour Control (PBC)

PBC refers to an individual's perceived control over one's action or intentions (Ajzen & Fishbein, 1980). PBC is measured with one's control beliefs and one's perceived power to control one's behavior intentions. It reflects the level of ease or difficulty in performing the behaviour and availability of the required resources for the same. Prior studies have suggested that the PBC has a positive influence on behavior intentions such as recycling (Yeow et al, 2014), and purchase intentions in context of green hotels (Chen & Tung, 2014), green products (Dilotsotlhe, 2021). Thus,

H5: Perceived behaviour control (PBC) will have an impact on purchase intentions towards green mobiles (PI)

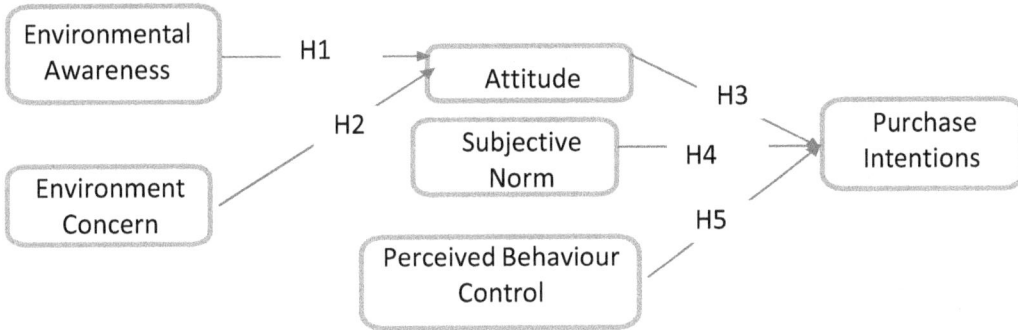

Figure 1 – Hypothesized model of the study

Research Methodology

Present study used a quantitative approach with a survey design. As the objective of the study is to develop a comprehensive model, the study used a structured questionnaire as a research instrument. A thorough literature review offered the constructs of the interest, which were adapted for the study. The questionnaire was prepared using a Google form and circulated using social media sites such as WhatsApp, LinkedIn and via emails.

Sampling

Primary data were collected from 213 respondents using a convenience sampling method from the city of Mumbai, a cosmopolitan city in India. The representative sample comprisedof 115 males (54%) and 98 females (46%); spread across age-groups – 77 respondents (36%) from 18-24 years, 90 from 25-40 years (42.3%) and 46 belonged to above 41 years (21.3%) (Refer Table no. 1). Additionally, the sample consisted of more of educated respondents with graduate (29.6%), post-graduate (55.4%) and professionally qualified (11.7%), likewise, majority were student (49.3%), salaried (41.78%) followed by business (5.16%) and homemakers (3.76%). The sample is equally spread in terms of gender, age groups andincome categories. Additionally, 78% of respondents are from generation Z & millennials which are important from most marketers' perspectives. Likewise, majority of the respondentsare well-educated, thus, would have a fairly good understanding of the environmental issues and more discerning. Also, over 60% of the respondents belong to higher income, thus allowing them to have resources to purchase green mobiles.

Research Instrument Design

A structured questionnaire was drawn up and selectively induced on respondents to ensure quality data was obtained. Using the framework of theory of planned behavior (Ajzen, 2005; 2012), the questionnaire adapted four constructs namely, attitude, subjective norm, the perceived behavior control and purchase intentions. The items were measured on a scale of 1- 7 (1 – strongly disagree and 7 strongly agree). Additionally, environmental concern was adapted from (Maichum et al, 2017 & Hu et al, 2010) and was measured with three-item statements on a scale of strongly disagree –

strongly agree on a 7-point scale. The construct, environmental awareness was taken and adapted from (Vazifehdoust et al, 2013; Kaufmann et.al., 2012) and measured with two items on the same scale.

To assess the content validity of the questionnaire, the questionnaire was pre-tested with a pilot study conducted amongst 30 post-graduate management students and it was fine-tuned further with the removal one item statement each from PBC and EA respectively.

Results and Discussion

Primary data collected herein was then analysed using SPSS 21.0 and AMOS 23.0. Firstly, the data was analysed using a Confirmatory Factor Analysis (CFA) to examine the reliability and validity of the constructs and Structural Equation Modelling (SEM) was used to test the directional hypotheses and validate the conjectured model.

The Measurement Model

CFA as the measurement model was used to examine the reliability and the validity of the constructs of the conjectured model. Composite reliability (CR), as shown in Table No. 2 measured the reliability of the constructs. All constructs namely, environmental awareness (EA) (CR =0.84), Environmental Concern (EC) (CR = 0.93), Attitude (Att) (CR = 0.87), Subjective Norm (SN) (CR = 0.95), Perceived Behaviour Control (PBC) (CR =0.91), and Purchase Intentions (PI) (CR = 0.93); have CR greater than 0.7, higher than the acceptable norm of 0.7 (Hair et al, 2010), thereby indicating that all constructs demonstrate robust reliability.

The validity of the constructs comprises of convergent and discriminant validity. The convergent validity measures the level of convergence of the items of the construct. This was examined using two criteria 1) factor loadings of the items statements should be higher than 0.6 and 2) the Average Variance Extracted (AVE) must be higher than 0.5 (Hair, Black, Babin, & Anderson, 2010). Refer Table No. 2 – all factor loadings of the item statements were above 0.6 and AVE of all constructs was greater than 0.5. This demonstrated convergentvalidity of the constructs.

The discriminant validity of the constructs refers to the extent to which the constructs differ from one another. This was assessed using Fornell and Lacker (1981) criteria – if the square- root of the AVE is higher than the correlations between the constructs, the constructs said to demonstrate the discriminant validity. As shown in Table No. 3, the diagonal values (the square-root values of AVE) are higher than off-diagonal values (the inter-construct correlations), thus the constructs demonstrated discriminant validity.

Results of SEM

The results of SEM assessed five directional paths referring to five hypotheses of the study:

H1 -Environmental Awareness (EA) □ Attitude (Att) (β =0.15, t-value = 3.817, p-value ≤0.01);

H2 - Environmental Concern (EC) □ Attitude (Att) (β =0.144, t-value = 2.857, p-value ≤0.004);

H3 - Attitude □ Purchase Intentions (PI) (β =0.378, t-value = 3.76, p-value ≤ 0.01);

H4 - Subjective Norm (SN) □ Purchase Intentions (β =0.357, t-value = 6.128, p-value ≤ 0.01)and

H5 - Perceived Behaviour Control (PBC) ☐ Purchase Intentions (PI) (β =0.268, t-value =4.226, p-value ≤ 0.01).

All five hypotheses were accepted as the p-value of all hypotheses were less than 0.01 and were found significant at 99% confidence level (Refer Table No. 4). Thus, the authors could now validate the hypothesized model with help of standardized estimates is shown in Figure2.

Further, the structural model was assessed using model fit indices such as Chi- Square/Degrees of Freedom (CMIN/df) = 2.734, Root mean square residual (RMR) = 0.114, Goodness of Fit Index (GFI) = 0.83, the comparative fit index (CFI) = 0.927 and Root mean square error of approximation (RMSEA) = 0.9 (see Table No. 5). All indices are nearing to the acceptable norms given Hair et al. (2010) and Byrne (1994), thereby indicating a larger sample size would lead more accurate indices.

Figure 2– Statistically validated model with regression estimates

Note - * indicates p-value ≤0.01

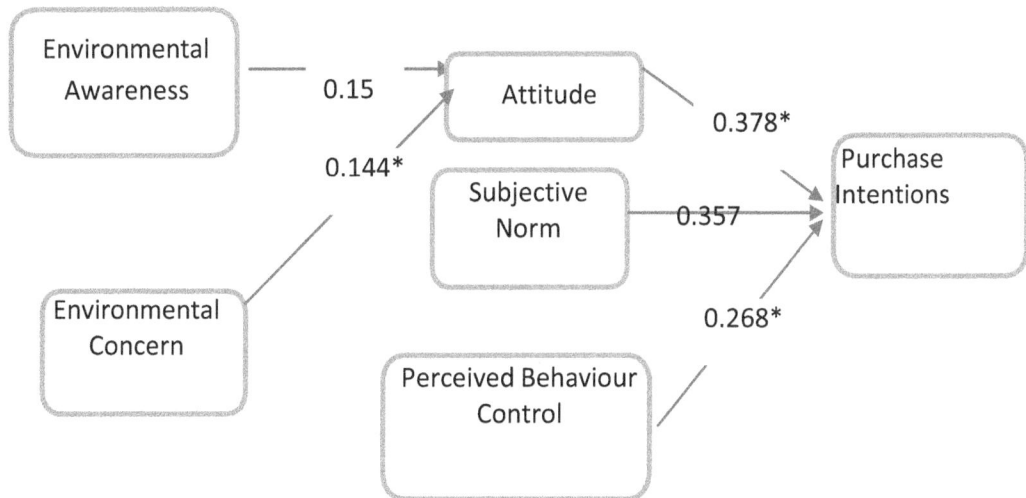

Discussion

The present study presented a model of determinants of purchase intentions towards green mobile handsets using the theory of planned behavior (TPB) in an Indian context. TPB is one of the widely used and parsimonious theoretical frameworks and has been deployed by numerous studies to propose a comprehensive model of behaviour intentions towards green products (Khan et al., 2019; Chen & Tung, 2014; Chen & Peng, 2012; Zhou et al., 2013; Han et al., 2011). Thus, the present study was hypothesized using the TPB. The proposed model demonstrated that attitude towards green products; subjective norm and perceived behavior control are significant determinants of the purchase intentions of green mobile handsets. The attitude was found to be stronger predictor of the behavior as seen in the theory (Azjen, 2012), followed by the subjective norm. Subjective norm measures an individual's level of confirmation to the reference group's normative beliefs. As the path of SN > PI is statistically validated in the conjectured model, it can be observed that respondents' group hasa significant influence on his/her purchase intentions. Additionally, as the PBC has been found to have a statistically significant impact on purchase intentions, it can be deduced that Indian consumers are better equipped to purchase green mobiles.

The study also examined the effect of environmental awareness and environmental concern on attitude, which were found statistically significant. As the p-value was less than 0.01, thus both were found to have a significant impact of attitude towards green mobile handsets. Thus, it is imperative and will help to build awareness of green mobiles and develop stronger concern towards environmental issues.

Therefore, the present study validates the theory of planned behavior with attitude, subjective norm and perceived behavior control having a positive impact on purchase intentions towards green mobile handsets. Furthermore, environmental awareness and environmental awareness have a positive effect on purchase intentions through a mediation of attitude towards green mobiles.

Implications of the study

The study highlights and suggests several measures to be taken by mobile manufacturers related to green concept. The mobile handset manufacturers should take some precautionary measures since in the beginning of the mobile designing, formation and "green" packaging. It includes the internal mobile parts to be made from the green supported materials which can be easily introduced e.g. handsets with built-in solar panels. A solar panel might be useful in places where the availability of energy is sporadic or depends on unsustainable diesel or electric generators in the developing world, where a handset manufacturer might focus on. Such generators are frequently utilized to power the mobile phone towers that transmit signals in remote regions. Even solar or wind power based mobile towers can be erected which can be planned since policy making with mobile manufacturers. Such manufacturers can be supported and provided with maximum subsidy for showcasing solar and even wind-powered towers supporting Government initiative. However, the mobile phone industry has a long way to go before it can be implemented.

Further, "green" phones need to be accompanied with proper recycling programmes or replacement cycles. There is a necessity to take such steps to make the people aware of the measures to be taken to dispose of old handset in an environmentally friendly way because the matter of waste mobiles is also highly concerned in the developing world. More people will be able to follow the major international events that are creating awareness about environmental degradation due to mobile handsets, comprehend its effects on individuals and communities, and be motivated to take meaningful action to raise awareness of the environmental hazards associated with disposing of mobile phones in the garbage. Such guidelines can be easily provided to the consumers. This is a crucial realization because manufacturers may need to start initiatives to raise public awareness of green products. However, it is a welcome shift that the government is attempting to raise public awareness of potential dangers by including such themes into the Indian curriculum for schools and universities.

The present study also offers several managerial implications for the marketing managers. Green marketing is not just about offering something to customers that demonstrate that the company is pursuing environmentally friendly approach, but something that truly delivers value/benefit to the customers. It's only when such value/benefit is made aware that helps to develop a favourable and a positive attitude towards green mobiles.

Positive attitude towards purchasing green mobile is a combination of both factors namely environmental awareness, and environmental concern. The study revealed that consumers with a medium to high level of awareness demonstrate a more positive attitude to environmentally friendly products when they are concerned about environmental issues. Similarly, customers with a positive/favourable environmental concern also impact their attitude towards green products.

Furthermore, the study highlighted the role of reference power and normative influence on attitude towards green products and their purchase intentions. Also, the study reveals the 'rub-off' effect that a positive attitude could have on the consumer, especially when their peers acknowledge and corroborate with the consumer on his/her favourable attitude towards green products. In the process, the attitude of both, the consumer and his/her peer group get further reinforced and slowly but surely tends to spread and gains momentum. Thus, marketers may build on role of group influence in this category. Moreover, the effect of perceived behavior control on purchase intentions reveal the role of making green mobiles available and accessible to the mass consumers so as to enable higher control over their intentions. Thus, the study provided the mobile handset marketers deep and valuable insights that will help them design their offering and marketing plan in line with the green consumer expectations. Therefore, marketers need to build awareness and concern towards green mobile handsets, which would result in higher purchase intentions. Moreover, marketers need to focus on role of group influence and making green mobiles accessible to the consumers to enable higher purchases.

The above in-turn has a reflux impact that further reinforces the organization's belief in pursuing green/environmentally friendly initiatives more resolutely, even if it amounts to absorb some higher costs, lower /strained margins and if need be, losses during the initial stages of the launch. This in many ways demonstrate organizations leadership style as the ownership is on the organisation to take first steps, as the future, the longevity and sustainability of the business all lies with the organisation as the primary owner of the business, to be then shared between the government and the customer. Secondary research amply indicates that organisations that have led from the front have seen far greater and faster success when it comes to green marketing.

Finally, the need of the hour today is green mobile handsets as this category has seen the fastest and deepest penetration in the Indian market, with a subscriber base of approx. 1.1 billion in a 1.3 billion population. In terms of facilitating green consumption, the role of government and policymakers is pivotal. The present study offered implications for making suitable environmental friendly policies and take lead in creating awareness and concern towards green products. Thus, all key stakeholders -industry, government and the end consumer will stand to benefit from this study leaving behind a sustainable and responsible industry.

Conclusion

The onset of Covid-19 pandemic has had its impact in many areas namely, changing lifestyle, consumer behavior, eating and living habits, going as far as in many cases, probably even rediscovering oneself. These has led a lot of consumers to a take step back and rethink on many of their pre-pandemic habits, what with the lockdown also forcing consumers to stay content with what they have and get, rather than what they wish they could have.

The above changes have now seen the rise of a different set of consumers and consumerism that is socially and self-conscious of what, when, and how they consume. Increasingly such consumers are seen to be drawn towards brands that have a purpose, particularly in the context of environment. Consumers are now willing to support the green cause and demonstrate positive purchase intentions to buy green products that genuinely support saving the environment.

The authors were inspired by the theory of planned behavior (Ajzen, 1985) which upon deeper study and subject research enabled to augment the model with additional determinants namely, environmental awareness and concern. The study revealed that awareness and concern over environmental issues are the basis on which positive attitude is formed leadingto a positive disposition towards green mobile handsets. The study also reveals that subjectivenorm – impact of peer group behavioural traits being appreciated and replicated holds good inthis study and similar observation is also made when reviewing the perceived behavioural control which is purely in the hands consumers as to how he /she conducts oneself in a given situation. Finally, purchase intentions towards green mobile handsets will be a result of environmental awareness, concern, a positive attitude towards green mobiles, subjective normand perceived behavior control.

Limitations and scope of further study

This study is limited to the city of Mumbai, although the city offers fair degree of diversity. Additionally, the study could possibly be short of authentic rural insights focus and attention was paid to capture as diverse an audience sample to ensure a robust study. The authors also believe a future study could consider other determinants namely, perception, consumer guilt, motivation and effect demographic variables such as age, gender, occupation, income etc. Additionally, government support and firm's initiatives are important in terms of developing positive dispositions. Thus, role of government and firm's initiatives could be explored in further studies.

References

Ajzen, I. (1985). From intentions to actions: A theory of planned behavior. In *Action control* (pp.11-39). Springer, Berlin, Heidelberg.

Ajzen, I. (2013). *Instrument Title: Theory of Planned Behaviour Questionnaire*. RetrievedSeptember 22, 2021, from www.midss.ie

Ajzen, I. (n.d.). *Instrument Title: Theory of Planned Behaviour Questionnaire*. RetrievedSeptember 22, 2021, from www.midss.ie

Ajzen, I. (n.d.). TPB Questionnaire Construction 1 Constructing A Theory OfPlanned Behavior Questionnaire.

Ajzen, Icek. (2012). The theory of planned behavior. *Handbook of Theories of Social Psychology: Volume 1*, 438–459. https://doi.org/10.4135/9781446249215.n22

Akhil, A. (2016). Green Marketing to meet consumer demands and sustainable development-Challenges and Opportunities. *International Journal of Advanced Trends in Engineering and Technology (IJATET)*, 1.

Alamsyah, D., Othman, N., & Mohammed, H. (2020). The awareness of environmentally friendly products: The impact of green advertising and green brand image. *Management Science Letters*, 10(9), 1961-1968.

Aries, E. J., Gold, C., & Weigel, R. H. (1983). Dispositional and situational influences on dominance behavior in small groups. Journal of Personality and Social Psychology, 44(4), 779.

Awan, A. G., & Wamiq, S. (2016). Relationship Between Environmental Awareness And Green Marketing. *Science International*, 28(3).

Barton, S. S., & Behe, B. K. (2017). Retail promotion and advertising in the green industry: An overview and exploration of the use of digital advertising. *HortTechnology*, 27(1), 99-107.

Bhatia, M., & Jain, A. (2013). Green marketing: A study of consumer perception and preferences in India. *Electronic Green Journal*, 1(36).

Bhavana, A., & Thiruchanuru, S. (2018). Green marketing: Gap analysis in the decision making process of a green consumer. *Journal of Business Management & Social Sciences Research*, 7(3), 50-57.

Biswas, A., & Roy, M. (2015). Leveraging factors for sustained green consumption behaviorbased on consumption value perceptions: testing the structural model. Journal of Cleaner production, 95, 332-340.

Booi Chen, T., & Teck Chai, L. (2010). Attitude towards the Environment and Green Products: Consumers' Perspective. *Management Science and Engineering*, 4(2), 27–39. www.cscanada.net%5Cnwww.cscanada.org

Chan, R. Y., & Lau, L. B. (2002). Explaining green purchasing behavior: A cross-cultural study on American and Chinese consumers. *Journal of international consumer marketing*, 14(2-3), 9-40.

Chen, C. C., Chen, C. W., & Tung, Y. C. (2018). Exploring the consumer behavior of intention to purchase green products in Belt and Road countries: An empirical analysis. *Sustainability (Switzerland)*, 10(3). https://doi.org/10.3390/su10030854

Chen, M. F., & Tung, P. J. (2014). Developing an extended Theory of Planned Behavior model to predict consumers' intention to visit green hotels. *International Journal of Hospitality Management, 36,* 221–230. https://doi.org/10.1016/J.IJHM.2013.09.006

Chen, T. B., & Chai, L. T. (2010). Attitude towards the environment and green products: Consumers' perspective. Management science and engineering, 4(2), 27-39.

Davis, M. H., & Gaskell, M. G. (2009). A complementary systems account of word learning: neural and behavioural evidence. *Philosophical Transactions of the Royal Society B: Biological Sciences, 364*(1536), 3773-3800.

Dilotsotlhe, N., & Akbari, M. (2021). Factors influencing the green purchase behaviour of millennials: An emerging country perspective. *Cogent Business & Management, 8.* https://doi.org/10.1080/23311975.2021.1908745

Eneizan, B., Alshare, F., Salaymeh, M., Enaizan, O., & Abdul-Latif, M. (2020). Green Marketing and Sustainability. *International Journal of Academic Management Science Research, 4*(4), 26-30.

Fishbein, M., Jaccard, J., Davidson, A. R., Ajzen, I., & Loken, B. (1980). Predicting and understanding family planning behaviors. In Understanding attitudes and predicting social behavior. Prentice Hall.

Ghorai, S., & Sengupta, S. (2021). Awareness of Green Marketing in Preventing Pollution of Environment.

Han, H., & Kim, Y. (2010). An investigation of green hotel customers' decision formation: Developing an extended model of the theory of planned behavior. *International journal of hospitality management, 29*(4), 659-668. https://doi.org/10.1016/j.tourman.2009.03.013

https://www.ibef.org/industry/telecommunications.aspx

https://www.investindia.gov.in/team-india-blogs/indian-economy-overview

https://www.weforum.org/reports/future-of-consumption-in-fast-growth-consumer-markets-india

India: value of mobile phone production 2021 | Statista. (n.d.). Retrieved November 1, 2021, from https://www.statista.com/statistics/809557/india-domestic-mobile-phone-manufacturing-value/

Jebarajakirthy, C., & Lobo, A. C. (2014). War affected youth as consumers of microcredit: An application and extension of the theory of planned behaviour. Journal of retailing and consumer *services, 21*(3), 239-248.

Johri, L. M., & Sahasakmontri, K. (1998). Green marketing of cosmetics and toiletries in Thailand. *Journal of consumer marketing.*

Joshi, Y., & Rahman, Z. (2015). Factors Affecting Green Purchase Behaviour and Future Research Directions. In *International Strategic Management Review* (Vol. 3, Issues 1–2). Holy Spirit University of Kaslik. https://doi.org/10.1016/j.ism.2015.04.001

Kabadayı, E. T., Dursun, İ., Alan, A. K., & Tuğer, A. T. (2015). Green purchase intention of young Turkish consumers: Effects of consumer's guilt, self-monitoring and perceived consumer effectiveness. *Procedia-Social and Behavioral Sciences, 207,* 165-174.

Kalafatis, S. P., Pollard, M., East, R., & Tsogas, M. H. (1999). Green marketing and Ajzen's theory of planned behaviour: a cross-market examination. *Journal of consumer marketing.* https://doi.org/10.1108/07363769910289550

Kassaye, W. W. (2001). Green dilemma. *Marketing Intelligence & Planning.*

Khare, A. (2015). Antecedents to green buying behaviour: a study on consumers in an emerging economy. *Marketing Intelligence & Planning.*

Kim, H. Y., & Chung, J. E. (2011). Consumer purchase intention for organic personal care products. *Journal of consumer Marketing.*

Laroche, M., Bergeron, J., & Barbaro-Forleo, G. (2001). Targeting consumers who are willing to pay more for environmentally friendly products. *Journal of Consumer Marketing, 18*(6), 503–520. https://doi.org/10.1108/EUM0000000006155

Liere, K. D. V., & Dunlap, R. E. (1980). The social bases of environmental concern: A review of hypotheses, explanations and empirical evidence. Public opinion quarterly, 44(2), 181-197.

Liu, H. T., & Tsaur, R. C. (2020). The theory of reasoned action applied to green smartphones: Moderating effect of government subsidies. *Sustainability, 12*(15), 5979.

Maichum, K., Parichatnon, S., & Peng, K.-C. (2017). Factors affecting on purchase intention towards green products: A case study of young consumers in Thailand. *International Journal of Social Science and Humanity, 7*(5), 330–335. https://doi.org/10.18178/ijssh.2017.7.5.844

Makhdoomi, U., & Nazir, U. (2016). Consumer purchase behavior towards green products. Journal of consumer marketing, 16(6), 558-575.

Medhi, M. (2015). A Study on the Green Marketing Practices Adopted by Various Companies In India. *International Journal of Marketing and Human Resource Management, 6*(3), 83-88.

Mitomo, H., & Otsuka, T. (2012). Rich information on environmental issues and the poor reflections on consumers' green actions: A behavioral economic approach. Telematics and Informatics, 29(4), 400-408.

Moisander, J. (2007). Motivational complexity of green consumerism. International journal of consumer studies, 31(4), 404-409.'

Mostafa, M. M. (2007). Gender differences in Egyptian consumers' green purchase behaviour: theeffects of environmental knowledge, concern and attitude. International journal of consumer studies, 31(3), 220-229.

Nam, C., Dong, H., & Lee, Y.-A. (n.d.). Factors influencing consumers' purchase intention of green sportswear. *Fashion and Textiles*. https://doi.org/10.1186/s40691-017- 0091-3

Paladino, A., & Ng, S. (2013). An examination of the influences on 'green'mobile phone purchases among young business students: an empirical analysis. *Environmental Education Research*, *19*(1), 118-145.

Paul, J., Modi, A., & Patel, J. (2016). Predicting green product consumption using theory of planned behavior and reasoned action. *Journal of retailing and consumer services*, *29*, 123-134.

Raghavan, L., & Vahanti, G. (2009). Going Green in India. *Landor*, 1-5.

Rahbar, E., & Wahid, N. A. (2011). Investigation of green marketing tools' effect on consumers'purchase behavior. Business strategy series.

Rehman, Z. U., & Dost, M. K. (2013, June). Conceptualizing green purchase intention in emerging markets: An empirical analysis on Pakistan. In The 2013 WEI International AcademicConference Proceedings (Vol. 1, pp. 101-102)

Singh, G. (2013). A study of evolution and practice of green marketing by various companies in India. *International Journal of Management and Social Sciences Research*, *2*(7), 49-56

Soonthonsmai, V. (2007, June). Environmental or green marketing as global competitive edge:Concept, synthesis, and implication. In EABR (Business) and ETLC (Teaching) Conference *Proceeding, Venice, Italy*.

Sujith, T. S. (2017). Awarness of Green Marketing and Its Influence on Buying Behaviour of Consumers in Kerala. *International Journal of Scientific Research and Management*, *5*(7), 6156-6164.

Tiwari, J. (2014). Green marketing in India: An overview. *IOSR Journal of Business and Management*, *1*(6), 33-40.

Van Liere, K. D., & Dunlap, R. E. (1981). Environmental concern: Does it make a difference howit's measured?. Environment and behavior, 13(6), 651-676.

Vazifehdoust, H., Taleghani, M., Esmaeilpour, F., & Nazari, K. (2013). Purchasing green to become greener: Factors influence consumers' green purchasing behavior. *Management ScienceLetters*, *3*(9), 2489-2500.

Vazifehdoust, H., Taleghani, M., Esmaeilpour, F., & Nazari, K. (2013). Purchasing green to become greener: Factors influence consumers' green purchasing behavior. *Management ScienceLetters*, *3*(9), 2489-2500.

Veleva, V., & Ellenbecker, M. (2001). Indicators of sustainable production: framework andmethodology. *Journal of cleaner production*, *9*(6), 519-549.

Whitefoot, K. S., & Donofrio, N. M. (Eds.). (2015). Making value for America: Embracing thefuture of manufacturing, technology, and work. National Academies Press.

Wijekoon, R., & Sabri, M. F. (2021). Determinants That Influence Green Product Purchase Intention and Behavior: A Literature Review and Guiding Framework. *Sustainability*, *13*(11),6219.

Winkler von Mohrenfels, H., & Klapper, D. (2012). The influence of mobile product information on brand perception and willingness to pay for green and sustainable products.

Wu, S. I., & Chen, J. Y. (2014). A model of green consumption behavior constructed by the theory of planned behavior. *International Journal of Marketing Studies*, *6*(5), 119.

Yadav, R., & Pathak, G. S. (2017). Determinants of Consumers' Green Purchase Behaviorin a Developing Nation: Applying and Extending the Theory of Planned Behavior. *Ecological Economics*, *134*, 114–122. https://doi.org/10.1016/j.ecolecon.2016.12.019

Table 1 – Demographic details of the sample

Variable	Details	Frequency	Percentage
Gender	Male	115	54.0
	Female	98	46.0
Age	18-24 years	77	36.2
	25-40 years	90	42.3
	Above 41 years	46	21.6
Income (in INR)	Less than 10 Lacs	85	39.9
	10 Lacs & Above - Below 15 Lacs	71	33.3
	15 Lacs & above - 20 Lacs	22	10.3
	Above 20 Lacs	35	16.4
Education	10th / 12th Pass	4	1.9
	Graduate	63	29.6
	Doctorate	3	1.5
	Post-graduate	118	55.4
	Professional Qualification	25	11.7
Occupation	Business	11	5.16
	Home Maker	8	3.76
	Salaried	89	41.78
	Student	105	49.30
	Total	213	100.00

Table 2 – Assessment of constructs reliability and convergent validity

Construct	Item	Factor Loading	AVE*	CR*
Environmetal Awarenes s (EA)	I am aware of green mobile handsets	0.78	0.72	0.84
	I am aware of the role of green mobile handsets in overall environmental sustainability	0.92		
Environmental Concern(EC)	I am very conscious of the global environmental issues	0.89	0.81	0.93
	It is very important to raise environmental consciousness to reduce pollution	0.91		
	I am conscious that purchasing green mobiles will contribute to reducing environmental pollution and leading to a sustainable future	0.91		
Attitude (Att)	Buying a green mobile handset is Extremely bad- Extremely Good	0.79	0.63	0.87
	Buying a green mobile handset is Extremely Unfavourable - Extremely Favourable	0.74		
	Buying a green mobile handset is Extremely Insignificant - Extremely Significant	0.80		
	Buying a green mobile handset is Extremely foolish - Extremely wise	0.86		
Subjective Norm (SN)	Purchasing a green mobile would make a good impression of me	0.86	0.78	0.95
	Purchasing a green mobile would cause me to be admired	0.85		
	Purchasing a green mobile would improve the way I am perceived by people around me	0.92		
	Most people who are important to me would want me to purchase a green mobile	0.94		
	Most people who are important to me would think that I should buy a green mobile	0.84		
Perceived Behaviour Control (PBC)	I have financial ability to purchase a green mobile	0.87	0.84	0.91
	I have resources to purchase a green mobile	0.96		
Purchase Intentions (PI)	If I can choose between green mobile and the conventional ones, I would prefer to buy thegreen version	0.83	0.77	0.93
	I have positive intentions toward buying agreen mobile because of its environmental benefits	0.84		
	I definitely will purchase a green mobile in my next purchase	0.93		
	I will consider switching to a green mobile for environmental reasons	0.91		

*Note – AVE – Average Variance Extracted, CR – Composite Reliability

Table 3 – Assessment of Convergent and Discriminant Validity

	EA	EC	Att	SN	PBC	PI
EA	**0.8505**					
EC	0.487	**0.9024**				
Att	0.438	0.386	**0.7959**			
SN	0.464	0.62	0.354	**0.8832**		
PBC	0.555	0.689	0.369	0.605	**0.91463244**	
PI	0.561	0.698	0.464	0.671	0.614	**0.879104943**

*Note – The highlighted diagonal values are the square roots of Average Variance Extracted (AVE) and off-diagonal are correlations between the constructs.

Table 4 – Path Analysis and Hypotheses Testing

Hypotheses	Path	Standardised Estimate	t-value	P-value
H1	Environmental Awareness --> Attitude	0.15	3.817	***
H2	Environmental Concern --> Attitude	0.144	2.857	0.004
H3	Attitude --> Purchase Intentions	0.378	3.76	***
H4	Subjective Norm --> Purchase intentions	0.357	6.128	***
H5	Perceived Behaviour Control --> Purchase intentions	0.268	4.226	***

*Note – P-value are less than 0.01, marked as ***

Table 5 – Model Fit Indices

Index	CMIN/DF	RMR	GFI	CFI	RMSEA
Observed Value	2.734	0.114	0.83	0.927	0.9

*Note - Chi-Square/Degrees of Freedom (CMIN/df), Root mean square residual (RMR), Goodness of Fit Index (GFI), the comparative fit index (CFI) and Root mean square error of approximation (RMSEA)

CHAPTER 5

PREDICTING CONSUMER DECISIONS USING MODIFIED TEMPORAL MOTIVATION
THEORY

Pranav Manjunath Bhat[1], Priyanshu M[2], S Shruti[3], Madhav Murthy[4]

Introduction

The volatility of markets is heavily influenced by the rapidly changing dynamics of consumerbehavior. Therefore, entities that can predict consumer behavior to a reasonable degree have better insights into market trends and can prepare accordingly. This advantage can give them an edge over their competitors and enable them to increase their returns on investment (ROI).The economic potential in being able to predict consumer behavior has motivated many researchers and economists to postulate several theories in the field and even borrow related theories from other fields. One theory that has shown enormous potential is Temporal Motivation Theory (TMT). Temporal Motivation Theory is an integrative motivational theorydeveloped by Piers Steel and Cornelius J. Konig. It is an amalgamation of expectancy theory, hyperbolic discounting, cumulative prospect theory, and need theory (Steel & König, 2006). According to it, motivation is a function of expectancy, value, delay, and differences betweenrewards and losses of choices presented. Temporal Motivation Theory finds application in theanalysis of procrastination, goal setting, strategic risk behavior, military deterrence, and unlikemost other theories, accounts for behavior over time but has not yet found application in consumer behavior.

This study proposes the application of a variation of the Temporal Motivation Theory value equation in modeling consumer behavior in an environment where multiple choices areavailable to a potential customer. Unlike machine learning algorithms which make generalizedpredictions, this study focuses on making personalized predictions. In addition, this will enablebusinesses to identify the most relevant factors influencing buying preferences of individuals,which in turn will help them tailor their products to make them more appealing to their potentialcustomers. Furthermore, businesses can benefit from TMT as it reveals the specific features ofthe product or aspects of the marketing strategy that requires fine-tuning, thus enabling them to bridge the gaps in their product-market fit and position their products that align with the needs of the target consumer segment. For service companies, this means identification of theareas in their service offerings that require refinement. Marketers can employ TMT to understand a competitor's performance in relation to theirs, and the insights from such an analysis can enable them in reducing churn rates.

Take for example, the consumer electronics industry. Products here have to be tailored to targetspecific demographics with specific interests. This requires enormous amounts of data and analysis and even within a particular demographic, certain features of a product are valued more than others. It

[1] Pranav Manjunath Bhat, Student, Department of ECE, BMS College of Engineering, Bull Temple Rd, Basavanagudi, Bengaluru, Karnataka 560019, India. E-mail: pranav.ec18@bmsce.ac.in
[2] Priyanshu M, Student, Department of ECE, BMS College of Engineering, Bull Temple Rd, Basavanagudi, Bengaluru, Karnataka 560019, India. E-mail: priyanshu.ec18@bmsce.ac.in
[3] S Shruti, Student, Department of ECE, BMS College of Engineering, Bull Temple Rd, Basavanagudi, Bengaluru, Karnataka 560019, India. E-mail: shruti.ec18@bmsce.ac.in
[4] Prof. Madhav Murthy, M. Tech (PhD), Assistant Professor, Department of Mechanical Engineering, BMS College of Engineering, Bull Temple Rd, Basavanagudi, Bengaluru, Karnataka 560019, India. E-mail: madhavmurthy.mech@bmsce.ac.in

will be difficult to collect enormous amounts of data for these purposes and even after that, it might be difficult to find out how and which features consumers of a particular demographic prioritize or why consumers of a particular demographic prefer a particular brand over others.

To achieve the objective of this study, which is to model consumer behavior with a reasonabledegree of accuracy using TMT, the theory was applied in two different cases – predicting customer retention in online food delivery services and consumer buying decisions in smartphones. Both these applications are characterized by the availability of two or more choices to the consumer.

This paper first gives an overview of various other studies in modeling consumer behavior using different methods and technologies such as artificial intelligence, predictive analytics, psychological modeling, and real-time modeling. The third section then explains Temporal Motivation Theory, along with its modified mathematical formula that is an attempt to model human decision making. The fourth section is the core of this study and is itself divided into two different parts – the first part deals with the application of TMT to predict customer retention in online food service apps and the second part deals with the application of TMT to predict buying decisions concerning smartphones belonging to a similar price range. Each subsection gives a description of the dataset followed by the application of TMT and the resultsand their analysis.

Related Work

Study	Domain/ Type	Objective/ Outcome
A Machine Learning-Based Method for Customer Behavior Prediction (Li et al., 2019)	ML/AI Modelling	This paper analyzes customer characteristics and attributes with historical purchase records using machine learning techniques such as decision trees, cluster analysis, and the Naive Bayes algorithm.
Machine Learning-Based Prediction of Consumer Purchasing Decisions: The Evidence and Its Significance? (Arandjelovic et al., 2018)	ML/AI Modelling	The Study was employed to model consumer purchase decisions using entirely data-driven methods, with no subjective judgments or assumptions made ahead of time.
A machine learning framework for customer purchase prediction in the non-contractual setting (Martínez et al., 2020)	ML/AI Modelling	The study uses the new set of consumer-relevant attributes to create a dynamic and data-driven framework for forecasting a customer purchase decision in the near future.
Predicting customer purchase behavior in the e- commerce context (Qiu et al., 2015)	ML/AI Modelling	The purpose of this study is to develop a predictive framework for customer purchasing behavior in an e-commerce setting. It presents a two-stage technique called CustOmer purchase pREdiction modeL(COREL).
Predictive Analytics forPredicting Customer Behavior (Asniar & Surendro, 2019)	Predictive Analytics	The solution entailed developing prediction models based on behavioral patterns discovered in behavioral data.
An Extended Model of Behavioral Process in Consumer Decision Making (Kanagal, 2016)	Psychological modeling	The model considers the relationship between communication sensitivity, enculturated individuality, and rational/economic decision-making for consumer decision making process.
Modeling real-time online information needs: A new research approach for complex consumer behavior (Grant et al., 2013)	Realtime Modelling	An additional basis for real- time customer requirement evaluation is offered, merging clickstream and user input data with an online information utility, to enable more efficient information provision.

The table above summarizes studies conducted in modeling consumer behavior. Significant contributions have been made by researchers in modeling and predicting consumer behavior in traditional business, digital business, and e-commerce environments. Machine learning, predictive analytics, data mining, and other behavioral modeling techniques are widely used topredict consumer decisions and model their behavior.

Machine learning techniques such as decision trees, cluster analysis, and Naive Bayes algorithms can be applied to analyze customer characteristics and attributes with historical purchase records. Further, the key factors influencing potential customers' purchase behavior can be examined by selecting models with high promotion degrees through a promotion graphto achieve accurate marketing (Li et al., 2019). Predicting consumer purchase decisions usingmeasurable features of the purchasing context can pose a challenge. To overcome this, Arandjelovic et al. (2018) proposed an entirely data-driven method with no subjective judgments or assumptions made ahead of time. The findings indicated that the random forest-based classifier significantly outperformed the standard naive Bayes technique, with a 10% improvement. Machine learning techniques can also be used to create a dynamic and data- driven framework for forecasting whether a customer would make a purchase at the companywithin a given period in the near future by using the new set of consumer-relevant attributes derived from the timings and values of prior transactions (Martínez et al., 2020). Predictive analytics techniques utilizing behavior informatics and analytics approach can be implementedto predict customer behavior by mapping transactional data into behavioral data and developing prediction models based on behavioral patterns discovered in behavioral data (Asniar & Surendro, 2019).

Kanagal (2016) offers an aggregate level framework of consumer preference behavioral processes- an extended stimulus-response model of consumer choice-making, which incorporates the impacts and interconnections of buyer psychology, distinct buyer attributes, and the impact of the buyer selection process on consumer decision making. The model considers the relationship between communication sensitivity, enculturated individuality, and rational/economic decision-making for the consumer decision-making process. Qiu et al. (2015) developed a predictive framework for customer purchasing behavior in an e-commercesetting. They presented a two-stage technique called CustOmer purchase pREdiction modeL (COREL) which predicts buyer motives by constructing a candidate product collection, and then it learns customer preferences for product attributes, which it then uses to select the candidate items that are most likely to be purchased. To create a dynamic and responsive online information service with cognitive lock-in benefits, an integration of all types of data is needed-merging of clickstream with user input data with online information utility can be employed for real-time customer requirement evaluation (Grant et al., 2013).

While there have been several attempts made using data analytics, machine learning/ artificial intelligence models, and other modeling techniques, none of them were able to predictconsumer behavior with very high accuracy. ML/AI Models can provide reasonable predictionaccuracy but they require huge training data to be fed in to obtain acceptable accuracy levels.

Several studies have been proposed using Temporal Motivation Theory (TMT) to study the factors concerning individual decision-making. However, no papers were found to study the application of TMT in modeling consumer decision-making.

Temporal Motivation Theory

Temporal Motivation Theory (TMT) is an integration of four motivational theories - hyperbolic discounting, expectancy theory, cumulative prospect theory and need theory. While temporal motivation theory does not include all features of the aforementioned theories, it does integratetheir most important features (Steel & König, 2006). Hyperbolic discounting accounts for behavior over time as discussed by Ainslie and Haslam (1992) in Choice over time (Loewenstein & Elster, 1992). The theory posits that while choosing from a variety of possiblerewarding activities, humans prefer performing activities that offer immediate rewards even when they are lesser than the ones in the distant future. Expectancy theory and theories derivedfrom it suggest that in an environment where multiple choices are presented to a person, the final decision is made by evaluating the probability of an outcome being achieved and the degree to which that outcome is valued (Vroom, 1965). CPT by Tversky & Kahneman (1992),a refurbished version of Prospect Theory by Kahneman & Tversky (1979) describes the value of choices and transformation of expectancy under uncertainty by employing cumulative decision weights. It allows different weighting functions to evaluate gains and losses when several outcomes are possible for a decision, under uncertain or risky circumstances (Tversky& Kahneman, 1992). Need theory explains how actions are influenced by the three needs-theneed for achievement, affiliation, and power. Since needs partly drive behavior and in turn become a representation of action, the resulting value of an action can be obtained by gaugingthe effect of each need (Steel & König, 2006).

The modified formulation of TMT for modeling consumer behavior is –

$$Value = \frac{Reward \times p(S)}{Impulsiveness \times Delay + 1}$$

Value: Value represents the extent to which a particular action meets and satisfies the needs ofan individual. In an environment where multiple actions are possible, the action with the highest value is usually performed.

Reward: Reward signifies the degree of satisfaction an outcome of action provides. If the desired reward is obtained, then that particular action's value increases. Reward is the sum of four constructs – belongingness, autonomy, brand preference, and competence.

Belongingness: Belongingness can be defined as the emotional need to be affiliated with a group or the desire for interaction and connectedness. A sense of belongingness is experiencedby consumers when they use the same product or brand as their peers, friends, and family. Thesocial setting in which the product is used and the people who use the product shape one's preferences and choices (Janssen & Jager, 2001).

Autonomy: Consumers' sense of autonomy can be defined as the ability to control their choicesand decisions. The sensation of having control over one's decisions leads to increased sentiments of competence and positive impact (André et al., 2018). Autonomy can also be characterized as the feeling of uniqueness imparted when choosing a particular product or brand over others. Consumers are motivated to differentiate themselves from the crowd by acquiring, using, and displaying consumer goods that aren't commonplace in the market (Tianet al., 2001).

Brand preference: Brand preference refers to how likely a customer is inclined to choose a certain brand's products over its competitors. Brand preference is closely linked to the attitudemeasurements based on one's beliefs about and the related relevance of product-specific attributes (Bass & Talarzyk, 1972). Brand preference contributes majorly to brand equity. Brands with higher levels of equity are known to produce significantly greater preference andpurchase intentions (Cobb-Walgren et al., 1995).

Competence: Competence is a measure of how well a certain purpose can be fulfilled by performing an action. This might be the utility of a certain product and its necessity in performing some other tasks or simply taking action to achieve a particular outcome.

Probability of Success (p(S)): Probability of success, p(S), represents the likelihood an event or an action will occur. An increase in the value is observed as the probability of success in acquiring the reward increases.

Delay and Impatience/Impulsiveness: Delay refers to the nearness or the amount of time required to complete an action. The motivation or value of an action is weakened by delay. Impatience or impulsiveness signifies a person's sensitivity to delay (Steel & König, 2006).

Individuals discount the value of delayed or uncertain outcomes based on the estimated time or the possibility of their occurrence when deciding between them. When presented with two rewarding actions – an action with a smaller reward that can be obtained quickly and an actionwith a larger reward but which can only be obtained in the comparatively distant future, an individual is likely to take action to obtain the smaller reward over the larger one. However, with time, the preference is likely to reverse and there is a tendency for the individual to take action to obtain the larger reward (Green & Myerson, 2004).

Fig. 1: Change in preference where the vertical axis (or Y-axis) denotes the discounted valueof future reward and the horizontal axis (or X-axis) denotes time

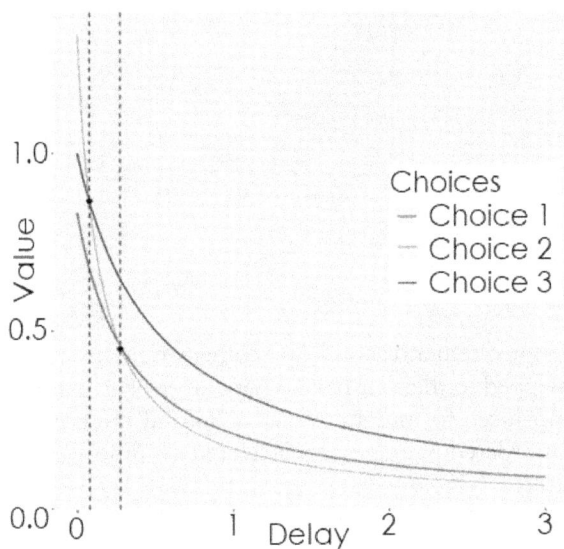

Fig. 1 portrays the inverse relation of delay with the value of performing a certain action. It depicts the rate of change of value concerning time between three given choices and how, intime, the value of a particular action might be superseded by another.

75

Methodology

Temporal motivation theory was tested in two different scenarios and applications. The study included the application of theory for predicting customer retention and consumer buying decisions based on given choices. Two different types of datasets were used – a secondary dataset of online food delivery preferences and a primary dataset for predicting consumer preferences in consumer electronics.

Secondary Data Analysis

Dataset Description

To test temporal motivation theory on customer retention, an online food delivery preferencesdataset sourced from Kaggle was used (Roshan B, 2020). The dataset, collected from 388 residents of Bangalore, has 55 attributes that take into account the customer demographics and the factors affecting their overall purchase decision. The output variable is a categorical variable that indicates whether a customer will opt for a food delivery app or not. To understand and gain insights into the demographics of the consumers, four variables – age, sex, marital status, and occupation were considered for demographic analysis. It is evident from Fig. 2 and and Fig. 3 that the vast majority of the respondents in the survey were between 20 and 30 years old, with most of those being students.

Fig. 2: Occupations of the respondents   **Fig. 3:** Age distribution of the respondents

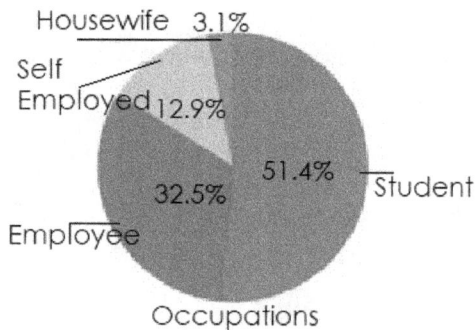

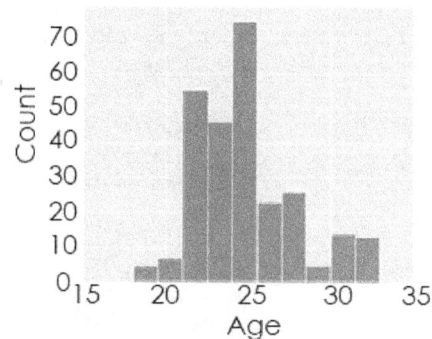

Feature Selection and Implementation of TMT

11 features were considered to make predictions about whether or not the customer would useonline food delivery apps again and the responses were mapped to the four reward parameters.The features selected mostly concern the competence of the apps used for ordering food onlineand the training provided to the delivery agents which ensures that ordered packages are delivered on time and the customer has a pleasant experience.

Features	Reward
Ordering ease	Competence
Restaurant choices	Autonomy
Number of offers	Competence
Good tracking	Competence
Late delivery	Negative Competence
Bad experience	Brand preference

Long delivery time	Negative Competence
Delivery person ability	Competence
Influence of restaurant rating	Belongingness
Politeness	Brand preference

The maximum time a customer is willing to wait was mapped to impulsiveness and the averagetime taken to deliver food in the city of Bangalore (45 minutes) was considered as the delay.

Delay	Impulsiveness
45 min	Maximum waiting time (30-60 min)

Results and Analysis

Monte Carlo Optimization was used to obtain the best weights of each of the four reward parameters. A value distribution plot was then plotted before the threshold for binary classification of the data was decided upon. This threshold was then used to predict whether ornot a respondent would use online food delivery apps again.

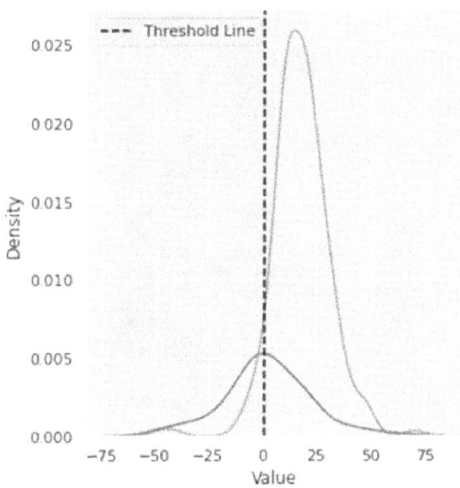

Fig. 4: Data distribution and the chosen threshold line at Value = 1

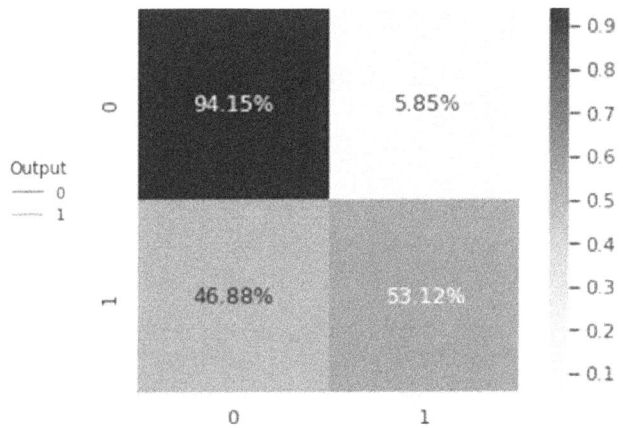

Fig. 5: Confusion matrix of the classification

It is evident from Fig. 4 that the majority of the respondents intend to use online food deliveryapps again. The best threshold for value was found to be 1. Even though the data samples thatcomprise the tails of the distribution are misclassified by the chosen threshold, it is evident thatin cases where overlapping distributions can be separated, greater accuracy can be achieved.

For threshold=1, the accuracy and F1-score of the predictions are given below. F1-score was considered to be an appropriate metric for predictions made using the TMT value equation dueto the imbalance in classes and because it accounts for both, true positives as well as true negatives, being the weighted average of precision and recall. The predictions made are fairlyaccurate, with reasonably high precision and recall as can be seen in F1-score.

Accuracy: 84.39%	F1-score: 90.19%

Primary Data Analysis

Dataset Description

A survey in the form of a questionnaire was designed to test the temporal motivation theory on consumer buying preferences concerning smartphones. The target demographic was the section of the population that has the highest penetration rate in smartphone usage (Vardhman R, 2021). The survey targeted college-going students and working professionals between the ages of 18 and 25. In this study, a purposive sampling technique was used to gather data that is reliable and germane. The questionnaire consisted of 17 closed-ended questions. Before the conduction of the actual survey, a pilot test of the questionnaire was conducted among 10 respondents. The final questionnaire was administered to 87 people.

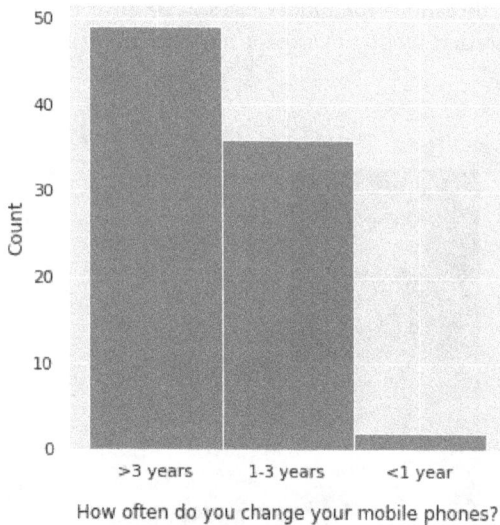

Fig. 6: Distribution plot of responses to how often, they change their phones

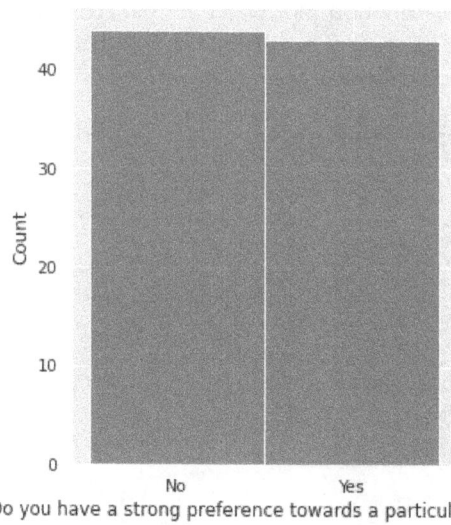

Fig. 7: Distribution plot of responses to test brand loyalty

From Fig. 6, it is gathered that majority of the respondents change their mobile phones every few years while only a few prefer frequent upgrading of their mobile phones, while Fig. 7 shows that almost 50% of the respondents have an inclination towards a particular brand of mobile phone. This inclination can either be due to a positive experience in the past or positive word of mouth.

Fig. 8 and Fig. 9 summarize brand and buying preferences. Even though brand preference for Motorola is smaller than for Realme, Motorola MotoG60 is observed to be a popular choice among the respondents, suggesting that respondents tend to change their preferences when presented with comparable specifications for the available choices.

Implementation of TMT

The questions asked were designed to help us gain a better insight into the buying preferences of the respondents. The answer to each question was mapped to one of the four reward parameters – feeling of autonomy, belongingness and competence, and brand preference. The quantified feeling of reward was then multiplied by the probability of success, which considersonly the number of options available to the consumer. This product was then divided into the product of impulsiveness/impatience and delay. Here, impulsiveness/impatience signifies the urgency in procuring a smartphone. Delay is the minimum amount of time required to completean action, which in this case is the time difference between placing an order for a phone and itis delivered. Respondents were then asked to choose between three brands of smartphones thatfall under the same price range, by comparing their specifications. The three brands chosen were Realme, Motorola, and Infinix. Two of these brands were chosen due to their popularity and the third was chosen to help us gain a better understanding of how buying preferences change in the presence of a brand that offers reasonably competent products but is not very well-known. Unreliable responses had to be weeded out and this was done by repeating questions that were phrased differently and then comparing the respondent's answers to that question with their answers to the original question.

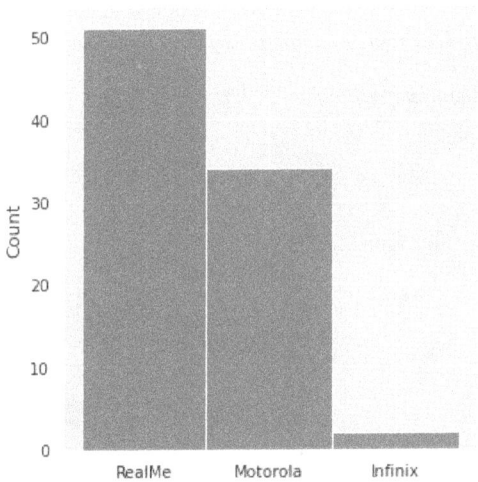

Among the three brands, which one do you prefer?

Fig. 8: Distribution plot of responses for their preferred brand based on the choiceavailable

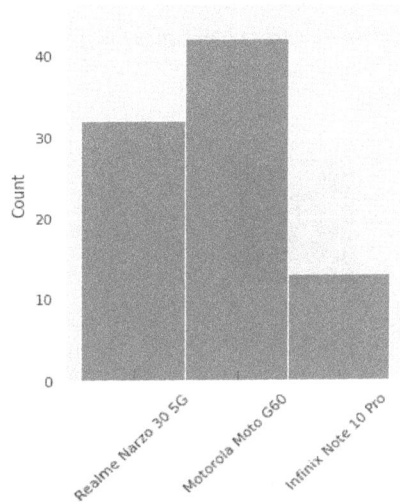

Which of the following phones is your preferred buying option?

Fig. 9: Distribution plot of responses to the preferred buying option

Results and Analysis

Fig. 10 depicts the confusion matrix obtained after analyzing and implementing the Temporal Motivation Theory value equation on primary data. The percentage of accurate classificationswas $\geq$ 50% for each class, going as high as 84.62% for the first class.

Accuracy	Weighted F1 Score
63.01%	63.20%

The general accuracy of the predictions was 63.01%, with a weighted F1-score of 63.02%. F1-score was considered to be an appropriate metric for predictions made using the TMT value equation due to the imbalance in classes and because it accounts for both, true positives as wellas true negatives, being the weighted average of precision and recall.

Fig. 11 depicts the change in preferences over time for different values of impulsiveness for adata sample. If an action is completed well before the time by which it is required to be completed, then impulsiveness may not have a significant impact on the choice made as there is no urgency. Hence, impulsiveness is ignored until delay surpasses it. However, when the importance of taking a certain action towards a particular outcome increases with time but the delay in being able to do so does not decrease appropriately, the value of that particular action decreases. This is reflected in Fig 7. For different values of impulsiveness for each of the three choices – Realme, Infinix, and Motorola – the variation of value in time (delay) is plotted. The plateaus that can be seen in the graph represent the maximum time a consumer might be willing to wait without that time bearing a negative impact on the action the consumer will take for which they require that product. Any delay beyond impulsiveness will decrease the value of the product to the consumer and the rate of decrease will depend on the feeling of reward for each product. As shown in the graph, the value of Infinix drops below that of Motorola after a delay of three units for certain values of impulsiveness. That signifies the increased likelihood of the consumer switching their buying preference from Infinix to Motorola. The values of all products to the consumer decrease with an increase in delay.

Fig. 10. *Confusion matrix of predictions vs. ground reality*   **Fig. 11:** *Preference changes over time for different*

of primary data   *values of impulsiveness [1,2,3]*

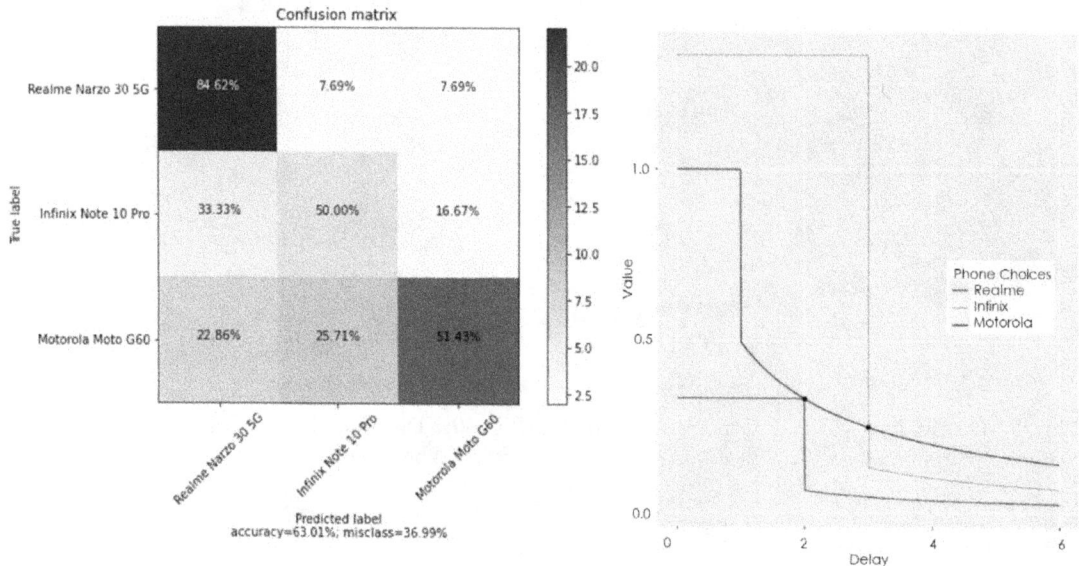

Conclusion

Many attempts have been made to model consumer psychology and consumer behavior. However, each model has its own set of disadvantages and inadequacies. While Temporal Motivation Theory is not perfect, it does integrate the features of many of its predecessors to help model consumer behavior to a reasonable degree as was observed in this study. The potential of the Temporal Motivation Theory in the field of consumer behavior is enormous and has already been identified (Steel & König, 2006).

The managerial implications of this are significant. TMT has shown that its application paves the way for easier identification of the more valuable features of a product to consumers and simultaneously identifies the reasons why a particular brand is preferred over others by a particular demographic.

This will allow the management of corporate entities to decide on removing certain features or adding fresh features to their products to make them more appealing to their target demographic. It will also aid marketers and organizations in creating value by developing a better understanding of their customer's perception of their products andappropriately optimizing their manufacturing processes, supply chains, and marketing and promotional strategies to enhance levels of customer satisfaction, encourage repeat purchases,and cement brand loyalty. Additionally, the fact that prediction models based on this theory require minimal data to work when compared to machine learning models is a major advantageas it eases data collection and analysis.

One important factor overlooked while modeling consumer behavior using the Temporal Motivation Theory is the influence of price on human decision-making. Factoring price into the equation might result in unreliable predictions unless it includes several other variables associated with it, such as the economic class a potential consumer belongs to, their spending patterns, etc. These variables are usually analyzed by marketers separately and Temporal Motivation Theory can be used just to analyze competing products belonging to a similar pricerange, which will help in isolating factors that are creating a huge positive impact or factors that might be adversely affecting the psychological value of a product to consumers. However,a deeper and more comprehensive study is required to decide how best to implement the Temporal Motivation Theory in various industries and to scale the reward factors appropriatelybased on consumer demographics.

References

Ainslie, G., & Haslam, N. (1992). Hyperbolic discounting. In G. Loewenstein & J. Elster(Eds.), *Choice over time: 57-92*. New York: Russel Sage Foundation.

André, Q., Carmon, Z., Wertenbroch, K., Crum, A., Frank, D., Goldstein, W., Huber, J., vanBoven, L., Weber, B., & Yang, H. (2018). Consumer Choice and Autonomy in the Ageof Artificial Intelligence and Big Data. *Customer Needs and Solutions*. https://doi.org/10.1007/s40547-017-0085-8

Stubseid, S., & Arandjelovic, O. (2018). Machine Learning Based Prediction of ConsumerPurchasing Decisions: The Evidence and Its Significance. *AAAI Workshops*.

Asniar, & Surendro, K. (2019). Predictive analytics for predicting customer behavior. Proceeding - 2019 International Conference of Artificial Intelligence and Information Technology, ICAIIT 2019. https://doi.org/10.1109/ICAIIT.2019.8834571

Bass, F. M., & Talarzyk, W. W. (1972). An Attitude Model for the Study of BrandPreference. *Journal of Marketing Research*. https://doi.org/10.2307/3149618

Cobb-Walgren, C. J., Ruble, C. A., & Donthu, N. (1995). Brand equity, brand preference, andpurchase intent. *Journal of Advertising*. https://doi.org/10.1080/00913367.1995.10673481

Grant, R., Clarke, R. J., & Kyriazis, E. (2013). real-time online information needs A newresearch approach for complex consumer *Journal of Marketing Management*. https://doi.org/10.1080/0267257X.2011.621440

Green, L., & Myerson, J. (2004). A discounting framework for choice with delayed andprobabilistic rewards. In *Psychological Bulletin*. https://doi.org/10.1037/0033- 2909.130.5.769

Janssen, M. A., & Jager, W. (2001). Fashions, habits and changing preferences: Simulation ofpsychological factors affecting market dynamics. *Journal of Economic Psychology*. https://doi.org/10.1016/S0167-4870(01)00063-0

Kahneman, D., & Tversky, A. (1979). Prospect Theory: An Analysis of Decision under RiskDaniel Kahneman; Amos Tversky. *Econometrica*.

Kanagal, N. (2016). An Extended Model of Behavioral Process in Consumer Decision Making. *International Journal of Marketing Studies*.https://doi.org/10.5539/ijms.v8n4p87

Li, J., Pan, S., Huang, L., & Zhu, X. (2019). A machine learning based method for customerbehavior prediction. *Tehnicki Vjesnik*. https://doi.org/10.17559/TV-20190603165825

Martínez, A., Schmuck, C., Pereverzyev, S., Pirker, C., & Haltmeier, M. (2020). A machinelearning framework for customer purchase prediction in the non-contractual setting. *European Journal of Operational Research*. https://doi.org/10.1016/j.ejor.2018.04.034

Qiu, J., Lin, Z., & Li, Y. (2015). Predicting customer purchase behavior in the e-commercecontext. *Electronic Commerce Research*. https://doi.org/10.1007/s10660-015-9191-6

Roshan, B. (2020). Online Food Delivery preferences - Bangalore Region. *Kaggle*. https://www.kaggle.com/benroshan/online-food-delivery-preferencesbangalore-region

Steel, P., & König, C. J. (2006). Integrating theories of motivationSteel, P., & König, C. J.(2006). Integrating theories of motivation. Academy of Management Review. https://doi.org/10.5465/AMR.2006.22527462.

Tian, K. T., Bearden, W. O., & Hunter, G. L. (2001). Consumers' need for uniqueness: Scaledevelopment and validation. *Journal of Consumer Research*. https://doi.org/10.1086/321947

Tversky, A., & Kahneman, D. (1992). Advances in prospect theory: Cumulativerepresentation of uncertainty. *Journal of Risk and Uncertainty*. https://doi.org/10.1007/BF00122574

Vardhman, R. (2021). Smartphone Users in India (Statistics & Facts) - 2021. *Findly*.https://findly.in/smartphone-users-in-india-statistics/.

Vroom, V. (1965). Work And Motivation - Vroom,Vh. *Personnel Psychology*.

CHAPTER 6

MARKETING 4.0: EMERGING TECHNOLOGIES THAT ARE REFINING DIGITAL MARKETING

Fathima Raj Kilimas[1], Ashish Chandra[2], Narendra Rustagi[3]

Introduction

Technology can be defined as the application of scientific knowledge to meet a specific practical need. This definition is an all-embracing one and is more relevant in a world which has seen its influence permeate every facet of the present-day life at a rapid pace. However, its influence can be embodied in the diverse industries that have emerged in this century. Certain industries are anticipated to change so much in the coming 20 years than they have in the last two centuries (Morrison, 2017). To counter the impact of technology and to ensure that they never lose sight of the race, industry giants are investing a huge chunk of their revenue on Research and Development; and its (R&D) part of the pie is always on the rise year-on-year (Loeb, 2018). The computational and analytical ability of AI systems are increasing faster than Moore's Law (Perrault, 2019). Such prowess has enabled the emergence of a multitude of streams rooted in Artificial Intelligence and related technologies.

Technology is an inevitable element of our everyday life. A report by We Are Social indicates that there are more than 5 billion unique mobile users, about 4.4 billion internet users. In India, the internet penetration rate is nearly 45% in 2021 (Statista, 2021). Another key metric to be kept in mind is the global social media users (3.6 billion in 2020). The wide array of analytics providers has enabled firms to efficiently target their customers by customizing the message and delivering personalized content. The oftenest used acronym "What You See Is What You Get – WYSIWYG" is a clear indication of the power information possesses on the internet. Further, digitalization has opened the avenue for new types of business models that are thriving on the rapid progress that the IT industry has attained over the last few decades (Milkau, 2019).

Efficiency, replication and zero incremental cost are the three pillars of any digital technology. Digital platforms are so ubiquitous that they have become a necessity to most organizations. Though an enhancer to business development, rapid changes in the technology and digital advancement are considered a major challenge for businesses today. This necessitates businesses to be ever more vigilant of the changing paradigms in the industry.

The VUCA world challenges the ability of organisations and managers to cater to the needs of the users. However, the accumulation of consumers in one platform (internet) is beneficial because the efforts that would have otherwise diverged into multiple channels is focused on a single channel to deliver a superior experience. Digital Marketing caters to the growing demands of users on the internet. Many emerging technologies are coming to the aid of both the firms and users to enable engagement and usefulness. Managers must possess a technology orientation to identify opportunities

---

[1] Mr. Fathima Raj Kilimas, Welingkar Institute of Management Development and Research, Bangalore, India.
E-mail: fathima.kilimas@welingkar.org
[2] Prof. Ashish Chandra, Professor of Healthcare Administration, College of Business, University of Houston-Clearlake, USA.
E-mail: chandra@uhcl.edu
[3] Dr. Narendra Rustagi, Howard University, USA. E-mail: nrustagi@howard.edu

while conforming with the required norms and practices to attain business success (Nikolaeva & Bicho, 2011).

Terminology

By the word 'technology' we intend to mean the word 'technology paradigm', as they have multiple technology applications. However, for the sake of simplicity the term technology has been used. In certain sections we have explicitly mentioned technology paradigm to avoid confusion. Emerging technologies are those that contains the following 5 attributes: radical novelty, fast growth, coherence, prominent impact and uncertain and ambiguous (Rotolo, 2015). We have used the term 'emerging technologies' to indicate those technologies which possess the 5 attributes and are garnering interests and innovation from the business community.

According to American Marketing Association, "Digital marketing is the use of digital or social channels to promote a brand or reach consumers". One of the reasons to focus on Digital Marketing is the rapid accumulation of users on the internet and the innovative potential it possesses. Another reason is that in the last few years, the ad budgets are tilting in favour of digital marketing over traditional media (Adgate, 2021). Such shift in budgets have led to innovations in the Digital Marketing industry, which can be capitalised by managers.

Further, refining is considered from the perspective of how certain technologies are transforming digital marketing in the process of creating, communicating, delivering, and exchanging products or services.

We intent address the following research objectives through this study: To study the various emerging technologies for their appropriateness in digital marketing decisions. The study the managerial implication, and current and future metrices that aid in improving customer experiences.

Significance of the Study

The technological, socioeconomic, and geopolitical trends have a profound impact on marketing, and are reshaping the field of marketing (Rust, 2020). Research indicates that integrating technology and marketing strategy in a VUCA aids in corporate success (Capon, 1987). Technology also has a deeper impact on marketing due to the declining costs and the implications they have on existing markets (Shugan, 2004). A study done on Belgian firms indicated that practitioners are to give special consideration to resources that aid in IT enabled marketing initiatives (Trainor, 2011).

Technological innovations and solutions compel marketers to stay ahead of the curve and provide opportunities to create, communicate, capture, and deliver value for and to customers (Grewal, et. al., 2020). There are studies evidencing that technology adoption in marketing is prevalent even among small businesses ((Bulearca & Bulearca, 2010; Durkin, McGowan, & McKeown, 2013; Harris & Rae, 2009; Kim et al., 2011; McGowan & Durkin, 2002; Simmons et al., 2008, 2011). Therefore, it is crucial for marketers from both large and small firms to keep themselves acquainted with the dominant technologies that have the deepest impact on marketing.

As customers are gearing up for interacting with virtual content, technologies are enabling firms to reach out to these customers via effective integration in the marketing strategies (Grewal et al. 2020a). Technologies help in transforming such interactions between consumers and firms and acts as an intermediary to build better relationships (Yadav & Pavlou, 2020). There is growing interest in understanding the implications of these technologies across domains as these improve customer experience and interactivity (Grewal et al. 2017, 2018). The pandemic is thought of as one of the reasons which quickened the pace of adoption and usefulness of technologies.

Mangers are continuously faced with challenges in their business environment and need to possess technology orientation (Nikolaeva & Bicho, 2011). Technology orientation is the continuous search for new technologies beyond the existing boundaries of business (Gatignon & Xuereb, 1997). Efficient technologies could lead to new business models which in turn could lead to competitive advantage, lowering costs, value addition, newer channels, and revenue models. (Wei et al., 2014; Zott et al., 2011; Clauss, 2017; Teece, 2010). Such an orientation could also lead firms out of their resistance toward innovation (Heidenreich & Talke, 2020). Therefore, it is necessary for managers to scout for better technologies.

Those firms that are early adopters in any technology tend to determine the 'rules of the game' is another reason managers need to continuously look out for newer options (Grewal, 2019). This study will potentially benefit the digital marketing practitioners who intend to take the lead in evaluating and adopting technological options for better resource allocation.

Approach to the Review

Literature review and In-depth interview have been used as the two research methods. Industry Reports and Academic journals were considered to understand some of the emerging technologies that are impacting the digital marketing environment. The shortlisting of technologies was based on AMA's definition of Marketing, which included creating, communicating, delivering, and exchanging. Further, the implications these technologies have on user engagement in digital marketing is considered.

We intend to study how each of these technologies impact decision making for managers and the possible metrics and dimensions that help in decision making. The various technologies are discussed with reference to their application and the complexities they pose to digital marketing. Further, potential metrics and future direction for each of these technologies are discussed too. Though not a comprehensive list, we intent to create a set of useful technologies and their implications which would help decision makers in the field of digital marketing.

Methodology

To gain an in-depth understanding of the various technology paradigms open-ended in-depth interviews were used for data collection for the current study. Research has indicated that in-depth open interviews enable researchers to understand the experiences concerning a phenomenon (Creswell, 1998) and an opportunity to understand it from their perspective (McCracken, 1988). We organised in-depth interviews with industry experts who were associated with the field of technology.

The questions were designed to understand how these experts used these technologies and the practical implications these had on creating, communicating, delivering, and exchanging value for their product or service. All participants were chosen based on the years of experience (minimum 20 years in the marketing domain of any technology company). The sample included 20 individuals with the above referenced requirements. An interview guide was developed, based on the review of the literature, and was utilized for the interviews. It included four main questions for each of these technological paradigms with associated probes in understanding the implication of these technologies in relation to creating, communicating, delivering, and exchanging value for their product or service. (McCracken, 1988).

The below referenced table contains the definitions of the key words (creating, communicating, delivering, and exchanging) of marketing (Tanner, J., & Raymond, M. A., 2012). Based on these the authors were required to rate the specific technology in terms of its relevance.

Even though the interview guide had associated probes, the questions that followed were based on the responses provided by these experts. In simple the responses to the main questions determined the direction of the probes (McCracken, 1988). The interviews were organised in a comfortable surrounding which was devoid of any distraction. Notes which were taken during the interview provided the basis for the results. The interviews ranged between half an hour to an hour.

Table 1: The definitions are taken from the book Marketing Principles (v 1.0)

Key Word	Definition
Creating	The process of collaborating with suppliers and customers to create offerings that have value
Communicating	Broadly, describing those offerings, as well as learning from customers.
Delivering	Getting those offerings to the consumer in a way that optimizes value
Exchanging	Trading value for those offerings

Literature Review and Theoretical Background

Based on a series of research reports and articles from Gartner, PwC, Forbes, etc., and a few academic journals a series of Twelve (12) technologies were initially considered for the study (PwC, 2018; Garfinkel, 2018; Rayome, 2019; Newman, 2019; Kotane, 2019; Marr, 2020; Stamford, 2021). These included 5G, Robotics, 3D printing, Drones, Digital Twins, Biometrics, Artificial Intelligence, Voice Assistants, Immersive Experiences (AR/VR/MR), Internet of Things (IoT), Blockchain and Big Data. The technologies were chosen based on their widespread acceptance and the potential for growth in mainstream business.

According to American Marketing Association, "Marketing is the activity, set of institutions and processes for creating, communicating, delivering, and exchanging offerings that have value for customers, clients, partners, and society at large". In accordance with this definition, the technologies that are aiding in the process of creating, communicating, delivering, and exchanging are considered for this study.

The industry experts were required to rate the relevance of each of these technologies to digital marketing on a scale of 1 to 10 in relation to creating, communicating, delivering, and exchanging value, 1 being the lowest and 10 being the highest. The cumulative points were averaged and nearest whole number was chosen based on two decimal points. The below referenced table categorizes each of these technologies in terms of their relevance to digital marketing as high, medium, and low. In a 10-point scale, technologies were scored *High* if they were rated between 8-10, as *Medium* if they were scored between 5-7 and as *low* for those that scored 4 or below.

Table 2: Impact of emerging technologies

Technology	Creating	Communicating	Delivering	Exchanging
IoT	*High*	*High*	*High*	*High*
AI	*High*	*High*	*High*	*High*
5G	Low	Low	High	Low
Blockchain	*High*	*High*	*High*	*High*
Robotics	Low	Low	Low	Medium
Biometrics	Low	Low	Low	Medium
3D printing	Low	Low	High	Medium
Immersive Experience	*High*	*High*	*High*	*High*
Drones	Low	Low	High	High
Voice Assistants	*High*	*High*	*High*	*High*
Digital Twins	Low	Low	Low	Medium
Big Data	*High*	*High*	*High*	*High*

Only those technologies that have a high impact on digital marketing have been considered for the study. Even though 5G, Robotics, 3D printing, Biometrics, Drones, and Digital Twins have implications on marketing, they are not considered in the present study as they have not scored consistently high across the various stages of digital marketing. Future studies could be organised to understand the implications of these technologies. Artificial Intelligence, Voice Assistants, Immersive Experiences (AR/VR/MR), Internet of Things (IoT), Blockchain and Big Data are considered because they have scored consistently high on the impact they have on the stages of marketing (digital marketing). The justification for the claims in the table are detailed in the coming paragraphs. The below referenced table provides the list of technologies that are shortlisted and their impact across digital marketing.

Table 3: Emerging Technologies that are shortlisted for the study

Technology	Creating	Communicating	Delivering	Exchanging
AI	*High*	*High*	*High*	*High*
Voice Assistants	*High*	*High*	*High*	*High*
Immersive Experience	*High*	*High*	*High*	*High*
IoT	*High*	*High*	*High*	*High*
Blockchain	*High*	*High*	*High*	*High*
Big Data	*High*	*High*	*High*	*High*

Potential Market Growth of the selected technologies

One of the criteria to consider something an emerging technology is that it needs to have fast growth (Rotolo, 2015). The below referenced bar graph give a glimpse into market potential of these technologies (Aslop, 2021; See, 2021; Statista Research Department, 2021; Vailshery, 2021; Marketers Media, 2022). It also indicates the market for all the chosen technologies are projected to significantly grow in the next few years. Though these technologies do not limit their impact on digital marketing, they can drastically transform digital marketing because of their direct implications.

The possibility of growth from the graph indicates higher innovation and better features in the future. Therefore, a carefully considered set of emerging technologies towards which decision makers could direct their budgets to complement their efforts is a necessity from the perspective of ROI. This paper intents to delve into such technologies trends that could aid digital marketers in their endeavours.

Graph 1: Technologies and their global market potential in USD (billions)

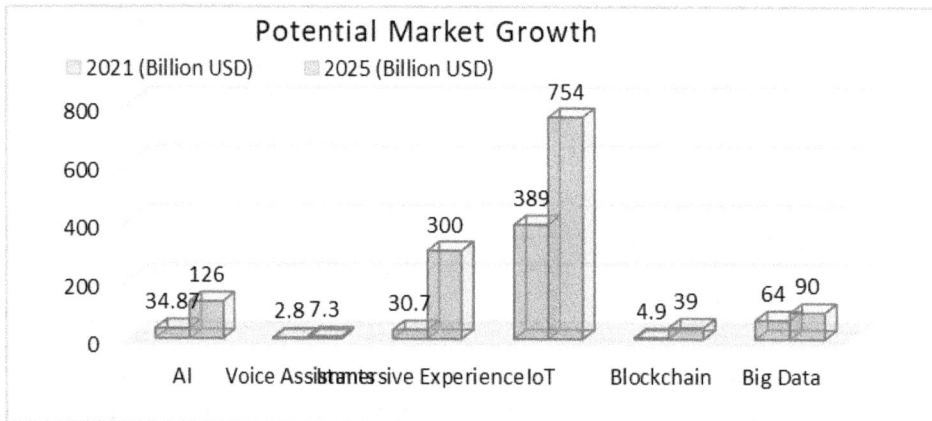

Potential Market Growth

■ 2021 (Billion USD)　　■ 2025 (Billion USD)

Bar values shown: AI 34.87, 126; Voice Assistants 2.8, 7.3; Immersive Experience 30.7, 300; IoT 389, 754; Blockchain 4.9, 39; Big Data 64, 90

[The data for IoT is from 2020 (reflecting as 2021) and the data for Immersive Experiences is projected to 2024 (reflecting as 2025)]

Technology Paradigms and their influence

In the following paragraphs each of the shortlisted technology paradigms are reviewed in brief to understand their real-world applications. We also review the managerial implications, important metrices and future directions of the shortlisted technologies, which we intent to be a useful collation for decision makers in the field of digital marketing. Each of the technology paradigms are categorized into three sub parts – introduction, business application & research, and managerial implications. The table below describes each of the technologies and the subcategories that have been considered for the study.

Table 4: Technology Paradigms and the subcategories

Technology Paradigms	Subcategories	Journals
AI	Cognitive Science, Robotics and Natural Interface Applications	Strong, A. I. (2016).
Voice Assistants	Interactive Voice Response [IVR] systems, smartphones, and smart speakers	Sezgin, E., Militello, L. K., Huang, Y., & Lin, S. (2020)
Immersive Experience	Virtual Reality, Augmented Reality, and Mixed Reality	Zhang, C. (2020)
IoT	Social Internet of Things, Semantic, Future Internet, Cloud, Evolved RFID-IoT integration	Atzori, L., Iera, A., & Morabito, G. (2017) (Only Third Gen is chosen)
Blockchain	Piracy, Data Security & Privacy	Jain, D., Dash, M. K., Kumar, A., & Luthra, S. (2021)
Big Data	E-Commerce, Data Analytics, Piracy, & Data Privacy	Cozzoli, N.,et. al (2022); & Jain, P., Gyanchandani, M., & Khare, N. (2016)

Artificial Intelligence

This term has caught the attention of individuals from the time when John McCarthy coined it in the mid-1950s; however, its implications are felt strongly by the firms and users alike in the last few decades. Though a single synthesizing idea is at least quite some years away, progress in achieving excellence in specific fields is stupendous. From Programmatic Advertising to Content Creation to building a better user engagement, AI has seen its applications in an array of industries, including digital marketing (van Esch, 2021).

Business Applications & Research: The growing research interests in the field Artificial Intelligence (AI) has led to a great many business applications. With concepts such as Computer Vision, AI planning, Deep Learning affecting the way we interact with machines, it has had far reaching consequences in attaining efficiency for a specific task and its permeating effect can be felt in numerous industries (Stanford University, 2016). The modus operandi of humans instructing a technology is reversed in some cases such as the Jennifer unit. Today, technology assists humans while minimizing error. The vast amount of data from such technologies helps in market research, customer engagement, new product development, service delivery innovation and relationship management (Davenport & Ronanki, 2018)

Managerial Implications of AI: Ensuring that one's website has the least bounce rates is one of the prime tasks of any digital marketer as it drags your position down in the Search Engine Result Page (SERP). AI technologies such as Machine Learning are useful in making websites responsive which helps in reducing bounce rate and improves navigation, both of which are crucial metrics when it comes to SEO. If not taken care, this can result in search engines considering the information irrelevant to the user. Personalizing websites, using AI based predictive analytics and other features, increases the effectiveness of Identity Resolution and Account Based Marketing (ABM) campaigns. With adequate AI features, marketers can give an ideal experience for those who reach our landing pages or websites and improve the probability of performing the desired action. Such personalization can also result in positive brand association. Machine Learning, Native Advertising, Chatbots, Programmatic Advertising, Omni-channel Integration, Email Marketing Automation, and many more digital technologies have teetered digital marketing time and again.

Online Analytics Processing which is enabled by cloud is a vital technology that is renovating Business Intelligence. With their ability to perform complex analytical function and provide predictive 'what if' solutions help in precision forecasting. Pre stored data with the help of dimensions and measures provide analysis at exceptional speed (Ivanov, 2019). Firms will have to learn to integrate various platforms to provide an Omni-channel experience to customers to capture the mind of the young audience. The quality of the displayed content is very crucial because about half of the consumers would desert if the content were displayed poorly.

As search engines get smarter, the black hat techniques will give way to white hat techniques in SEO. This means that quality and relevance of content will play a crucial role. A paper on Digital Content Marketing indicates that some of the antecedents that play a crucial role in the mind of the consumer are the functional motive, hedonic motive, and authenticity motive. The paper also suggests that companies can begin with cognitive, emotional, and behavioral engagement and then move to gaining brand trust and brand attitude, which could ultimately result in Brand Equity (Hollebeek, 2019).

As users more users are adopting mobile phones for finding information, new advances such as Accelerated Mobile Pages (AMP) and Progressive Web Apps (PWA) have become useful. Though, some Search Engine companies have claimed that such advancements do not have an impact on Search Engine Results Pages (SERP). However, Search Engine Land's periodic table for the year 2019 has included them among the factors that will impact SEO.

Therefore, as marketers, it is paramount to ensure that content delivered on the digital media will have to be authentic and relevant. As individuals get saturated with promotions and advertisements via the digital media and the efficiency of Click through Rates (CTR) rapidly declining, content (in terms of text, image, video, and voice) will be a powerful force that will drive traffic to one's website for any kind of action. This indicates that marketers will have to create content that increases engagement with the users, while at the same time being authentic, else pay the price of being blocked by the search engines and lose all the traction gained until then. Therefore, investments in relations to such applications will translate into useful results for marketers.

Voice Assistants

Voice Assistants Market can be categorized into smart speakers, personal assistants, laptop, smartphones, tablets, set-top box, wearable, and healthcare (Moreno, 2022). Research by PWC in 2019 indicates that 65% of the individuals between the age group 25 and 49 speak at least once a day to their voice enabled devices; within the 18 to 24 age categories, it was at 59% (PricewaterhouseCoopers, 2018). The intense competition between Amazon Echo, Apple Homepod and Google Home can only be justified by the fact that about 30% of the searches in 2020 was not on a screen-based device.

Business Applications & Research: An Adobe report says that more than one third of the customers believe that voice ads are less intrusive and more engaging (Abramovich, 2019). As adoption rose it led to an equivalent rise in innovation in this technology. One example is China's iFlytek, which can translate English into Mandarin and Mandarin into multiple other languages at 98% efficiency (Synced, 2017). Considering that the number of voice searches are rising, marketers can effectively run advertising campaigns. Researchers are trying to understand how voice assistants affect the behaviour of users while shopping online via voice (Mari, 2021). Further, research in terms of how certain users make decision using smart devices are also explored (Dellaert, 2020).

Managerial Implications of Voice Assistants: To build better experiences managers are finding innovative ways to use this technology. In the coming years (or months), to ensure that your page appears in the SERP (Search Engine Result Page), marketers will also have to optimize their websites for the spoken language; this ensures that the voice queries are captured and attended to. A 'call request' campaign can be run through these devices where the devices would run an advertisement and at end ask a polar question requesting the user to choose to receive a call (or not) from the specific advertiser.

Adequate techniques must be incorporated to counter the needs of voice search which can puncture the way Search Engine Optimization (SEO) currently functions. This means that purely text-based optimization would be insufficient going forward. Research has indicated that SEO and SEM will play a part in the way search queries are displayed for voice queries. Therefore, synchronous tools and techniques which provide integration for all formats of search queries must be introduced and incorporated. Since the spoken language is different from the written language, for at least some of the languages, digital marketers will have focus on a new keyword and not limit themselves to short or long tail keywords.

Marketers will have to take measures to ensure that voice-based search queries are captured and addressed to. Some measures that could be taken include – to ensure that the websites are secured (HTTPS), using of schema markup language (structed data) to be informative and relevant, to make mobile websites that are user friendly and fast, a detailed FAQ section which captures the questions that people might ask to a voice assistant, optimizing the content on one's website for local SEO and many more. As the voice assistants get smarter, we could develop apps that trigger push notifications onto user mobile and making the search and purchase experience delightful.

Immersive Experiences

Immersive Experiences include Augmented Reality, Virtual Reality and Mixed Reality. Augmented Reality (AR) is used to add an item to the physical environment, while Virtual Reality (VR) creates its own environment and Mixed Reality (MR) is a hybrid of both. By 2022, smart clothing is expected to be shipped in quantities exceeding three (3) crores; about two and a half (2.5) crore units of AR headsets and about four (4) crore VR headsets are expected to be sold within the same period (Liu, 2019). Further, AR can be used to foster a powerful customer brand relationship; one such example is 'shopping on the go'.

Business Applications & Research: Progress in the field of human and computer interaction is indicating that traditional sensory interactions such as visual and auditory inputs are no more the limit of upcoming purchase interfaces (Scholz, 2018). Today, Shoppers are able to better experience their physical world with the help augmented reality that provides context specific information leading to better purchase experiences (Heller et al. 2019; Hilken et al. 2020; Jessen et al. 2020). The same revolution is taking place in the Virtual Reality space too (Flavián et al. 2019; Sample et al. 2020).

Managerial Implications of Immersive Experiences: Immersive Experiences can become useful when you want to show a product prior to customer experiencing the product. In some cases, even before the product is ready, for example in the real estate sector, which could use the virtual experience to give a glimpse into how their projects will look upon completion. During the Covid-19 pandemic the positive impact of such Immersive Experiences was studied in detail by researchers especially in marketing tech (Ekmeil, 2021). Rather than using brochures and drab websites, such technologies can increase the likelihood of customers' openness toward advance booking.

For digital marketers, these technologies can be used to increase customer delight. For example, a company like IKEA uses the Augment Reality technology to see how the furniture will look in one's living room or any other space, with the help of mobile phone's camera. With technologies such as depth perception and others coming to their aid the experience is only going to get better in the future. This reduces the effort needed, from the perspective of the customer, to imagine how a variety of products will look in their desired space and choose optimally.

Many companies from the eye-ware industry have also used this technology to go so far as to suggest what kinds of frames suit the user's face structure; customer can also try and choose from the numerous options available online. From the perspective of the marketer, it reduces the replacement costs, warehousing costs and more importantly increases the digital customer delight, which is crucial to a successful digital campaign. From smart helmet to smart glasses, digital marketers across industries will have come up with innovative solutions to optimize user experiences on digital platforms.

The Microsoft HoloLens and Bosch Rexroth, which has used the mixed reality experience using devices, applications, and other solutions to ensure that training and guidance can be provided remotely. Meta, Microsoft, Nvidia, Epic Games, Apple and others have invested a lot of resources into bringing better experiences to the immersive experience space (Sinha, 2022). Even in India, the leading companies are offering services to help in the development of metaverse (The Hindu, 2022). Though such platforms will take time to consolidate, mangers will have to take the lead in developing such spaces to capture audiences who will move towards such platforms. This shift could be looked upon as the next evolution of social media and social commerce. In the future, such technologies can be used to aid effective marketing campaigns and may provide an opportunity for ad spaces in the non-premium segments.

Internet of Things (IoT)

According to a survey the number of devices connected to the Internet of Things (IoT) will become 30.9 billion by 2025. (Statista, 2021). The academic research in the field of Internet of Things is vast and there is research pointing to the application of this technology in digital marketing from creation to exchanging (Perera, 2019). Behavioural Surplus which is indication of the amount of data that is being generated has drastically increased because of sensor based devices and these have helped marketers make sense of the available data (Kilimas, 2021).

Business Applications & Research: Today, visual is the most frequently used form of interface between a customer and the machine. In one survey by Kissmetrics, 93% of consumers consider visuals to be the key deciding factor in a purchase decision (Rogers, 2014). However, Sensory Enabling Technologies (SET), an application of IoT, will enable the customer to break the barrier of limiting oneself to the visual experience. It provides a multisensory experience that captures the environment of the product and render it through the online platform. SET of the future will use a combination of visual, haptic, auditory, olfactory, and gustatory techniques to simulate real life experience via the internet (Petit, 2018). For managers, this translates into users having higher product knowledge and better purchase decisions.

Managerial Implications of IoT: The array of interminable devices such as wearable devices, electronic devices, headphones, digital assistants, smartphones, and many more are part of Internet of Things (IoT) revolution. Concepts such as Industrial Internet of Things and others have played their role in the way industry seeks and analyses information. IoT is likely to change some business models of firms which desire to incorporate the huge amount of data that are captured via these technologies. But as there is going to be an avalanche of data coming in old metrics and dimensions might become irrelevant for technologies like SET. New ways of measuring and analyzing how people perceive the quality of visual, haptic, auditory, olfactory, and gustatory interfaces, how they respond to the various triggers, etc., will come into the picture.

A world of possibilities exists for sectors such as the FMCG (Fast Moving Consumer Goods), which can effectively utilize these monitoring systems to identify sensory triggers. In some cases, digital marketers might be able to create a retail experience at home, with trials, which is more likely to increase the chances of the customer purchasing online. The application of this technology can increase the effectiveness and efficiency of Click-through-Rates (CTR) and Impression campaigns, which are losing traction, due to the avalanche of advertisements.

Blockchain

From the time Satoshi Nakamoto released the bitcoin whitepaper in 2009, blockchain and its applications have been widely debated. Concepts such as smart contracts, which avoid all the cumbersome processes in between, could become widely used with the help of this technology. The properties of Blockchain – transparency, immutability, and security, if extended to marketing can widely influence multiple platforms and generate new revenue models.

Business Applications & Research: Companies such as Mastercard and Visa have offered the option to send money through a Blockchain, in the local currency. However, its applications are not limited to one sector (Harvey, 2018). Maersk, a shipping company has made use of the Blockchain technology, with the help of IBM and government authorities, and real time sensors to provide fast, cost-effective services (Furr, 2019). Another, important element of Blockchain is avoiding piracy. KODAKOne, a company by Kodak facilitates the management of image rights for photographers using KodakCoin. Its application extends even to advertising, as the authenticity of content improves it will have a proportional growth in advertising, as counterfeit and duplication will become highly regulated (Harvey, 2018). Even in social media, companies such as Keybase are providing authentication mechanism of valid accounts, which could be used to efficiently targets customers and avoid unnecessary budget spends on fake accounts.

Managerial Implications of Blockchain: Blockchain is revolutionizing security on the online space. With the advent of Blockchain based firms, the digital marketing industry will become highly competitive and customer centric. New ecosystems might emerge with various forms of crypto currencies. Researchers have been continuously exploring the use cases for finance and marketing in general and nowadays even in the field of digital marketing (Thangam, 2021).

Personalization and security would become the key driver to increase Blockchain adoption in the future. Though barriers such as technological, governance, organizational and societal exists for the adoption of this technology, the rising costs of fake data and hacking will drive certain keystone industries to adopt blockchain based technologies. When issues related to privacy might become irrelevant, there could be huge shifts in online consumer behaviour. As fake products and services, with their glorified hyperboles vanish, authentic and useful products will gain traction and thereby open wide the new era of online consumer behaviour.

In 2019, advertisers globally lost about $5.8 billion because of online fraud, this could be countered via Blockchain based advertising according to a Gartner report (Panetta, 2019). Currently, companies such as Meta and Google dominate the digital ads space. Though the traditional bid-based advertising might still exit, new forms where individuals get paid directly by firms for allowing ads on their websites could emerge. This would drive companies to make products and services that would have to be fundamentally useful to the society. And advertising campaigns might shift from purely promotional to information-based campaigns, where trust could lead the race.

Big Data

As an economist article had quoted in the previous decade, 'data is the next oil'. Information is a crucial element in guiding people towards decision making, and meaningful data is information. To meet the rising demands of the users, search engines such as Google and to provide highly relevant information. The popularity of Google's 'micro-moments' is a clear hint to the way people use their devices to seek information for basic necessitates.

Business Applications & Research: Google is continuously updating its algorithm to counter black hat techniques, fake information, and phishing websites. It is said that, on average, Google releases 11 updates per year. The Panda Update was to reinforce trust globally by countering such concerns. Search Engine Optimization (SEO) and Search Engine Marketing (SEM) are two methods that affect the way content reaches the user. Though data enables such firms to understand user preferences and help in providing better experiences, the idea of surveillance capitalism triggers concerns related to privacy. In a paper titled "Automated Serendipity" the authors are concerned about the power search engines and aggregators possess to push individuals into echo chambers and filter bubbles (Richard, 2018).

Just as any other technology it has its pros and cons too. However, from the perspective of marketers the availability of digital data has created better measurement metrices with the help of better technology (Pauwels et. al, 2009). From the managerial perspective useful applications of big data leads to innovative and better marketing solutions (Grishikashvili & Meadows, 2014). Companies such as Netflix, Google, Amazon, Apple, and many more have started focusing on economies of scope, where user data becomes powerful to determine preferences and, in some cases, recommend the perfect experience.

Managerial Implications of Big Data: Marketers are required to make meaningful and practical analysis using the data retrieved from a plethora of sources and deter information overload and misinterpretation. Predictive Analysis and Big data will play a huge role here, as the amount and diversity of data will increase. Though Big Data can answer the 'what' of the problem, the 'why' will require sufficient help from the field of cognitive science. Account based platforms, Multitouch Attribution and Identity Resolution that are reaching the trough of disillusionment in the Gartner Hype Cycle for Digital Marketing 2021 and are expected to have innovative solutions arising out of them (Stamford, 2021).

Concerns related to the ethical use of data has gained prominence with the rising data privacy breaches. The data breach by Cambridge Analytica is an example of how complex algorithms can collect data without the approval of the individual. This is where, protocols like the General Data Protection Regulation (GDPR) and others could affect the way data is collected and used (Ghosh, 2018). The fines for noncompliance are high and it becomes crucial for managers to be aware and adhere to the data regulation policies of the state.

Amalgamation of These Technologies

The power of technologies amplifies when they come together and aid in reducing discomfort, increasing frictionless experiences, and boosting loyalty (Dekimpe et al., 2020). As technologies come together, understanding customer requirements becomes essential for better customer service. Large quantities of useful data from multiple technology sources aid to efficiently understand customer and help in customizing the product as per customer needs. It can also be used to target ideal customers with products they are likely to buy. With the appropriate combination of technology marketers can match the products to the digital persona (online personality created from such data) and thereby improve digital sales.

As investments keep pooling towards means to combine the transformative power of multiple technologies, marketers need to complement it with their efforts to incorporate it within their firms. A combination of technologies can aid in understanding the customers better and providing effective personalization, which can help in unplanned purchase too (Davis, 2019). As the adoption of technologies increase, their potential must be proactively understood and managed, especially in relation to sustainability (Dodman, D., 2016; Han, J., et. al., 2017).

Value Addition to Digital Marketing

Industry giants such as General Electric, Microsoft and Accenture have come together to innovate new technologies and finding new ways of using their resources (Iansiti, 2014). New techniques to progress Conversion Rate through improved User engagement (UX) and Visual Experience is gaining popularity. The advent of automation and search technologies are providing added advantage to marketers who can now track data on a real time basis and improve efficiency which could also help in advocacy, an essential element in the digital era (Kartajaya, 2019).

Mobile marketing, an important element of digital marketing has been continuously developing with its own set of advancements. It has become a norm for companies to make their websites mobile responsive and incorporate Accelerate Mobile Pages (AMP) or Progressive Web Application (PWA) into their strategy. Micro-moments and use of devices to seek information through voice must be given due consideration by firms wishing to be in the race, especially in the coming decades. A Call to Action (CTA) is an action that results in a desired outcome such as purchase or downloading a material. When such proliferating technological advancements occur, it becomes the responsibility of marketers to generate superior - CTA.

An able guide to ensure that any firm achieves such prowess is to ensure your digital marketing technologies are focused on SMART which is an acronym for - Specific, Measurable, Attainable, Relevant and Time-bound - as introduced by George Doran in 1981 (Doran, 1981). Techniques such as SMART will provide ample guidance for Digital Marketers to hold on to in the ever-changing horizon of technology. In our Volatile, Uncertain, Complex and Ambiguous (VUCA) world, marketers will have to assemble their forces of innovation to face the rising challenges. In our fast-paced world, rather than galvanizing customers to act (which will only decrease the effectiveness of such techniques), we must incorporate relevant technologies into the ecosystem of digital marketing. Aspects of behaviour when technologies do not limit themselves to the visual arena will have to be studied and deciphered.

As machine and human interaction increase, we will treat machines as copartners. As the digital and the real world gets more and more tangled and create a new world, the expertise required to create, communicate, deliver, and exchange via marketing will require awareness about shifting technological landscape. This will aid decision makers in the digital marketing arena to get a peek into the decision-making process of the digital customer; this is primordial according to prominent concepts such as design thinking. New metrices and dimensions will have to be introduced to calculate customer interaction, to predict usage and buying behaviour. In the future, metrics such 'Reality Index' – a measure of the resemblance to reality, Ease of use, any lag associated with technology could be used to develop and market the product or service effectively.

Directions for Future Research

In this paper we have reviewed only a limited set of technologies based on their ability to impact digital marketing directly and their relevance across the marketing stages. As this is a continuously evolving field other technologies which have not been part of the study can be considered for future research. This study limits the practical applications of these technologies to digital marketing; technologies that impact other areas of marketing could be another direction for future research. The impact and managerial implications of these technologies in other domains such as supply chain, finance, etc., could be studies too. Furthermore, each of these technologies and their implication on businesses could be studied in detail.

References

Abramovich, Giselle (2019). Voice Ads Are More Engaging Than Other Formats, Consumers Say. Retrieved on July 5, 2021 from https://blog.adobe.com/en/publish/2019/02/19/adobe-voice-report-feb19

Adgate, Brad. (2021). Agencies Agree; 2021 Was A Record Year For Ad Spending, With More Growth Expected In 2022 retrieved on February 1, 2022 from https://www.forbes.com/sites/bradadgate/2021/12/08/agencies-agree-2021-was-a-record-year-for-ad-spending-with-more-growth-expected-in-2022/?sh=11ad87fd7bc6

Aslop, Thomas. (2021). VR and AR market size 2024. Statista. Retrieved on March 3, 2022 from https://www.statista.com/statistics/591181/global-augmented-virtual-reality-market-size/

Atzori, L., Iera, A., & Morabito, G. (2017). Understanding the Internet of Things: definition, potentials, and societal role of a fast evolving paradigm. *Ad Hoc Networks, 56*, 122-140.

Bulearca, M., & Bulearca, S. (2010). Twitter: a viable marketing tool for SMEs?. *Global Business & Management Research, 2*(4).

Capon, N., & Glazer, R. (1987). Marketing and technology: a strategic coalignment. *Journal of marketing, 51*(3), 1-14.

Clauss, T. (2017). Measuring business model innovation: conceptualization, scale development, and proof of performance. *R&d Management, 47*(3), 385-403.

Cozzoli, N., Salvatore, F. P., Faccilongo, N., & Milone, M. (2022). How can big data analytics be used for healthcare organization management? Literary framework and future research from a systematic review. *BMC health services research, 22*(1), 1-14.

Creswell, J. W., & Miller, D. L. (2000). Determining validity in qualitative inquiry. *Theory into practice, 39*(3), 124-130.

Davenport, T. H., & Ronanki, R. (2018). Artificial intelligence for the real world. *Harvard business review, 96*(1), 108-116.

Davis, M. Krystle. (2019). 5 Content Marketing Stats That Will Help You Reach Your Audience. Retrieved on July 1, 2021 from https://www.forbes.com/sites/forbescontentmarketing/2019/03/01/5-content-marketing-stats-that-will-help-you-reach-your-audience/#5c094c606d8b

Dekimpe, M. G., Geyskens, I., & Gielens, K. (2020). Using technology to bring online convenience to offline shopping. *Marketing Letters, 31*(1), 25-29.

Dellaert, B. G., Shu, S. B., Arentze, T. A., Baker, T., Diehl, K., Donkers, B., ... & Steffel, M. (2020). Consumer decisions with artificially intelligent voice assistants. *Marketing Letters, 31*(4), 335-347.

Dodman, D. (2016). Environment and urbanization. International Encyclopedia of Geography: People, the Earth, Environment and Technology: People, the Earth, Environment and Technology, 1-9.

Donnelly, Gordon. (2019). 33 Voice Search Statistics to Prepare You for the Voice Search Revolution. Retrieved on July 5, 2021 from https://www.wordstream.com/blog/ws/2018/04/10/voice-search-statistics-2018

Doran, G. T. (1981). There's a S.M.A.R.T. way to write management's goals and objectives. *Management Review*, 70, 35.

Durkin, M., McGowan, P., & McKeown, N. (2013). Exploring social media adoption in small to medium-sized enterprises in Ireland. *Journal of Small Business and Enterprise Development*.

Econsultancy. (2017). *Conversion Rate Optimization Report 2017*. Retrieved on July 7, 2021 from https://econsultancy.com/reports/conversion-rate-optimization-report/

Ekmeil, F. A. R., Abumandil, M. S. S., Alkhawaja, M. I., Siam, I. M., & Alaklouk, S. A. A. (2021, March). Augmented reality and virtual reality revolutionize business transformation in digital marketing tech industry analysts and visionaries during Coronavirus (COVID 19). In *Journal of Physics: Conference Series* (Vol. 1860, No. 1, p. 012012). IOP Publishing.

Flavián, C., Ibáñez-Sánchez, S., & Orús, C. (2019). The impact of virtual, augmented and mixed reality technologies on the customer experience. *Journal of business research, 100*, 547-560.

Furr, Nathan & Shipilov, Andrew. (2019). Digital Doesn't Have to Be Disruptive. *Harvard Business Review*. July-August 2019, pp.94–103.

Garfinkel, Jennifer. (2018). Gartner Identifies the Top 10 Strategic Technology Trends for 2019. Retrieved on July 4, 2021 from https://www.gartner.com/en/newsroom/press-releases/2018-10-15-gartner-identifies-the-top-10-strategic-technology-trends-for-2019

Gatignon, H., & Xuereb, J. M. (1997). Strategic orientation of the firm and new product performance. *Journal of marketing research, 34*(1), 77-90.

Ghosh, Dipayan. (2018). How GDPR Will Transform Digital Marketing. *Harvard Business Review, May 21, 2018*.

Grewal, D. (2018). Retail marketing management: The 5 Es of retailing. Sage.

Grewal, D., Ahlbom, C. P., Beitelspacher, L., Noble, S. M., & Nordfält, J. (2018). In-store mobile phone use and customer shopping behavior: Evidence from the field. *Journal of Marketing*.

Grewal, D., Hulland, J., Kopalle, P. K., & Karahanna, E. (2020). The future of technology and marketing: A multidisciplinary perspective. *Journal of the Academy of Marketing Science, 48*(1), 1-8.

Grewal, D., Hulland, J., Kopalle, P. K., & Karahanna, E. (2020). The future of technology and marketing: A multidisciplinary perspective. *Journal of the Academy of Marketing Science, 48*(1), 1-8.

Grewal, D., Hulland, J., Kopalle, P. K., & Karahanna, E. (2020). The future of technology and marketing: A multidisciplinary perspective. *Journal of the Academy of Marketing Science, 48*(1), 1-8.

Grewal, D., Noble, S. M., Roggeveen, A. L., & Nordfalt, J. (2020). The future of in-store technology. *Journal of the Academy of Marketing Science, 48*(1), 96-113.

Grewal, D., Roggeveen, A. L., & Nordfält, J. (2017). The Future of Retailing &. *Journal of Retailing, 93*(1), 1-6.

Grishikashvili, K., Dibb, S., & Meadows, M. (2014). Investigation into big data impact on digital marketing. *Online Journal of Communication and Media Technologies, 4*(October 2014-Special Issue), 26-37.

Han, J., Meng, X., Zhou, X., Yi, B., Liu, M., & Xiang, W. N. (2017). A long-term analysis of urbanization process, landscape change, and carbon sources and sinks: A case study in China's Yangtze River Delta region. *Journal of Cleaner Production, 141*, 1040-1050.

Harford, Tim. (2017, March 4). BBC radio [Audio podcast]. Retrieved on February 7, 2021 from https://www.bbc.co.uk/programmes/p04tz7rg

Harris, L., & Rae, A. (2009). Social networks: the future of marketing for small business. *Journal of business strategy.*

Harvey, Campbell; Moorman, Christine & Castillo Toledo, Marcos. (2018). How Blockchain Will Change Marketing As We Know It. SSRN Electronic Journal. doi: 10.2139 /ssrn.3257511

Heidenreich, S., & Talke, K. (2020). Consequences of mandated usage of innovations in organizations: developing an innovation decision model of symbolic and forced adoption. *AMS Review, 10*(3), 279-298.

Heller, J., Chylinski, M., de Ruyter, K., Mahr, D., & Keeling, D. I. (2019). Touching the untouchable: exploring multi-sensory augmented reality in the context of online retailing. *Journal of Retailing, 95*(4), 219-234.

Hilken, T., Keeling, D. I., de Ruyter, K., Mahr, D., & Chylinski, M. (2020). Seeing eye to eye: social augmented reality and shared decision making in the marketplace. *Journal of the Academy of Marketing Science, 48*(2), 143-164.

Hollebeek, Linda & Macky, Keith. (2019). Digital Content Marketing's Role in Fostering Consumer Engagement, Trust, and Value: Framework, Fundamental Propositions, and Implications. *Journal of Interactive Marketing.* 27-41.

Iansiti, Marco & Lakhani, Karim. (2014). Digital Ubiquity: How Connections, Sensors, and Data Are Revolutionizing Business. *Harvard Business Review.* November 2014, p 92.

Ivanov, Mykola. (2019). The digital marketing with the application of cloud technologies. *SHS Web of Conferences 65.* doi: 10.1051/shsconf/20196504019

Jain, D., Dash, M. K., Kumar, A., & Luthra, S. (2021). How is blockchain used in marketing: a review and research agenda. *International Journal of Information Management Data Insights, 1*(2), 100044.

Jain, P., Gyanchandani, M., & Khare, N. (2016). Big data privacy: a technological perspective and review. *Journal of Big Data, 3*(1), 1-25.

Jessen, A., Hilken, T., Chylinski, M., Mahr, D., Heller, J., Keeling, D. I., & de Ruyter, K. (2020). The playground effect: How augmented reality drives creative customer engagement. *Journal of Business Research, 116*, 85-98.

Johnson, Steven (2010). *Where Good Ideas Come From.* New York, USA: The Penguin Group.

Joy, Rason. (2016). 5 Reasons Why Fresh Content is Critical for Your Website and SEO. Retrieved on July 20, 2021 from https://seositecheckup.com/articles/5-reasons-why-fresh-content-is-critical-for-your-website-and-seo

Kantar IMRB, ICUBE on Digital Adoption and Usage Trends. (2018). Report of the Kantar IMRB, ICUBE on Digital Adoption and Usage Trends. Retrieved from https://imrbint.com/images/common/ICUBE%E2%84%A2_2019_Highlights.pdf

Kartajaya, H., Kotler, P., & Hooi, D. H. (2019). Marketing 4.0: moving from traditional to digital. *World Scientific Book Chapters*, 99-123.

Keynes, Milton. (2019). Strategy Analytics: 2018 Global Smart Speaker Sales Reached 86.2 Million Units on Back of Record Q4. Retrieved on July 4, 2021 from https://news.strategyanalytics.com/press-release/devices/strategy-analytics-2018-global-smart-speaker-sales-reached-862-million-units

Kilimas, Fathima Raj., & Lalithan, Lanna (2021). The Changing Landscape of the Digital Consumers and its implications. *Empirical Economic Letters, 20*(3), 115-124.

Kim, H. D., Lee, I., & Lee, C. K. (2013). Building Web 2.0 enterprises: A study of small and medium enterprises in the United States. *International Small Business Journal, 31*(2), 156-174.

Kotane, I., Znotina, D., & Hushko, S. (2019). Assessment of trends in the application of digital marketing. *Scientific Journal of Polonia University, 33*(2), 28-35.

Liu, Shanhong. (2019). Augmented Reality (AR) - Statistics & Facts. Retrieved on July 5, 2021 from https://www.statista.com/topics/3286/augmented-reality-ar/

97

Loeb, Walter. (2018). Amazon Is The Biggest Investor In The Future, Spends $22.6 Billion On R&D. Retrieved on July 3, 2021 from https://www.forbes.com/sites/walterloeb/2018/11/01/amazon-is-biggest-investor-for-the-future/#75bfb3f1f1db

Mari, A., & Algesheimer, R. (2021). The role of trusting beliefs in voice assistants during voice shopping.

Marketers Media. (2022). Voice Assistant Market Forecasted to Reach USD 7.30 Billion by 2025 | Voice Assistant Market Growth Analysis and Industry Forecast. Retrieved on March 2, 2022 from https://news.marketersmedia.com/voice-assistant-market-forecasted-to-reach-usd-730-billion-by-2025-voice-assistant-market-growth-analysis-and-industry-forecast/89060831

Marr, Bernard. (2020). Future Tech Trends: The 4 Technologies That Will Change Marketing Forever. Retrieved on March 6, 2022 from https://www.forbes.com/sites/bernardmarr/2020/03/06/future-tech-trends-the-4-technologies-that-will-change-marketing-forever/?sh=b438c271a4a7

McCracken, G. (1988). *The long interview* (Vol. 13). Sage.

McGowan, P., & Durkin, M. G. (2002). Toward an understanding of Internet adoption at the marketing/entrepreneurship interface. *Journal of Marketing Management, 18*(3-4), 361-377.

Milkau U. Value Creation within AI-enabled Data Platforms. Journal of Creating Value. 2019;5(1):25-39. doi:10.1177/2394964318803244

Moreno, Theresa. (2022). Voice Assistant Market Expected to Reach $7.30 Billion by 2025 retrieved on February 1, 2022 from https://speechdat.org/2022/01/20/voice-assistant-market-expected-to-reach-7-30-billion-by-2025-voice-assistants-market-growth-analysis-and-industry-forecast/

Morrison, Nick. (2017). Rapid Technological Change Is The Biggest Threat To Global Business. Retrieved on July 3, 2021 from https://www.forbes.com/sites/nickmorrison/2017/02/09/donald-trump-is-not-the-biggest-threat-to-global-business/#3eb8d5531b73

Newman, Daniel. (2019). Top 10 Digital Transformation Trends For 2020. Retrieved on July 29, 2021 from https://www.forbes.com/sites/danielnewman/2019/07/14/top-10-digital-transformation-trends-for-2020/#100101da76be

Nikolaeva, R., & Bicho, M. (2011). The role of institutional and reputational factors in the voluntary adoption of corporate social responsibility reporting standards. *Journal of the Academy of Marketing Science, 39*(1), 136-157.

Pauwels, K., Ambler, T., Clark, B. H., LaPointe, P., Reibstein, D., Skiera, B., ... & Wiesel, T. (2009). Dashboards as a service: why, what, how, and what research is needed?. *Journal of service research, 12*(2), 175-189.

Perera, M., Haller, A., & Adcock, M. (2019). A Roadmap for Semantically-Enabled Human Device Interactions. In *SAW SemStats@ ISWC*.

Perrault, R., Shoham, Y., Brynjolfsson, E., Clark, J., Etchemendy, J., Grosz, B., Lyons, T., Manyika, J., Mishra, S., & Niebles, J.C. (2019). The AI Index 2019 Annual Report. *AI Index Steering Committee, Human-Centered AI Institute, Stanford University.* 65-66. Retrieved on February 2, 2022 from https://hai.stanford.edu/sites/default/files/ai_index_2019_report.pdf

Petit, Olivia & Velasco, Carlos & Spence, Charles. (2018). Digital Sensory Marketing: Integrating New Technologies into Multisensory Online Experience. *Journal of Interactive Marketing.* May 2019. doi: 10.1016/j.intmar.2018.07.004

PricewaterhouseCoopers. (2018). Report of PricewaterhouseCoopers on Consumer Intelligence Series: Prepare for the voice revolution. Retrieved on February 8, 2022 from https://www.pwc.com/us/en/advisory-services/publications/consumer-intelligence-series/pwc-voice-assistants.pdf

Puthiyamadam, Tom. (2017). How the Meaning of Digital Transformation Has Evolved. *Harvard Business Review. May 29, 2017.*

PwC. (2018). The Essential Eight Your guide to the emerging technologies revolutionizing business now. Retrieved on July 1, 2021 from https://www.pwc.com/gx/en/issues/technology/essential-eight-technologies.html

Rayome, Alison DeNisco. (2019). Top 10 emerging technologies of 2019. Retrieved on July 10, 2021 from https://www.techrepublic.com/article/top-10-emerging-technologies-of-2019/

Richard Fletcher & Rasmus Kleis Nielsen (2018) Automated Serendipity. *Digital Journalism,* 6:8, 976-989.

Rogers, Shaylee. (2014). Tips: The visual generation and the e-commerce revolution. Retrieved on July 7, 2021 from https://realbusiness.co.uk/tips-the-visual-generation-and-the-e-commerce-revolution/

Rotolo, D., Hicks, D., & Martin, B. R. (2015). What is an emerging technology?. *Research policy, 44*(10), 1827-1843.

Rust, R. T. (2020). The future of marketing. *International Journal of Research in Marketing, 37*(1), 15-26.

Sample, K. L., Hagtvedt, H., & Brasel, S. A. (2020). Components of visual perception in marketing contexts: A conceptual framework and review. *Journal of the Academy of Marketing Science, 48*(3), 405-421.

Schawbel, Dan. (2015). 10 New Findings About The Millennial Consumer. Retrieved on July 6, 2021 from https://www.forbes.com/sites/danschawbel/2015/01/20/10-new-findings-about-the-millennial-consumer/?utm_campaign=Forbes&utm_source=TWITTER&utm_medium=social&utm_channel=Entrepreneurs&linkId=11842324#5ffdc4ef6c8f

Scholz, Joachim & Duffy, Kat. (2018). We ARe at home: How augmented reality reshapes mobile marketing and consumer-brand relationships. *Journal of Retailing and Consumer Services*. doi: 10.1016/j.jretconser.2018.05.004

See, Arne von. (2021). IoT global annual revenue 2019-2030. Statista. Retrieved on March 4, 2022 from https://www.statista.com/statistics/1194709/iot-revenue-worldwide/

Sentance, Rebecca. (2018). The future of voice search: 2020 and beyond. Retrieved on July 4, 2021 from https://econsultancy.com/the-future-of-voice-search-2020-and-beyond/

Sezgin, E., Militello, L. K., Huang, Y., & Lin, S. (2020). A scoping review of patient-facing, behavioral health interventions with voice assistant technology targeting self-management and healthy lifestyle behaviors. *Translational Behavioral Medicine, 10*(3), 606-628.

Shugan, S. M. (2004). The impact of advancing technology on marketing and academic research. *Marketing Science, 23*(4), 469-475.

Simmons, G., Armstrong, G. A., & Durkin, M. G. (2008). A conceptualization of the determinants of small business website adoption: Setting the research agenda. *International Small Business Journal, 26*(3), 351-389.

Simmons, G., Armstrong, G. A., & Durkin, M. G. (2011). An exploration of small business website optimization: enablers, influencers and an assessment approach. *International Small Business Journal, 29*(5), 534-561.

Sinha, Disha. (2022). Top 10 companies working on metaverse and its developments in 2022. Retrieved on March 4, 2022 from https://www.analyticsinsight.net/top-10-companies-working-on-metaverse-and-its-developments-in-2022/

Stamford, Conn. (2021). Gartner Identifies Five Technologies to Have a Significant Impact on Digital Advertising in the Next Two to Five Years. Retrieved on March 5, 2022 from https://www.gartner.com/en/newsroom/press-releases/2021-09-02-gartner-identifies-five-technologies-to-have-a-signif

Stanford University, Artificial Intelligence and Life in 2030. (2016). *One hundred Year Study on Artificial Intelligence*. Retrieved on February 4, 2022 from https://ai100.stanford.edu/2016-report

Statista (2021). Internet of Things (IoT) and non-IoT active device connections worldwide from 2010 to 2025 (in billions). Retrieved on October 11, 2021from https://www.statista.com/statistics/471264/iot-number-of-connected-devices-worldwide/

Statista (2021). Internet of Things (IoT) connected devices installed base worldwide from 2015 to 2025 (in billions). Retrieved on October 12, 2021from https://www.statista.com/statistics/471264/iot-number-of-connected-devices-worldwide/

Statista Research Department. (2016). Internet penetration rate in India from 2007 to 2021. Retrieved on October 12, 2021 from https://www.statista.com/statistics/792074/india-internet-penetration-rate/

Statista Research Department. (2021). Big data market size revenue forecast worldwide from 2011 to 2027. Statista. Retrieved on March 1, 2022 from https://www.statista.com/statistics/607716/worldwide-artificial-intelligence-market-revenues/

Statista Research Department. (2021). Blockchain technology market size worldwide 2018-2025. Statista. Retrieved on March 1, 2022 from https://www.statista.com/statistics/647231/worldwide-blockchain-technology-market-size/

Statista Research Department. (2021). Forecast revenue big data market worldwide 2011-2027. Retrieved on March 1, 2022 from https://www.statista.com/statistics/254266/global-big-data-market-forecast/

Strong, A. I. (2016). Applications of artificial intelligence & associated technologies. *Science [ETEBMS-2016], 5*(6).

Sullivan, Danny. (2016). 5 Google now handles at least 2 trillion searches per year. Retrieved on July 3, 2021 from https://searchengineland.com/google-now-handles-2-999-trillion-searches-per-year-250247

Synced. (2017). Will iFlytek Voice Input's 98% Accuracy Kill the Keyboard? Retrieved on July 5, 2021 from https://syncedreview.com/2017/11/16/will-iflytek-voice-inputs-98-accuracy-kill-the-keyboard/

Tanner, J., & Raymond, M. A. (2012). Marketing principles. *Houston: Flat World Education*.

Teece, D. J. (2010). Business models, business strategy and innovation. *Long range planning, 43*(2-3), 172-194.

Thangam, D., Malali, A. B., Subramaniyan, S. G., Mariappan, S., Mohan, S., & Park, J. Y. (2021). Blockchain Technology and Its Brunt on Digital Marketing. In *Blockchain Technology and Applications for Digital Marketing* (pp. 1-15). IGI Global.

The Hindu. (2022). Top 10 Trusted Metaverse Development Companies in India 2022. Retrieved on March 10, 2022 from https://www.thehindu.com/brandhub/pr-release/top-10-trusted-metaverse-development-companies-in-india-2022/article65204298.ece

Trainor, K. J., Rapp, A., Beitelspacher, L. S., & Schillewaert, N. (2011). Integrating information technology and marketing: An examination of the drivers and outcomes of e-Marketing capability. *Industrial marketing management, 40*(1), 162-174.

Vailshery, Lionel Sujay. (2021). Global IoT revenue forecast 2025, by segment. Statista. Retrieved on March 4, 2022 from https://www.statista.com/statistics/976045/iot-revenue-forecast-worldwide/

van Esch, P., & Stewart Black, J. (2021). Artificial intelligence (AI): revolutionizing digital marketing. *Australasian Marketing Journal, 29*(3), 199-203.

Wei, Z., Yang, D., Sun, B., & Gu, M. (2014). The fit between technological innovation and business model design for firm growth: evidence from C hina. *R&D Management, 44*(3), 288-305.

Yadav, M. S., & Pavlou, P. A. (2020). Technology-enabled interactions in digital environments: A conceptual foundation for current and future research. *Journal of the Academy of Marketing Science*, *48*(1), 132-136.

Zhang, C. (2020). The why, what, and how of immersive experience. *IEEE Access*, 8, 90878-90888.

CHAPTER 7

MARKETING GAME CHANGERS: CAPITALIZING THE MICRO-MOMENT THROUGH AUGMENTED REALITY

Uday Salunkhe[1], D. Narasimha Murthy[2], Vijaya Kumar. B.[3]

Introduction

Imagine that you are watching a live stream Bollywood song with a colorful festive backdrop when you suddenly get attracted to the dress worn by your favorite actor. You pause the scene, take a close look at the dress, and start wondering if this is the dress you should wear for an upcoming evening party. Now comes Augmented Reality (AR), which will create your 3D image and put the dress on you virtually. You can then visualize yourself with this dress and moving around in the party hall backdrop. You can further customize the dress and place an order to be ready for the party just in time. All these are possible due to the advancements in technology, specifically what is called augmented reality.

Since the spread of the COVID-19 pandemic in 2019 across the globe impacting the lives and behavior of the vast majority, the innovation and penetration of digital technologies coupled with a "cautious spending" consumer have redefined the basics of consumer behavior towards purchasing (Salunkhe, et al., 2021). The traditional brick and mortar are being gradually replaced by online business, with most companies facing the challenge of attracting and providing a compelling customer experience online (Smink. Et al., 2020). The increased virtual shopping cart abandonment is forcing companies to rethink their marketing strategies by focusing on providing an innovative customer experience. Most of the shopping cart abandonment happens due to the online customers finding it hard to visualize how the product fits into their personalized interests and needs. To augment customers in their decision to go ahead with the purchase, companies are using the recent changes in technological innovations like Artificial Intelligence focusing more on the interaction between customers and the virtual products, by enabling a near-real environment for the customers to feel and experience (Hilken, et al., 2017).

Consumers always have access to a large amount of data right at their fingertips, thanks to the development and acceleration of the use of the Internet. The 2020 penetration rate of the Internet worldwide is over 62%, with more than half the number being in Asia [Internet World Statistics, 2020]. This access to information has created a new behavior in consumers, pushing them to turn to their mobile devices for personalized information, useful advice, and provide the necessary motivation to make their decisions. Consumers increasingly depend on the devices for all kinds of decision-making, ranging from career choices, buying houses, choosing life partners, to small-time purchases of everyday groceries (Gevelber, 2017). They expect the information to be available at their fingertips, always, anywhere, and the data must be personalized based on their consumption habits.

[1] Prof. Dr. Uday Salunkhe, Group Director, Welingkar Institute of management development & research, Lakhamsi Napoo Road, Matunga, Mumbai, Maharashtra 400019, India. E-mail: director@welingkar.org

[2] Dr. D. Narasimha Murthy, Professor and Dean, Marketing, Welingkar Institute of Management Development & Research, India. E-mail: dn.murthy@yahoo.co.in

[3] Vijaya Kumar. B., Research Scholar, Department of Marketing, IFIM, Electronics City, Bengaluru, Karnataka India 560100. E-mail: vijay.bhimarao@gmail.com

This impulsive action of the consumers to turn to their devices to know, go, do, and buy is what Google has described as micro-moments (Ramaswamy, S, 2017).

The topic of augmented reality is nascent but is evolving at a rapid pace. Companies like Google, Facebook, and Microsoft are investing heavily in building up the technologies and applications for mobile devices to support the blending of augmented reality in consumers' daily lives. The increased use of the Internet for shopping during the COVID-19 pandemic is driving the usage and adoption of these new digital technologies. Augmented reality is foreseen to be driving the complete consumer shopping experience online through their mobile devices (Salunkhe, et al. 2021).

However, the current studies are not specifically addressing how the changes in digital technologies like augmented reality are influencing the consumers in their critical moments of making purchase decisions. The literature review also didn't address how companies should plan their marketing strategies to capture the moment of purchase decision-making to provide an attractive value proposition of their products to influence consumers to make the purchase. The use of augmented reality helps guide the customers with valuable information they need through their shopping process, supporting them to make the decisions when they arrive at the moment of making purchase decisions.

The following research questions were proposed for this review:

- How do companies capitalize the micro-moments to influence consumers with ideas and information about their products and services?

- How can companies assist in the consumer's lookout for information than resorting to coercive advertisements?

- How can augmented reality play a key role in reaching out to customers during micro-moments?

This review is intended to accomplish a systematic study of the key upcoming applications of augmented reality during the consumer's micro-moments that can have a profound influence on the way consumers make purchasing decisions. The second purpose of this review is to help the top management of companies and marketers understand how they can build a compelling experience of their products to their customers using augmented reality and more importantly decide on when and how much to invest in these technologies to stay ahead in the competition.

The penetration of augmented reality in online shopping is increasing at a rapid pace thereby creating opportunities for introducing newer business models to attract customers. This research focuses on evaluating how companies offer innovative online shopping experiences using augmented reality to be competitive. The research will also potentially spur future research on this topic that can have a larger impact on rules defining the business today.

The remainder of this article is organized as follows. We will first describe the research methodology used in this study. We will then describe Hawkins Sterns impulse buying behavior, micro-moments, and augmented reality, the key terminologies used in this study through literature surveys. We will develop a conceptualization and description of how companies should capitalize the micro-moments through augmented reality. Finally, based on our analyses and discussions, we present our conclusions and the opportunities for future research.

Research Methodology

Leonard (2000, 2003) has articulated the importance of reviewing existing literature in marketing research to gain a good understanding of the current state-of-the-art developments and to plan a company's marketing strategies based on the current trends. Since the key topics of our study involve micro-moments and augmented reality, which is nascent, we have evaluated the publications in the last 6 years (2015 onwards) for our literature research review, with very few exceptions of citing reputed researchers from their earlier research.

As the topics in this research span impulse buying, micro-moments, and augmented reality, the relevant works of literature are spread across several research areas that include technology, marketing, business, and data science. The primary source of information for micro-moments is the Google website. We did a keyword search for micro-moments on Google (https://www.google.com), which resulted in over 50-page hits of all the articles published within Google itself. We reviewed the search results and chose 16 google webpages for our literature review. In addition, there were about 9 other non-Google sites and blogs that were relevant to our literature review. The search on "augmented reality" and "impulse buying" were done separately on the Google Scholar website (https://scholar.google.com/). After carefully reviewing the search results, we picked 19 publications on "augmented reality" and "impulse buying" from the Google Scholar website. In addition, we searched for our keywords in the following online journal databases for augmented reality, impulse-buying, and micro-moments: Elsevier Science Direct, IEEE Xplore, Wiley InterScience, ABI/INFORM database, Harvard Business Review.

In total, we finalized 54 publications in the areas of our interest for further analysis. The full content of the publications was reviewed, key points documented, and the publications that were not relevant to our research areas were excluded. The general guidelines used are as follows:

- The publication should have an in-depth evaluation of one of our three keyword searches – "augmented reality", "micro-moments", and "impulse buying"

- Publications should be relevant to marketing, technology, or purchasing. Publications on online consumer behavior, mobile purchases, and trends in marketing strategies were considered for our review.

After a thorough review of the publications, 41 papers from various journals, blogs, webpages from Google on micro-moments were considered for our literature review. A list of the final publications selected is shown in table 1, containing the source of the article, title, and the methodology used in the article.

Illustration of Key Concepts

Impulse Buying Theory

Hawkins Stern in 1962 defined the impulse buying theory, wherein consumers purchase without prior planning. Stern's theory differed from other consumer behavior theories like the Theory of Motivation and Maslow's Hierarchy of Needs, arguing that consumer purchases are also influenced by economic, personality, time, location, and cultural factors (Stern, 1962). Stern's analysis indicated that impulse buying was also exhibited by the same shoppers buying the same item under different circumstances.

For this paper, we will limit our discussion to two classifications of impulse buying: Suggestion Impulse Buying and Planned Impulse buying. Suggested impulse buying indicates a consumer visualizing the need for the product even though it is the first time the consumer is seeing the product and has no prior knowledge of the product. The "need" for the product gets generated by the consumers upon seeing the product. This buying behavior is commonly capitalized by online providers by displaying adjacent products to the products being viewed. Most commonly, the "people who bought this product also bought/viewed" label shows up during online shipping, trying to influence the "suggestion buying impulse" of the consumers.

Table 1: Studies on Micro-Moments, and Augmented Reality		
Author(s)	Research Focus	Methodology
Alessio Rossi	How one beauty brand is predicting intent to drive growth	Qualitative
Boudet, J., et al.	The Future of Personalization – and how to get ready for it.	Qualitative
Brioxr.com	How AR/VR Will Revolutionize Marketing in The Automotive Industry?	Conceptual
Chilamov, A	Bringing Augmented Reality App to your Retail App	Conceptual
Dalton & Gillham	Seeing is believing: How virtual reality and augmented reality are transforming business and the economy	Quantitative
Deyan. G.	67+ Revealing Smartphone Statistics for 2020	Conceptual/ Quantitative
Gevelber, L	Micro-Moments Now: Why you should be the adviser consumers are searching for?	Qualitative
Goldman Sachs	Virtual & Augmented Reality. Understanding the race for the next computing platform	Quantitative
Google.com	Augmented Reality – A new way for your Devices to be Helpful	Qualitative
Hawkins Stern	The significance of Impulse Buying Today	Conceptual
Hilken, T., et al.	Augmenting the eye of the beholder: Exploring the strategic potential of augmented reality to enhance online service experiences	Qualitative
Hogg, S	Customer Journey Mapping: The Path to Loyalty	Quantitative
Internet World Statistics	Internet Users Distribution in the World, 2020 Q1	Quantitative
Joei Chan	Why and How Marketers Should Leverage Micro-Moments Marketing	Conceptual
Jonathan Locaste	WTF is Micro-Moment Marketing? Learn More About This New Consumer Behavior and What It Means for Brands	Conceptual
Ken Wheaton	Ask a researcher: Why shoppers are turning to search for ideas and inspiration	Quantitative
Leonard, M	Marketing Literature Review	Conceptual
Lisa Gevelber	Micro-Moments Now: 3 new consumer behaviors playing out in Google search data	Qualitative
Lisa Gevelber	Micro-Moments Now: Why you should be the adviser consumers are searching for	Qualitative
Marr, B	The 10+ Best Real-World Examples of Augmented Reality	Conceptual
Mueller, H	What are micro-moments?	Conceptual
Murthy, N., & Bhimarao, V	Internet of Things (IoT) - Is IoT a Disruptive Technology or a Disruptive Business Model?	Conceptual
Porter & Heppelmann	Why Every Organization needs an Augmented Reality Strategy? AR will become the new interface between humans and machines	Conceptual/ Quantitative
Ramaswamy, S	Micro-Moments are multiplying—are you ready for the future of marketing?	Qualitative
Ramaswamy, S	How Micro-Moments Are Changing the Rules?	Qualitative
S. Rajappa and G. Raj	Application and scope analysis of Augmented Reality in marketing using image processing technique	Quantitative

Author(s)	Research Focus	Methodology
Salunkhe, U., Murthy, N., and Bhima Rao, V	Consumers in Crisis – Emerging Market Challenges	Qualitative
Smink, A., et al.	Shopping in augmented reality: The effects of spatial presence, personalization, and intrusiveness on app and brand responses	Qualitative
Souza, E.	9 Augmented Reality Technologies for Architecture and Construction	Conceptual
Stephen O' Mahony	A Proposed Model for the Approach to Augmented Reality Deployment in Marketing Communications	Qualitative
Suzanne Scacca	Designing For Micro-Moments	Quantitative
Sweller, J., et al	Cognitive Load Theory, Explorations in the Learning Sciences, Instructional Systems and Performance Technologies	Conceptual
ThinkwithGoogle.com	How People Use Their Devices	Quantitative
ThinkwithGoogle.com	How shoppers find ideas and inspiration	Quantitative
ThinkwithGoogle.com	Micro-Moments Now: New consumer behaviors you need to know	Quantitative
ThinkwithGoogle.com	Winning the consumer electronics shopping moments that matter	Quantitative
ThinkwithGoogle.com	The Basics of Micro-Moments	Conceptual
ThinkwithGoogle.com	Your Guide to Winning the Shift to Mobile	Conceptual
Tusikhai, T.	3 Types of AR Applications Disrupting the Automotive Industry	Conceptual
Wheaton, K	Ask a researcher: Why shoppers are turning to search for ideas and inspiration.	Qualitative
Wollam, M.	The Role of Augmented Reality in Construction	Conceptual

On the other hand, the Planned Impulse Buying indicates that the consumers plan to purchase a product but decide to purchase only after seeing the product at the point of purchase by evaluating certain criteria like cost, discounts, and aesthetics. The planned impulse buying behavior is increasingly demonstrated by online shoppers. They compare the cost with other similar products, evaluate the discounts offered across multiple online sites before making the purchase.

What are Micro-Moments?

Google coined the term micro-moments to describe the reflexive, yet intent-driven interactions of the consumers that can be capitalized by the brands to influence consumers' decisions (Ramaswamy, 2015). Micro-moments are the instantaneous action by the consumers to reach out to their devices to get some information, to act, to discover, or to purchase something. Consumers make critical decisions and establish bias in these moments. Examples of micro-moments can be instant price comparison when consumers are viewing a product in the store that they like but want to compare the prices online before making the purchase. Another example is selecting a restaurant for dinner. Consumers who decide to eat out grab their device to review the menu across several restaurants in a locality even before stepping out of the house (Scacca, S. 2018).

The 4 micro-moments as illustrated by Google (Ramaswamy, 2015) are I-want-to-know moments, I-want-to-go moments, I-want-to-do moments, and I-want-to-BUY-moments. Every consumer will go through these intent-driven moments of decision-making and preference-shaping.

The micro-moments reflect the consumer's journey in their purchase process. The search trends and click-stream analysis combined with the prior usage habits of the consumers provide valuable information to the companies about the common buying habits of the consumers.

The key of micro-moments marketing is for the companies to understand this consumer journey and capture the attention of the consumers in that few seconds of their micro-moments (Lacoste, 2016).

In those seconds, the companies should deliver compelling ideas to positively influence consumers in buying their products and services.

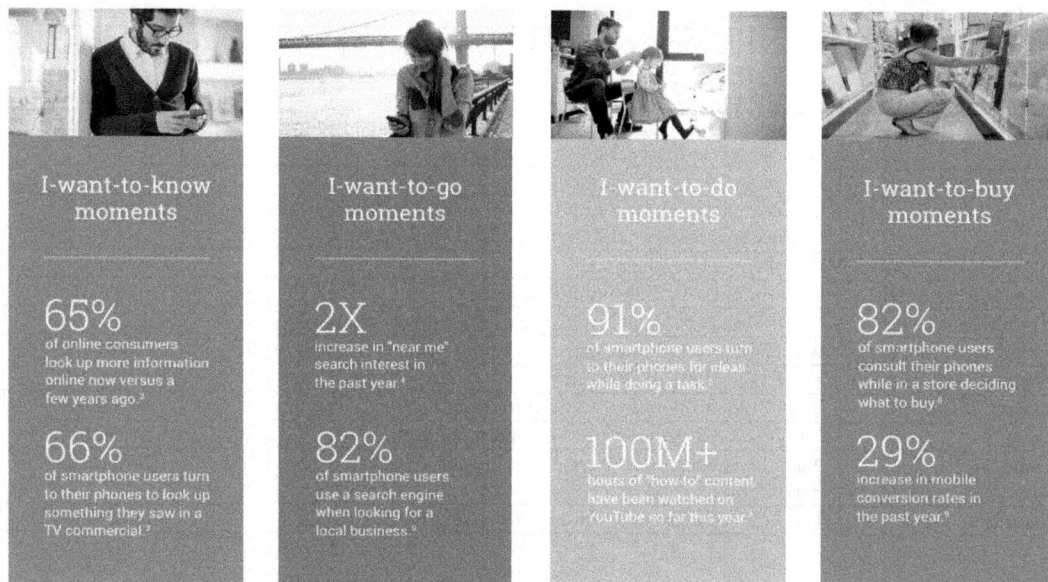

Figure 1: The 4 micro-moments (Source: Ramaswamy, S (2015)

Are Micro-Moments all about Consumer Behaviour?

According to Deyan, 2020, here are some interesting facts about smartphone users across the world.

- There are about 3.5 billion smartphone users in the world, almost half the world population carrying a smartphone.

- 87% always have their smartphone at their side, day and night.

- Over 70% of YouTube traffic comes from smartphones.

- An average smartphone user checks the phone about 58 times a day.

- 80% of shoppers use a mobile phone while in a physical store.

Today's consumers expect to get information anywhere, anytime, and at any place (Gevelber, 2017). The expectation is also that the information must be personalized for their browsing behaviors. These consumers are curious, demanding, and have very little patience. Consumers are turning towards smartphones for instant information, be it significant or otherwise, curious to gain more knowledge before making decisions. They are also demanding that the data that is being presented to them should be personalized, even if their search query is incomplete or not accurate for the information they are looking for. Finally, consumers make decisions at that moment based on the data they see on their devices, right-then and right-there (Gevelber, 2017).

Why are Consumers Increasingly "Searching" for Ideas?

According to Wheaton (2017), consumers "search" for information if they want more of something but are not sure of what are available that will fit their need. Many times, consumers don't even know how to start looking for information. They are looking for suggestions to their specific needs from other consumers who openly share their opinions and experiences online. Consumers are also looking for ideas on alternatives that can help them understand and make decisions. The Internet has become an open, easily accessible, and trustable source of information to the consumers during micro-moments.

Wheaton adds that Google's Ads Research and Insights team has identified that consumers use the word "idea" in their search extensively. Some of the example searches are "Virtual birthday party ideas", "Valentine's Day Ideas", "Tattoo ideas", and so on, indicating that oftentimes consumers don't know what exactly they are looking for, but are depending on their search to help them with "ideas" that are personalized for their preferences. The Google research team has published that 91% of Internet users turn to their ideas for phones for ideas in the middle of a task signifying the micro-moments that are critical touchpoints in today's consumer journey.

What is Augmented Reality (AR)?

The advent and penetration of the Internet have enabled the collection of huge amounts of data (Murthy & Bhimarao, 2015). Rendering back these data onto consumer's devices are mostly in a 2-dimensional format. It is not easy many times for the users to mentally translate these 2-D images into 3-D. AR superimposes the digital information onto a real physical environment, enabling a superior consumption of the information, enabling faster decision making.

Figure 2 – Benefits of 3D visualization

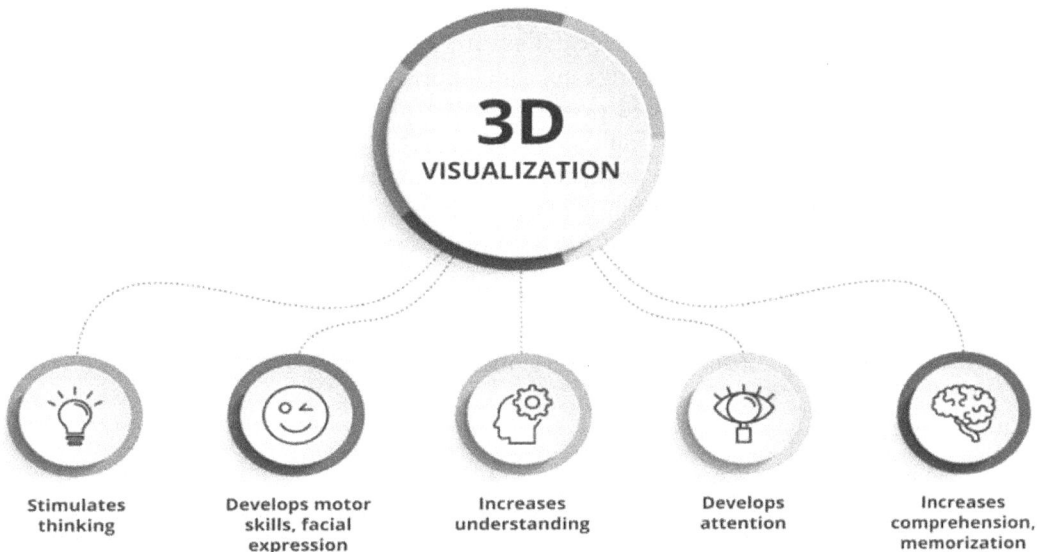

Source: itechcraft.com

According to Google (Google, 2020), Augmented Reality (AR) superimposes digital content and information on the physical world, to create an immersive live experience for the consumers. Porter

& Heppelmann (2017) in their publication in HBR describe that the real world is three-dimensional, whereas the digital world is two-dimensional images. Augmented reality is a set of technologies that closes the gap between the real and digital worlds by superimposing digital data and images on physical objects. AR eliminates the need for consumers to imagine or interpret the 2D data as 3D images, thereby helping them to absorb information, make quick decisions, and execute efficiently.

Figure 3: Economic Contributions of AR

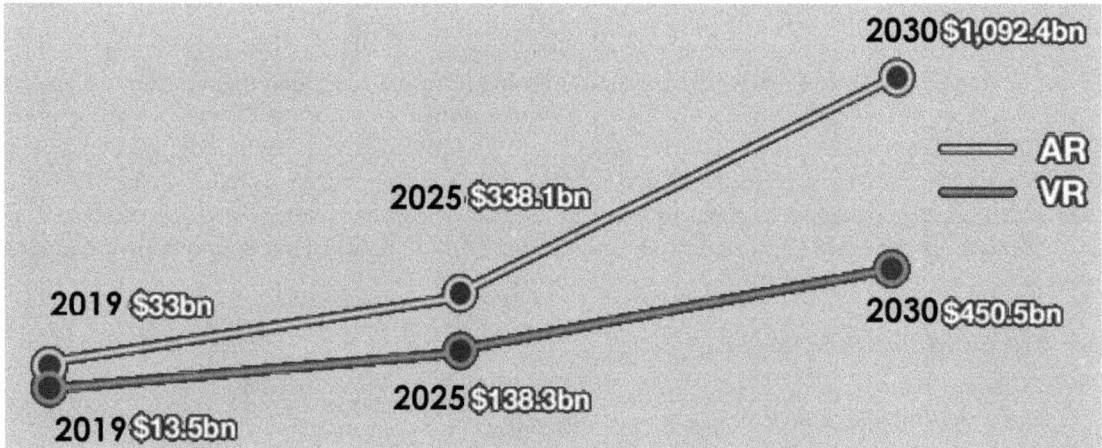

Source: Dalton & Gillham, 2019

Potential of Augmented Reality for Businesses

The adoption of AR in businesses has a profound economic impact on the businesses (Dalton & Gillham, 2019). Companies can create personalized experiences for the customers, speed up product development, and improve employee safety. The use of AR technologies will accelerate the company's innovation and forward-thinking capabilities, thus attracting critical technical and business talent for its growth. With the increased penetration of highspeed connectivity through 5G, the performance of the technologies will significantly improve. The latency will be substantially reduced thus providing an enjoyable viewing experience to the consumers. The cost of headsets will get cheaper, the requirement of local processing is substantially reduced as most of the compute is pushed out to the cloud, thus making the rollout of AR technologies more attractive and cost-effective.

AR is also estimated to provide a larger boost to the GDP. It is estimated that the combined AR & VR impact on the economy is at $1.5 trillion by 2030, with AR contributing to over 70% of the impact. Figure 2 shows the impact of AR on the global economy through 2030.

Cognitive Workloads

The cognitive load theory, which was developed by John Sweller, a psychologist in 1988 describes how human brains store and process information. Sweller (2011) has illustrated that the memory in the human brain can be classified into working memory and long-term memory. The processing of any new information happens in the working memory, but the retention of information happens in the long-term memory. Information can be stored in the long-term memory only after being processed and understood by the working memory. The working memory also referred to as short-term memory experiences "cognitive loads". The demand to process information depends on our

108

mental capacity, which is extremely limited both in terms of its size and retention. These limitations will hinder the learning process impacting the task completion and varies based on individuals. As an illustration, let us consider the famous English adage "A picture is worth a thousand words". Applying Sweller's cognitive load theory to this adage, we can infer that reading a thousand words from a book will involve mind mapping of the subject in the minds of the reader, which will increase the cognitive load on the working memory. However, listening or watching someone say the same 1000 words is less stressful to the working memory as it saves the brain from reading the letters, translating the letters to words, which are then mind mapped to create a pictorial (3D) representation in the working memory. However, a visual image that can describe these 1000 words is very easy to comprehend by the working memory, thereby reducing the cognitive load.

The concept of reducing the cognitive load on the working memory using imaging technology like augmented reality is used extensively in marketing when the consumers are at the cusp of making a purchase decision. Each page that the consumer browse increases the cognitive load and impacts the capability of the brain to process further information. Augmented reality, which can render a 360-degree view of the product including its appearance and usage will help reduce the cognitive workload on the brain to a large extent, thus helping the consumers to make faster purchase decisions.

Augmented Reality Influencing Micro-Moments

"I want it NOW" (Chen, 2021) is the instant gratification that today's buyers want. The increased use of smartphones to research a product, compare alternatives, seek feedback, and the hurry to complete the task is driving consumers to make purchase decisions faster. Google research has found that smartphone users are 50% more likely to make an instant purchase while reviewing a product more than a year ago (Gevelber, 2017), terming these consumers as the "right now" consumers.

The concept of micro-moment is a game-changer for both the buyers and marketers (Chen, 2017). For marketers, it is important to act at the "I-want-to-buy" moment of the consumers. This I-want-to-buy moment is when the consumers already have a preference, their expectations are high, and are in a hurry to make decisions (Ramaswamy, 2015). This is the moment that marketers should harness the power of augmented reality in marketing and influencing the consumers to make the final purchase.

AR is a promising technology for marketers since it allows the amalgamation of the consumers themselves in the spatial presence, providing a real experience of the virtual world (Smink, et al., 2020). An example is fitting an eye lens frame to the user's facial attributes. AR allows the consumers to take a picture of themselves, and on their mobile device fit several frames that are available on the virtual shelves of the store to their face. Embedding haptic into augmented reality, consumers can even feel the touch of the virtual product. AR thus fulfills the critical consumer need of seeing themselves in the virtual world and "experiencing the product" as if in a real environment.

Theoretical Framework

Augmented Reality Application

The AR application provides a total product experience by enabling interaction with a virtual product like in a real environment, including the touch and feel of the product. The AR application simulates a real environment for the customers, an experience as if they are physically touching and interacting with the product (Smink, et al., 2020. This provides a richer understanding of the product features unlike in a static product or picture of the product online that will not support customers to experience the product. Hence AR applications have an edge in the key micro-moments over traditional online marketing applications in inspiring customers at the I-want-to-buy moments.

Figure 4: AR Influencing I-Want-To-Buy moment

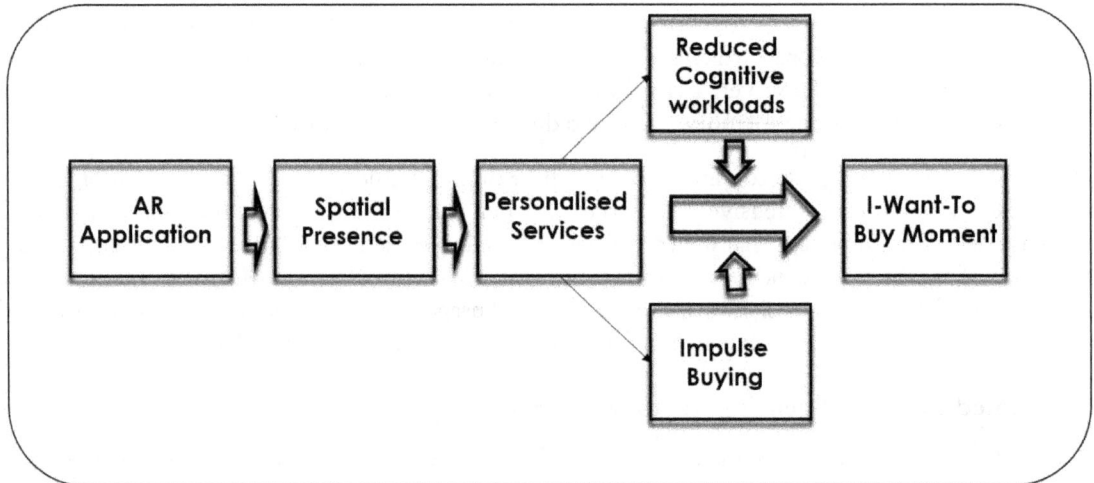

Spatial Presence

Spatial presence indicates how effectively the customers interact with the virtual objects with a feeling that they are interacting with the objects in their real-world as shown in figure 3. The higher the control the customers have in interacting with the virtual objects, the higher is the spatial presence (Hilken, et al., 2017), indicating that the customers can make changes to the location, size, look, feel, and other attributes of the object. The higher the spatial presence, the lesser is the discrepancy in the customer's understanding of the actual object (Smink, et al., 2020). The higher spatial presence inspires a positive mindset in the customers to go ahead with the purchase.

Personalized Services

Personalization is the key to marketing success (Boudet, et al., 2019). Technological innovations are enabling marketers to create personalized and customized services to cater to each customer's requirements (Salunkhe, et al., 2021). Advancements in camera sensors coupled with artificial intelligence are enabling the facial recognition of customers. Personalized content for each customer can be delivered based on previous purchase habits. Advancement in technologies using machine and deep learning has enabled emotion detection, wherein the system can offer products based on customers' emotions and reactions while interacting with the product (Boudet, et al., 2019). The personalized marketing strategies allow customers to experience the virtual product in real-time or in the customer's physical world, thus enabling the customers to visualize the product to meet their needs as compared to showing them a 2D picture or a movie with some other character using the product. Personalization induces positive persuasive behavior in the customers (Smink, et al., 2020), thereby increasing the relevance of the product for customers' needs.

Figure 5: A Model for the Approach to Augmented Reality Deployment in Marketing

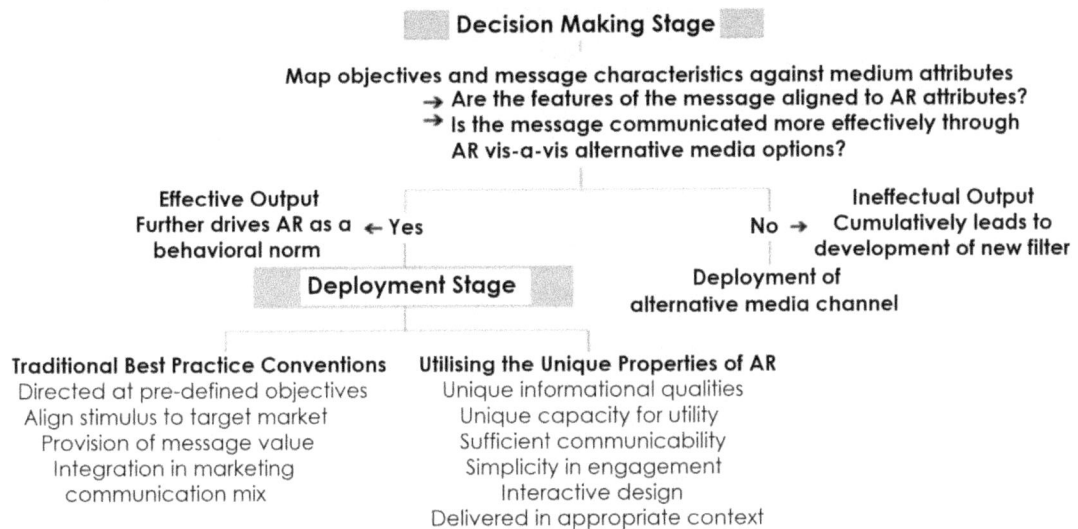

Decision Making Stage

Map objectives and message characteristics against medium attributes
→ Are the features of the message aligned to AR attributes?
→ Is the message communicated more effectively through
AR vis-a-vis alternative media options?

Effective Output		Ineffectual Output
Further drives AR as a ← Yes	No →	Cumulatively leads to
behavioral norm		development of new filter

Deployment Stage

Deployment of
alternative media channel

Traditional Best Practice Conventions
Directed at pre-defined objectives
Align stimulus to target market
Provision of message value
Integration in marketing
communication mix

Utilising the Unique Properties of AR
Unique informational qualities
Unique capacity for utility
Sufficient communicability
Simplicity in engagement
Interactive design
Delivered in appropriate context

Source: O' Mahony (2015)

If the prospective brand adopter has decided to implement AR in a communications campaign subsequent to the considerations examined under the decision-making stage, the focus turns to the execution of the stimulus. A predominant finding of the research is the need to conceive the deployment of AR on two dimensions, which are thus reflected in the proposed model. On one dimension, adherence to established best practice conventions is highlighted. Established conventions of the marketing communications discipline are important determinants of message effectiveness irrespective of medium, and AR does not form an exception in this regard, despite the singular nature of the phenomenon. On another dimension, the singularity of its nature is acknowledged in respect of deployment. A number of considerations tied to the properties of the phenomenon must be made; these are not necessarily unique to AR deployment, but they are factors worthy of particular attention.

The deployment of AR for marketing has produced extraordinary results in positively motivating the consumers during the purchase decision-making process. Deployment of AR requires the same set of well-defined principles as normally employed in any marketing communications (O' Mahony, 2015).

With the rapid advancements in technological innovations, companies must continually innovate their marketing strategies to provide a compelling personalized experience to customers using digital technologies. The key is to induce positive persuasive emotion in the customers at the time of making the purchase. Augmented reality provides this capability of positive persuasiveness by enabling the customers to experience the virtual product in their physical environment. Thus, customers are sure of what they are purchasing, and thereby by they have higher confidence in the product.

Industry Examples of Augmented Reality driving Marketing

Augmented reality, when combined with the increasing penetration of mobile devices and easy access to the Internet, offers endless possibilities for marketers to provide very compelling personalized content to consumers. The increasing adoption of digital technologies by consumers is driving marketers to offer an innovative experience to customers. Augmented reality is gaining popularity as the key marketing tool across all segments of the industries (HBR 2017). The AR market for construction is projected to be growing at 63% in the next seven years (Wollam, 2021).

Figure 6: Who is investing the most in Augmented Reality?

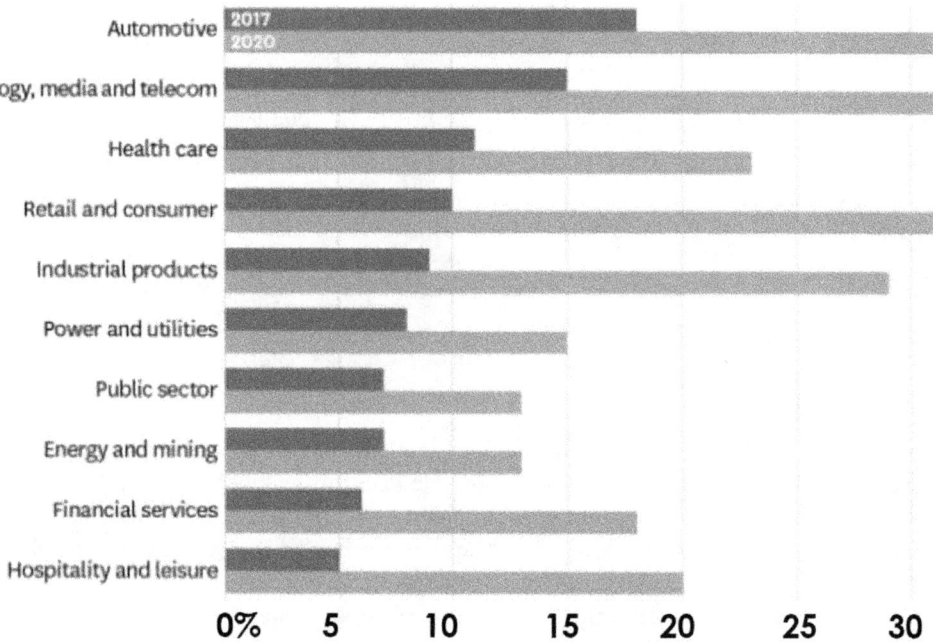

Source: Augmented Reality in the Real World, HBR Staff, Nov-Dec 2017

Automotive Industry

A car reflects one's personality. Often consumers have a dilemma before making the final purchase since the investment is high and they are not sure if they are evaluating all the options before making the purchase. Consumers also demand a lot of personalization in the car like the seats, entertainment sets, interiors, wheels, etc.

Automotive companies have started using augmented reality to provide the personalized experience that customers are looking for at the time of making the purchase (Brioxr.com). Virtual showrooms that can help the customers get an immersive experience of the vehicle they are purchasing are being deployed. The virtual showrooms not only provide the customers with the ability to personalize the accessories in the car but will also provide them the ability to virtually test drive the car in different terrains.

The entire experience is provided on the customers' handheld devices. Customers can get the complete experience of the visit to a car showroom, view cars of different models and colors, complete the test drive, and customize to their preferences. AR creates a unique bonding between the customers and their cars, thus providing a positive motivation for the customers to go forward with the purchase.

Figure 7: How AR/VR Will Revolutionize Marketing in The Automotive Industry?

Source: Brioxr.com

Figure 8: Global Automotive AR Market Growth

Each year from 2020 to 2026, the AR automative market is expected to grow 30 %

$2 Billion   **$10 Billion**

2019   **2026**

Source: Tusikhai, 2021

The global automotive AR market is expected to reach $10 billion by 2026, with a 30% growth year-on-year from 2020 through 2026 (Tusikhai, 2021).

Retail & Consumer Industry

Consumers prefer trying on a product before making the final purchase (Marr, B), be it purchasing a new dress, sunglasses, or even home furniture. The current pandemic has accelerated the use of digital technologies for making purchases online. This change in consumers' behavior towards online purchases is believed to endure even after the world returns to normality. This trend of shopping online is forcing companies to increasingly invest in technologies that can reach customers in their homes (Salunkhe, et al., 2021).

Using AR, companies enable consumers to interact, and visualize a virtual product in their physical world, as if the product is right with them. Advancements in haptics are helping consumers even touch and feel the product, thereby allowing consumers to personalize the product to their preferences.

One of the common marketing strategies used by clothing stores is to provide a "fitting room" AR application to consumers. Consumers can use their cell phone to browse through the catalog, select clothes that fit the event they are attending, and "try them on". The AR applications provide a 360 view of the dress, so consumers can request alternations before delivery. More and more consumers are preferring the fitting room app so that they easily and effortlessly try many dresses while making the purchase. The personalization of the product to suit consumers' needs aids the consumers to make the "buy" decision.

Figure 9: Virtual fitting rooms for trying out dresses while making the purchase

Source: Chilamov, 2021

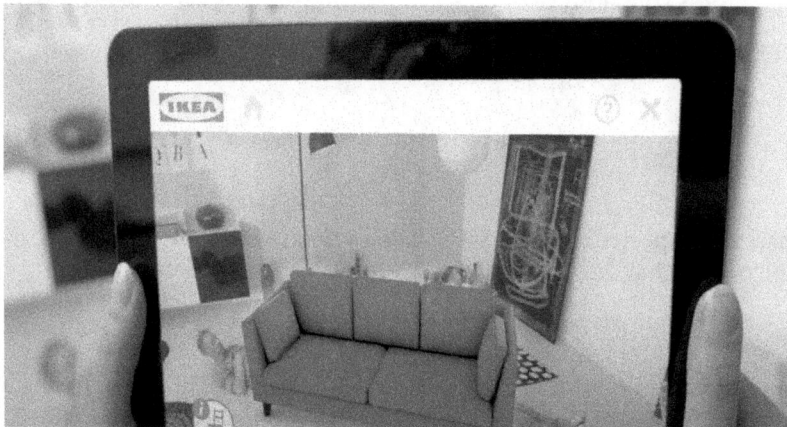

Figure 10: Using AR to visualize furniture in the room

Source: Place IKEA furniture in your home with augmented reality - YouTube

The concept of fitting rooms is extensively being used by retailers, a smaller list being those who sell dresses, shoes, cosmetics, sunglasses, and frames. Ikea, a furniture manufacturer has used AR to let the customers try placing furniture in their homes before making the purchase.

The retail AR market is expected to reach $1.6 billion by 2025 (Goldman Sachs, 2016). The numbers continue to grow and with the pandemic, companies are increasingly resorting to using AR for their marketing campaigns.

Construction Industry

The construction industry, being one of the older professions in the world has been a pioneer in using AR in its marketing strategies, especially to help consumers to decide at their purchasing mico-moments. With the help of AR, a 3D image of the actual building is built much before any work happens on-site (Souza, 2019). Users can rotate, zoom in to a particular area, and view the details of the planned construction. AR helps the consumers to gain all the information they need in the project by allowing them to virtually walk inside the building, move around, and suggest changes to the floor plan early in the project planning phase. The selection of the type of product for construction, the color combinations, and the design can be adjusted to the customer's preference, driving increased customer satisfaction, and stimulating them to make the purchase right at their "buy" micro-moments.

Figure 11: Use of Augmented Reality in Construction Industry

Source: Souza, 2019

Conclusions and Future Directions

This research paper after extensive literature review has proved that consumers are increasingly using online for making purchases. The online shopping trend is likely to continue post-pandemic. The micro-moments describe the behaviors of consumers at various stages of their purchase process, from need generation to information search, to evaluate alternatives, to making the actual purchase, to post-purchase dissonance.

The cognitive workload theory indicates that consumers have a shorter working memory, and it is important for the companies to recognize the micro-moments and plan their marketing strategies to meet consumers' needs. The marketing strategies must provide a personalized shopping experience to the consumers at each of the micro-moments.

The use of disruptive technologies like augmented reality is transforming the ways consumers perceive the need for products. Companies must create a compelling experience for the consumers, wherein the consumers sitting at home and using their mobile device can experience the virtual product in real life, like the product is in their physical environment. Consumers will then have the positive motivation to make the purchase and show greater satisfaction in using the products.

Companies may find it a bit overwhelming to keep track of the consumer's journey through all these micro-moments. Understanding the consumer's journey will involve mapping how the companies' products fit the consumer's preferences, expectations, and fulfill their needs. The following steps are recommended for the companies to evaluate to understand consumer's journey and capitalize on the micro-moments:

1. Identify the value proposition of the products: The companies need to identify the value their products are offering to the consumers. The product value proposition should meet consumers' needs and goals for the consumers to show interest in the product. The value proposition should also define the moments of delight and the pain points that the consumers experience in their journey of evaluating the product.
2. Define the target audience: The target audience and the value proposition should be clearly defined in the marketing strategy. For example, if the consumers are looking for a simple lawnmower, the company can't market their expensive brands to such consumers.
3. Define the touchpoints with the consumers: Companies must decide how to reach out to their consumers. Given the increased adoption of mobile devices for online purchases, the companies need to define the vehicle and the process for reaching out to the consumers. Mobile advertising is increasingly becoming popular to reach out to online shoppers. Marketing strategies should evaluate using the current technologies to reach out to consumers.
4. Capitalize on the "I-want-to-BUY" moments: Marketing strategies should use technologies like augmented reality to provide the consumers a real-world experience of the virtual products in their physical environment. These experiences will introduce a positive persuasive motivation to the consumers in their I-want-to-buy moments, thereby influencing their decision to go ahead with the purchase.

Technologies continue to evolve, and competition will take advantage of the newer technologies to create a compelling product experience for the consumers. Companies have to periodically evaluate the relevance of their marketing strategies given the changing consumer behavior and invest in changing their marketing mix to reach out to the consumers are their micro-moments to stay in the league and gain a competitive advantage.

References

Boudet, J., Gregg, B., Rathje, K., Stein, E., Vollhardt, K. (2019). The Future of Personalization – and how to get ready for it. McKinsey & Company. Retrieved from The future of personalization--and how to get ready for it | McKinsey

Brioxr.com. How AR/VR Will Revolutionize Marketing In The Automotive Industry? Retrieved from How AR/VR will Revolutionize Marketing in the Automotive Industry - BRIOXR

Chan, J. (2021). Why and How Marketers Should Leverage Micro-Moments Marketing. *Mention*. Sept 30, 2021. Retrieved from How Marketers Can Use Micro-Moments for Major Marketing (2021 Update) (mention.com)

Chilamov, A (2021). Bringing Augmented Reality App to your Retail App. *Eastern Peak*. Retrieved from Augmented Reality in Retail: Benefits and Use Cases of AR Retail Apps (easternpeak.com)

Dalton & Gillham (2019). Seeing is believing: How virtual reality and augmented reality are transforming business and the economy. *PWC Research*. Retrieved from Seeing is believing: PwC

Deyan, G. (2020). 67+ Revealing Smartphone Statistics for 2020. *Techjury*. Retrieved from https://techjury.net/blog/smartphone-usage-statistics/#gref

Gevelber, L. (2017). Micro-Moments Now: Why you should be the adviser consumers are searching for? *Think with Google*. Retrieved from https://www.thinkwithgoogle. com/consumer-insights/consumer-mobile-search-buying-behavior/?utm_medium= social&utm_campaign =thinkwithgoogle&utm_source=email&utm_content=consumer-mobile-search-buying-behavior

Gevelber, L. (2017). Micro-Moments Now: 3 new consumer behaviors playing out in Google search data. *Think with Google*. Retrieved from https://www.thinkwithgoogle.com/consumer-insights/consumer-trends/micro-moments-consumer-behavior-expectations/

Goldman Sachs (2016). Virtual & Augmented Reality. Understanding the race for the next computing platform. *Equity Research January 2016*. Retrieved from https://www.goldmansachs.com/insights/pages/technology-driving-innovation-folder/virtual-and-augmented-reality/report.pdf

Google.com (2020). Augmented Reality – A new way for your Devices to be Helpful. Retrieved from: https://arvr.google.com/ar/

Hilken, T., de Ruyter, K., Chylinski, M., Mahr, D., & Keeling, D. I. (2017). Augmenting the eye of the beholder: Exploring the strategic potential of augmented reality to enhance online service experiences. Journal of the Academy of Marketing Science, 45, 884–905. https://doi.org/10.1007/s11747-017-0541-x

Hogg, S. (2018). Customer Journey Mapping: The Path to Loyalty. *Think with Google*. Retrieved from https://www.thinkwithgoogle.com/consumer-insights/consumer-journey/customer-journey-mapping/

Internet World Statistics, (2020). Internet Users Distribution in the World, 2020 Q1. Retrieved from https://www.internetworldstats.com/stats.htm

Lacoste, J. (2016). WTF is Micro-Moment Marketing? *Inc.com*. Retrieved from https://www.inc.com/jonathan-lacoste/wtf-is-micro-moment-marketing.html

Leonard, M. (2000). Marketing Literature Review. Journal of Marketing, Vol. 64, Issue. 4, pp. 110-121.

Leonard, M. (2003). Marketing Literature Review. Journal of Marketing, Vol. 67, Issue. 2, pp. 140-150.

Marr, B. The 10+ Best Real-World Examples of Augmented Reality. Bernardmarr.com. Retrieved from The 10+ Best Real-World Examples Of Augmented Reality | Bernard Marr

O' Mahony, S. (2015). A Proposed Model for the Approach to Augmented Reality Deployment in Marketing Communications. Procedia - Social and Behavioral Sciences. 175. 10.1016/j.sbspro.2015.01.1195.

Mueller, H. (2019). What are micro-moments? *Formstack*. Retrieved from (1) New Messages! (formstack.com)

Murthy, N., & Bhimarao, V. (2015). Internet of Things (IoT) - Is IoT a Disruptive Technology or a Disruptive Business Model? *Indian Journal of Marketing*. August 2015. ISSN: 0973-8703. Volume. 45. Pages. 18-27

Porter, M., & Heppelmann, J. (2017). Why Every Organization needs an Augmented Reality Strategy? AR will become the new interface between humans and machines. *Harvard Business Review*. Nov-Dec 2017. https://hbr.org/2017/11/why-every-organization-needs-an-augmented-reality-strategy

Rajappa, S., Raj, G. (2016). Application and scope analysis of Augmented Reality in marketing using image processing technique. In: 2016 6th International Conference - Cloud System and Big Data (2016)

Ramaswamy, S. (2015). How Micro-Moments Are Changing the Rules? *Think with Google*. https://www.thinkwithgoogle. com/marketing-resources/micro-moments/how-micromoments-are-changing-rules/#:~:text=Micro%2 Dmoments%20occur%20when% 20people,are%20made%20and%20preferences%20shaped.

Ramaswamy, S. (2017). Micro-Moments are multiplying—are you ready for the future of marketing? *Think with Google*. Retrieved from https://www.thinkwithgoogle.com/ marketing-resources/micro-moments/future-of-marketing-machine-learning-micro-moments/

Rossi, A. (2018). How one beauty brand is predicting intent to drive growth. Think with Google. Retrieved from https://www.thinkwithgoogle.com/marketing-strategies/data-and-measurement/customer-needs/

Salunkhe, U., Murthy, N., and Bhima Rao, V. (2021). Consumers in Crisis – Emerging Market Challenges. Transnational Marketing Journal, August 2021. 9 (2). PP. 219-238. ISSN: 2041-4684 (Print) | ISSN 2041-4692 (Online). DOI: https://doi.org/10.33182/tmj.v9i2.1575

Scacca, S. (2018). Designing for Micro-Moments. Smashing Magazine. Retrieved from https://www.smashingmagazine. com/2018/08/designing-for-micro-moments/

Smink, A., Reijmersdal, E., Noort, G., and Neijens, P. (2020). Shopping in augmented reality: The effects of spatial presence, personalization, and intrusiveness on app and brand responses. *Journal of Business Research*. 118 (2020) 474–485. https://doi.org/10.1016/j.jbusres.2020.07.018

117

Souza, E. (2019). 9 Augmented Reality Technologies for Architecture and Construction. *Archdaily*. Retrieved from https://www.archdaily.com/914501/9-augmented -reality-technologies-for-architecture-and-construction

Stern, H. (1962). The significance of Impulse Buying Today. *Journal of Marketing*, 26, 59-62.

Sweller, J., et al. (2011). Cognitive Load Theory, Explorations in the Learning Sciences, Instructional Systems and Performance Technologies 1, DOI 10.1007/978-1-4419-8126-4_2, *Springer Science+Business Media, LLC* 2011

Tusikhai, T. (2021). 3 Types of AR Applications Disrupting the Automotive Industry. Softeq.com. Retrieved from 3 Types of AR Applications Disrupting the Automotive Industry (softeq.com)

Wheaton, K. (2017). Ask a researcher: Why shoppers are turning to search for ideas and inspiration. *Think with Google*. Retrieved from https://www.thinkwithgoogle.com/ consumer-insights/shopping-behavior-data-inspiration/

Wollam, M. (2021). The Role of Augmented Reality in Construction. Retrieved from Augmented Reality in Construction | Wollam Construction

CHAPTER 8

EXPLORATORY STUDY ON VALUE CREATION ALONG THE SUPPLY CHAIN OF ELECTRIC VEHICLES: AN OPINION MINING APPROACH

Dakshina Murthy R.A[1], Madhumita Guha Majumder[2], M. Khurrum S. Bhutta[3]

Introduction

We are witnessing a surge in the demand for electric vehicles, in the domestic as well as globalmarkets on account of greater concern for the environment and advancement in technology. Every country is committed to reducing its carbon footprint over the next decade in order to address the issues of global warming, deterioration in air quality, especially in the cities due toheavy pollution, and depletion of resources. EVs have the advantage of high performance andfuel efficiency along with very low emissions and long operating range, making them a viablealternative to fuel-based vehicles. As the automobile industry goes through an exciting phase of transformation with the adoption of EVs, it can be very interesting, from an academic viewpoint, to understand, assess, and analyse the various strategies and operational challengesfaced by the various stakeholders, as drastic changes in the management of supply chain are envisaged for the manufacture and servicing of EVs as compared to fossil fuel-based conventional vehicles.

The Growth of the EV Market in India

Five years after the introduction of the Faster Adoption and Manufacturing of EV (FAME) scheme, the number of EVs on the road so far is miniscule. According to data extracted from the Vaahan database, more than 57,000 two-wheelers and over 5,000 four-wheelers were soldin the year 2021-22; including three-wheelers and buses, a total of 121,915 EVs have been soldso far, which accounts for 1.65 percent of the total vehicles sold. When compared with the previous year's total of 168,311 units or 0.77 percent of the total vehicles sold, it is obvious that EV sales have doubled. According to the consulting firm RBSA, EV sales are expected togrow at a CAGR of 90 percent in this decade to touch USD 205 billion by 2030.

Two-wheelers are one of the most used modes of transportation. Therefore, many two-wheeler manufacturers are focusing on diversifying their portfolios by developing and introducing electric versions of their products, resulting in better choices for consumers. These EVs are onpar with conventional vehicles in terms of cost, style, and convenience.

According to the white paper titled 'EV–Ready India' (WEF, 2019), the electric four-wheelermarket in India is projected to grow at a compounded annual growth rate of 34.5 percent fromUSD 71.1 million to USD 707.4 million during the period 2017 to 2025, with government initiatives and subsidies playing an active role in this growth. Another factor influencing this growth is the arrival of

[1] Prof. Dr. Dakshina Murthy R.A, Sr. Associate Dean – Operations, Prin. L.N. Welingkar Institute of Management Development & Research, No. 102 & 103, Electronic city Phase 1, Hosur Road, Bengaluru 560 100, India. E-mail: dakshina.murthy@welingkar.org
[2] Prof. Dr. Madhumita Guha Majumder, Professor & Program Head – Research & Business Analytics, Prin. L.N. Welingkar Institute of Management Development & Research, No. 102 & 103, Electronic city Phase 1, Hosur Road, Bengaluru 560 100, India. E-mail: madhumita.majumder@welingkar.org
[3] Prof. Dr. M. Khurrum S. Bhutta, Professor of Operations, College of Business, 1 Ohio University, Athens, Ohio, USA E-mail: bhutta@ohio.edu

the world's largest electric vehicle manufacturer, Tesla, in India which is expected to boost the adoption of EVs immensely. The Make in India initiative by the Indiangovernment will also aid in increasing the demand for EVs and their components that would increase India's GDP by 25 percent over the next few years.

According to the Ministry of Power, Government of India, there are over 0.75 million EVs onthe road and 1,028 EV charging stations. Delhi, Telangana, Karnataka, and Chandigarh are theleading states in India in terms of the number of charging stations. By 2030, the government aims to transition India into a 100-per cent electric-vehicle nation and has proposed that two- wheelers of engine capacity below 150cc sold in the country after March 31, 2025, and three- wheelers sold after March 31, 2023, should be EVs. This study aims to review and analyse howvarious stakeholders in the EV sector are gearing up to meet the aforementioned objectives ofIndia achieving close to 100 percent adoption of EVs by 2030. The specific measures taken toachieve these objectives include subsidies, tax exemptions and the installation of the required capacity and infrastructure through capital investments by the manufacturers.

The Growth of the Global EV Market

The global electric vehicle market is expected to grow at a CAGR of 26.8 percent with total sales growing from 4,096,000 units to around 30,756,000 units by 2030, according to a reportby MarketsAndMarkets.com. Another report titled 'Global EV Outlook 2021', pegs China as the leader with 2.3 million EVs in actual use (5.2 percent), followed by Europe and the US (1.2and 1.1 million EVs respectively). In Norway, 56 percent of all vehicles are electric; the corresponding numbers for Iceland and the Netherlands are 25.5 percent and 15 percent respectively. EV sales reached new heights in the year 2020, reaching 10 million units, 41 percent higher than in 2019. (IEA, 2021). Europe had the highest share of new electric car registrations in 2020 with 1.4 million registrations, followed by China with 1.2 million, and theUnited States with 295,000. The increase in electric car registrations in Europe, where the number more than doubled from 2019, can be attributed to stimulus measures introduced by many European governments through tax rebates and subsidies, installation of EV charging stations and incentives offered for early adoption of EVs. Similar growth was also witnessed in the Asia Pacific and North America markets as well.

Value creation through adoption of EV

The industry is experiencing a shift, as there is considerable scope for value creation as well asseveral advantages of adopting EVs over conventional, fossil fuel-based vehicles. EVs offer better and comfortable rides for consumers, as they are lighter in weight with fewer components. Advanced composite material could provide for weight reduction of 25 percent for chassis parts and up to 35 percent for body parts. The use of bio-degradable resins and fibres could result in a further reduction of 25 percent. Additionally, as the running cost in terms of the energy required for every kilometre reduces drastically from INR 7-8 per km to INR 0.8-0.9 per km, this would bring huge savings for consumers. The most crucial outcome of the adoption of EVs is the reduction in air pollution when compared to conventional vehicles, which is essential not only for the safety and health of the consumers, but ultimatelyof the plant. Air pollution, which is caused in large part by transportation, has been rendering certain cities as non-liveable, with inhabitants suffering from various pulmonary diseases. It is,therefore, important to tackle these high levels of air pollution.

Literature Review

Early adopters found both hedonic and symbolic attributes of EVs and are pro-environmental (Schuitema et al, 2013). They were mainly influenced by enhanced fuel economy, decreasing pollution, etc. The EV market is growing slowly due to barriers such as range anxiety, chargingtime, and high purchase cost (Carley et al, 2013; Hidrue et al., 2011; Melliger et al., 2018; Hackbarth & Medlener, 2013). However, there is great potential for the growth of the EV market, with the expectation of reaching the USD 470 billion mark, along with abundant benefits (WEF, 2019; Filla & Klingebiel, 2014). Governments can play an important role by promoting knowledge and understanding of the various benefits from the adoption of EVs (Jin& Slowik, 2017).

The adoption of EVs would depend on the development of technologies for improving efficiency and reliability; financial support in the form of government subsidies, and other socio-financial elements. The carbon outflows of battery electric vehicles utilizing grid-mix power are approximately half of those from fuel cell vehicles (Wolfram & Lutsey, 2016). Battery technology is, therefore, considered very crucial for the success of EVs (Andwari et al.2017).

There have been several innovations in battery design aimed at increasing the range and reducing the charging time which would facilitate the quicker and greater adoption of EVs in the future. The safe dispersal of used batteries without affecting the environment is a crucial issue. There is great scope for further research and innovative practices towards safer disposaland handling of used batteries (Idiano, 2019). Battery cost and its frequent replacement could dent the economic viability of EVs (Speirs et al., 2014; Jin & Slowik, 2017) due to which the market share of EV is still at 0.1 %. There is a need to recycle the battery, instead of making new ones and identifying locations that can reduce the environment impact while studying thelife-cycle cost and economic feasibility contributing to "circular value chains" with considerable challenges to ensure continuous supply as well as recovery of basic materials andother useful materials (Liu et al, 2021; Mossali et al, 2020).

As EVs are environmentally friendly and reduce carbon dioxide emissions, all stakeholders including governments, are keen on introducing EVs to replace the present fuel-based vehicles.(Masurali, 2018; Kumar & Padmanaban, 2019; Fanchao, 2017). As per the National Electric Mobility Mission Plan 2020, installing adequate charging infrastructure all across India is keyto the adoption of EVs by consumers; other requirements include offering unique solutions to different ranges of vehicles in India (Kesari, 2019; Kumar & Dash, 2013). People committed to sustainability efforts with greater concern for ecological balance are the early adopters of EVs (Bhalla, 2018).

Unconventional challenges confronted by the Indian EV divisions, advancements in battery technology, and charging methodologies addressing speed and strength are the key facilitatorsfor the speedier adoption of EVs. The challenge is installing the infrastructure for charging anddealerships across India. (Kumar & Alok, 2020; Gujarathi et al., 2018).

India needs strategies to overcome its dependency on the international markets to meet its electric vehicle (EV) component needs, particularly battery cells (Gode et al., 2021). In order to obviate the overdependence on global supplies for battery components and materials, NITI Aayog, the Government of India's chief think tank, started the National Program on Advance Chemistry Cell (ACC) which aims to enhance battery capacity and formulate and launch the Phased Manufacturing Programmes. While it is still in a nascent stage in terms of the adoptionof EVs, a lot is desired to ensure the transition to EVs. This requires many stakeholders to takethe necessary steps in this direction. Government policies to facilitate the quicker adoption andensuring the availability of required infrastructure, as well as industry action towards the installation of the infrastructure and the adoption of the required technologies are critical. In this paper, the status and the preparedness of the various stakeholders towards transformation from predominant fossil fuel-based vehicles to EV is elucidated.

While it is still in nascent stage regarding adoption of EV by the consumer, lot is desired to ensure the transformation to EV which requires many stakeholders to take necessary steps in this direction. The Government policies to facilitate the quicker adoption and ensuring the availability of required infrastructure and the role of industry to install the infrastructure and adapt required technologies are critical. In this paper, the status and the preparedness of the various stakeholders towards transformation from predominant fossil fuel-based vehicles to EV is elucidated.

Research Methodology

This is an exploratory research focused on the electric vehicle market in India and the purpose of this research is to draw insights into the scope and growth of EVs in the Indian market as well as the various challenges involved. One of the focal points of our study is understanding the perceptions of the Indian corporates, because they are considered as key stakeholders in the EV industry, and another is to draw insights about value creation in the supply chain of electric vehicles, and the issues and challenges that must be addressed for faster adoption of EVs. This study aims to understand the potential electric vehicle market, identify issues and challenges, and analyse the opinions of key stakeholders in order to draw insights and actionable points.

This research was conducted through secondary data obtained by collating the views of stakeholders from various journals, news articles, websites, snapshots, and snippets. In order to ensure that only the latest data was captured for analysis, news items/snippets appearing in industry magazines, periodicals, websites, as well as websites related with the automobile sector were collated. The data collected provided the overall opinion of the stakeholders of the EV industry, and were categorized into three groups; manufacturers; perspectives, issues and challenges, and business opportunities, and was analysed using text mining techniques.

Text Mining Techniques

Text mining is a machine learning technique which is used to obtain summarised information from any kind of published material, or from any kind of conversational communication extracted from social media (Trinko et al., 2021). It helps researchers in deep-diving into texts and mining concepts in the form of keyword identification, category extraction, sentiment extraction, concept correlation, and so on. As the present research is based on secondary, unstructured data published in various media channels, we have adopted the text mining technique which appears to be the most appropriate for extracting data about the potential and challenges of the EV market in India. In this technique, information pertinent to research interests is extracted from the text and analysed for each category (Gupta & Lehal, 2009; Pennebaker et al. 2003; Ramanathan & Meyyappan, 2013).

The key technique used in the present study, is to extract the sentiments of the authors of various write-ups, using Sentiment Analysis, which is also referred to as Opinion Mining. Valence Aware Dictionary and sEntiment Reasoner (VADER), a lexicon and rule-based sentiment analysis, has been used to extract the categories of sentiments. The method not only extracts positive and negative sentiments, it also analyses the intensity of sentiments (Archak et al. 2011; Pang & Lee, 2008). For example, if 'bad' and 'horrible' are to be classified, the method would not only identify them as negative sentiments, but it would also assign more negativity towards 'horrible' compared to that of 'bad'. Positive, negative, and neutral scores, produced by the method, indicate the proportion of reviews that fall under these categories. Finally, it produces a compound score which lies between -1, the most negative sentiment, and +1, the most positive sentiments. This compound score finally categorises the sentiments of review text as follows:

Compound Score ≥ 0.05 = Positive Sentiment

Compound Score ≤ -0.05 = Negative Sentiment

-0.05< Compound Score < 0.05 = Neutral Sentiment

Results

In this study, analysis was carried out in three phases, namely, category extraction, sentiment analysis, and text link analysis.

Phase I - Category Extraction

Firstly, the key themes were extracted from stakeholders' views and opinions and categorised into various aspects of the EV business as shown in Figure 1. As seen in Figure 1, the stakeholders spoke about various aspects of EVs such as the sector, the product, concerns about revenue, power source mainly battery, infrastructure etc. The overall opinion of stakeholders was categorized into three groups: manufacturers' perspectives, issues and challenges; and business opportunities. Manufacturers' perspectives may include categories like the EV industry, vehicles, accessories, supplies, the economy, and so on. Issues and challenges encompass categories including infrastructure, installation, cost, purchase, parts, point, charging coverage, parking, and a few others. Business opportunities are captured in terms of revenues, consumers, cities, environment, locations, international trade, research, service coverage, and residential users.

Figure 1: Categories Extracted

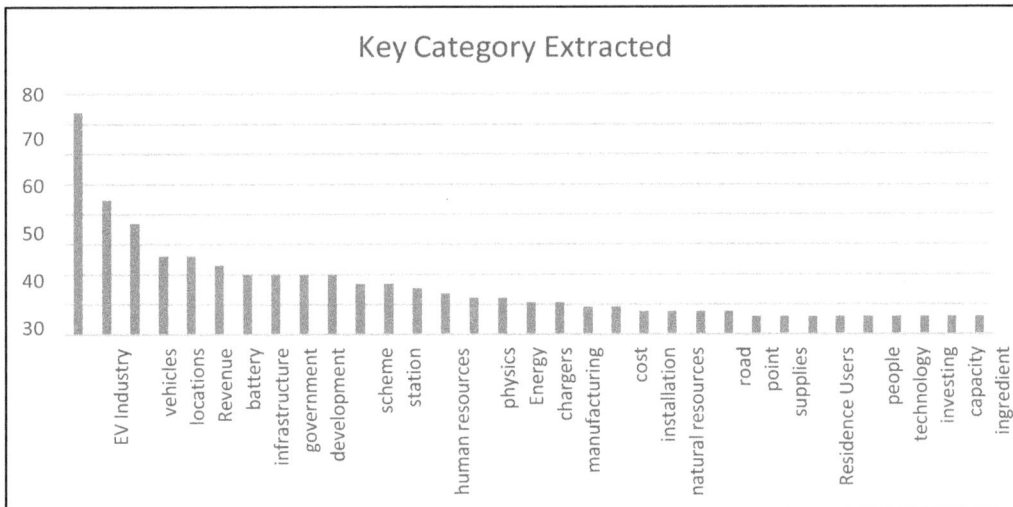

Source: Authors' own

Figure 2: Overall Positive and Negative Sentiments

Figure 2: Overall Positive and Negative Sentiments

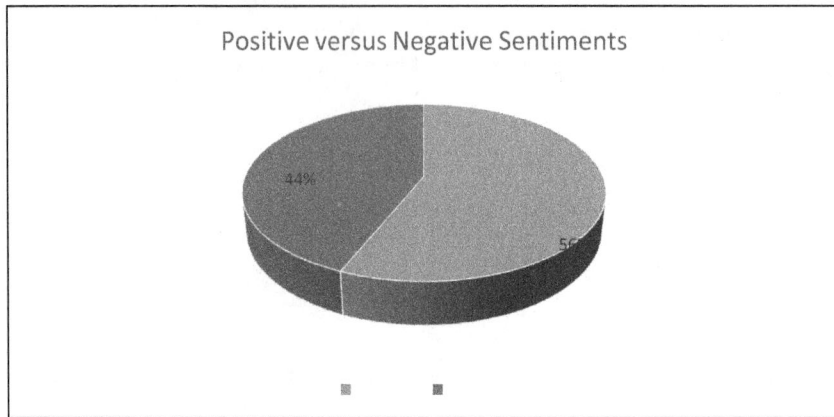

Source: Authors' own

Phase II - Sentiment Analysis

In the second phase of analysis, we extracted positive and negative sentiments from the data using VADER's sentiment analysis. The opinions from stakeholders were subjected to sentiment analysis and the sentiments were broadly catalogued as Positive and Negative. The distribution of positive and negative sentiments in terms of percentages is depicted in Figure 2.

On further analysis of the different sentiments in terms of *attitude* towards the product and the industry, *budget, competence, feeling,* and *functioning* of the product, *sentiment polarity* was observed across these groups. The results are shown in Figure 3.

Figure 3: Sentiment Polarity across Sentiment Type

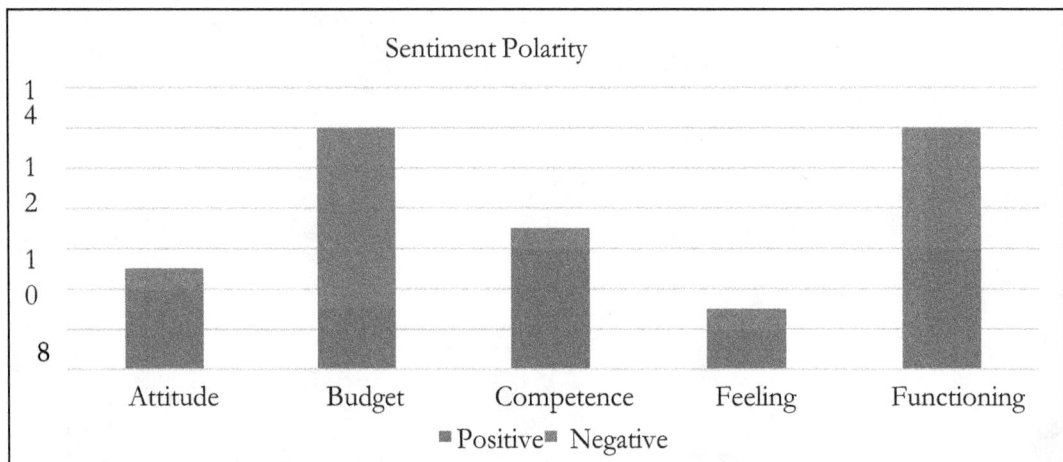

Source: Authors' own

124

Phase III - Text Link Analysis

Using Text Link Analysis, the concept web and concept map were derived to establish the link between the various concepts derived from stakeholders' opinions and to establish the connections between these concepts. These webs and maps reveal three focal themes from stakeholder views, which were further classified as manufacturers' perspectives, business opportunities, and issues and challenges.

Manufacturers' Perspectives

First, we extracted two concept maps, namely, 'concept map of EV' and 'concept map of scheme', which are depicted in Figures 4 and 5 respectively. They essentially indicate the manufacturers' perspectives in the analysis. Figure 4 highlights the challenges identified by the manufacturers. A second concept map was further been extracted to observe their views on certain government schemes and this is presented in Figure 5.

Figure 4: Concept Map of EVs

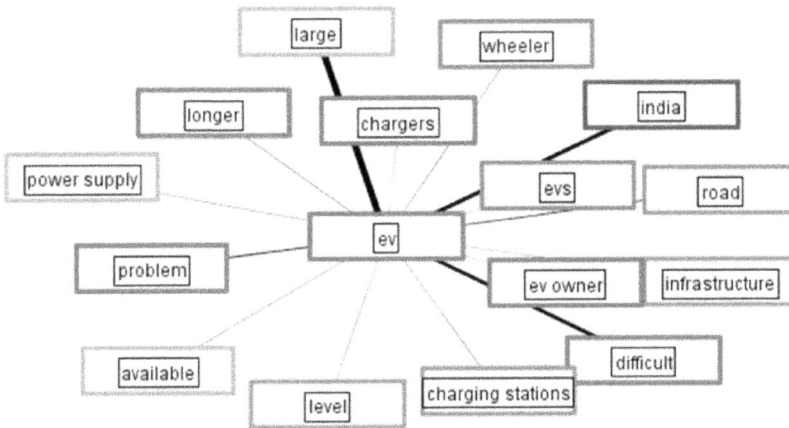

Source: Authors' own

Figure 5: Concept Map of the Scheme

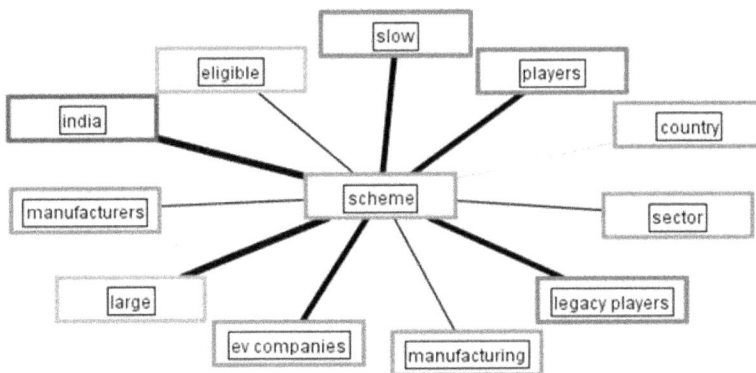

Source: Authors' own

Business Opportunities

The stakeholders of the EV industry highlighted the potential of the EV industry. The study extracted these opportunities in the form of concept webs, which are presented in Figures 6 through 10.

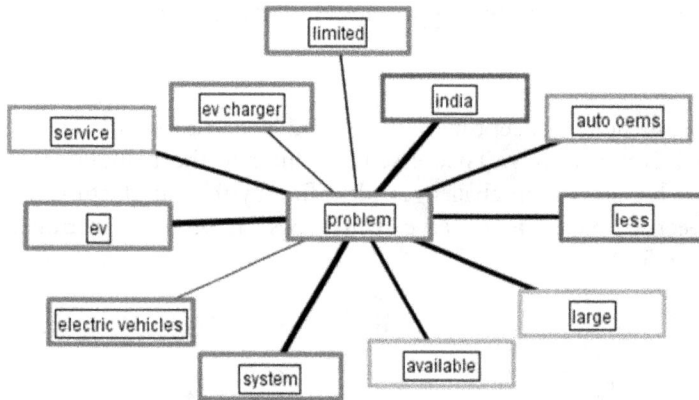

Figure 6: Concept Map of the Problem

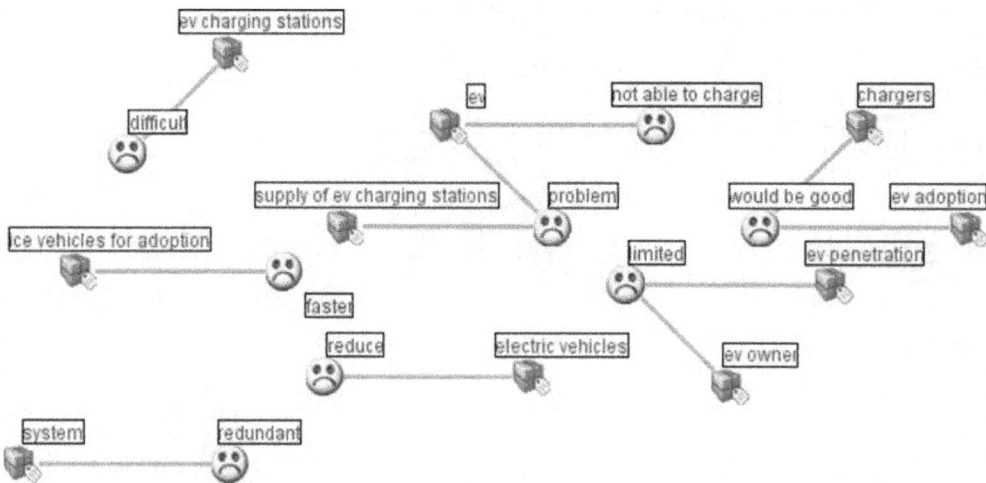

Figure 7: Concept Web - Challenges

Figure 8: Concept Link - Resale Value

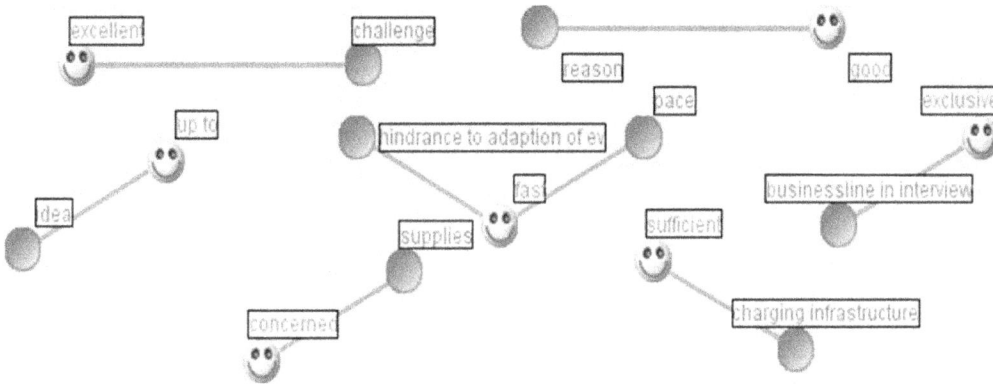

Figure 9: Opportunity Concept Web 1

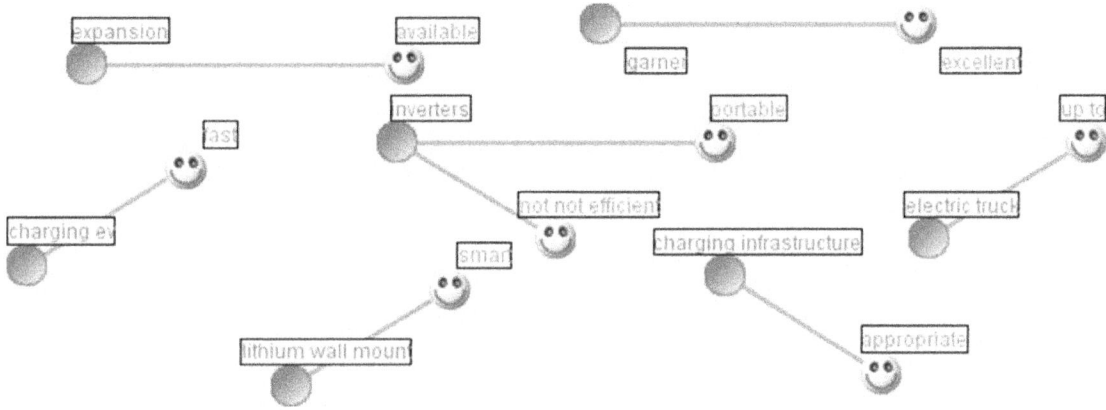

Figure 10: Opportunity Concept Web 2

Issues and Challenges

Using the text mining algorithm, we extracted the key challenges that stakeholders perceive about the EV industry. The map in Figure 11 shows *'problem'* as the central theme and how it is related to other concepts. The thickness of the line indicates the strength of the relationship between the concepts.

The study extracted a concept web of challenges, shown in Figure 12, which indicates the reasons for the low adoption of EVs. We further developed a concept link of resale value from the opinion of the experts, which is shown in Figure 13.

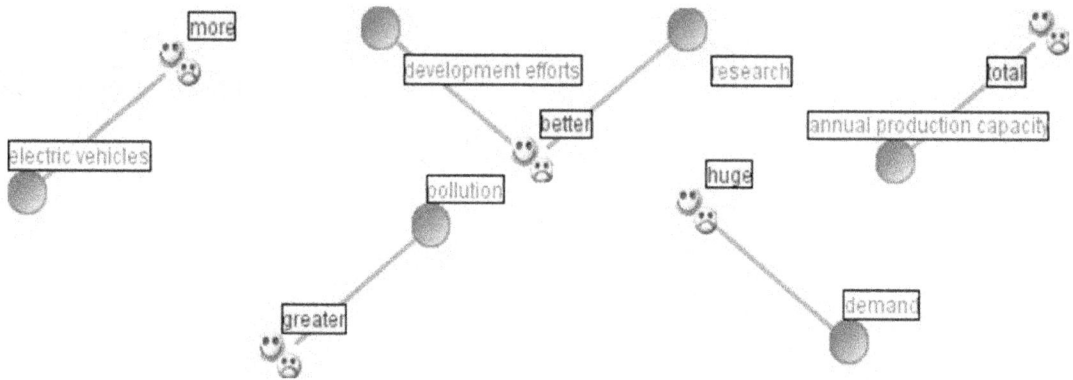
Figure 11: Opportunity Concept Web 3

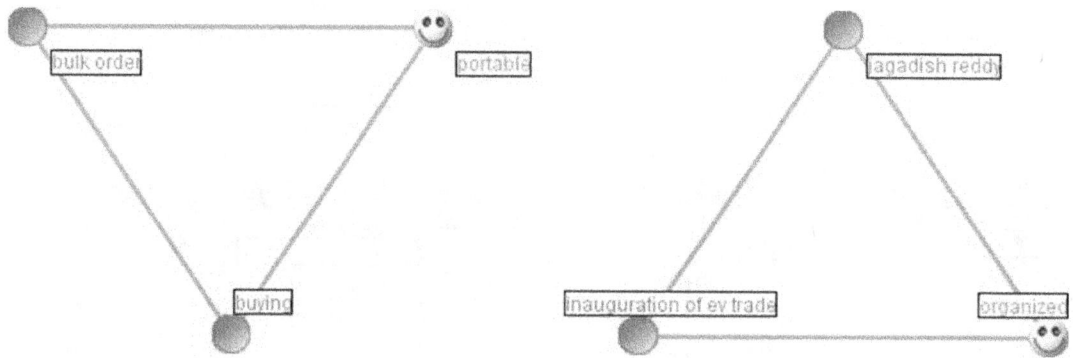
Figure 12: Opportunity Concept Web 4

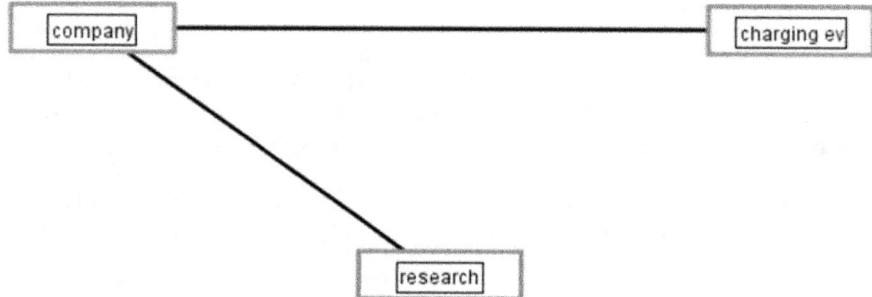
Figure 13: Opportunity Concept Web 5

Discussion

Two-wheelers are one of the most used modes of transportation, and many two-wheeler manufacturers have been focusing on diversifying their product portfolio by developing and introducing different versions of EVs. Consumers, therefore, have the luxury of choice of various EV models, which are on par with conventional vehicles in terms of cost, style, and convenience.

Category Extraction

As we categorised the key concepts extracted in Figure 1, we observed that even though the stakeholders are primarily concerned with the EV industry as a whole, they did, however, express certain concerns such as location, infrastructure, battery and charging points and many more. This indicate that despite being optimistic about the future of the EV industry, they are also sceptical about the growth in this sector.

Sentiment Analysis

The analysis of the overall positive and negative sentiments of the stakeholders (shown in Figure 2), on various aspects of EVs and the EV business, reveals that stakeholders have a balanced opinion about the product and its potential for business, as the 44 precent negative views recorded are almost balanced by the positive views (56 percent). This is probably because stakeholders opine that the business opportunities outweigh the issues and challengesin achieving the growth of this sector in India. Further, sentiment polarity reveals (shown in Figure 3) that stakeholders are highly positive about the competence of the product, which hasprobably generated a positive attitude towards the product and the industry. However, the figure also indicates that the stakeholders are highly sceptical about the expenses incurred in using the product, in terms of the purchase costs and maintenance of the product.

EV Manufacturers' Perspectives

Manufacturers are key stakeholders in the successful deployment and adoption of EVs. They are required to install the required infrastructure for manufacturing, which requires huge capitalinvestment. The present study analyses the views of the manufacturers in order to deduce theirperspective on EVs and the business through extracting certain concept maps.

The concept map of EV, as depicted in Figure 4, indicates that the key concern of manufacturersin India about electric vehicles. The industry is still in its nascent stage in *India*, and the *charging infrastructure* must be developed. India needs to manufacture efficient *charging mechanisms* and batteries for the vehicle. Presently, India does not have any lithium-ion batterymanufacturers even though it is the most significant cost element. Unless the infrastructure formanufacturing batteries is established, it will be very difficult to bring down the overall cost ofEVs. One of the key opinion of the EV manufacturers is that the scale of operations is low dueto supply chain constraints and low production capacity, which prevents them from achievingeconomies of scale, resulting in higher costs of production.

The concept map of Scheme in Figure 5 reflects a recent *scheme* announced by the Governmentof India, which allocated INR 259.38 billion to boost the country's automobile manufacturingsector and to encourage the EV start-up ecosystem. However, stakeholders feel that this scheme will benefit the larger, legacy players, who have been the very players urging to go *slow* on EVplans till now.

The Society of Manufacturers of Electric Vehicles, India's largest industry body representing EV companies echoed the same sentiment adding that most of India's current small and medium EV manufacturers, and new start-ups may not qualify for the scheme, which offers incentives for electric vehicles and hydrogen fuel cell vehicles of all segments, along with incentives for advanced automotive technological components of vehicles, CKD/SKD kits, vehicle aggregates of two-wheelers, three-wheelers, passenger vehicles, commercial vehicles and tractors. The scheme does not have much in terms of supporting the charging infrastructurein the country which is one of the areas that need special focus. Charging infrastructure is not growing at the same rate as the fleets (two- and three-wheelers). To meet the demand for charging infrastructure for the existing 4-5 million two- and three-wheeler EVs, the country needs about 100,000 charging points at a ratio of 1:50 according to one of the key EV manufacturers.

Another key automotive industry body, the Society of Indian Automobile Manufacturers (SIAM) opined that the scheme shows the government's commitment to support the Indian auto industry by incentivising battery-electric and hydrogen vehicles, and a selected list of autocomponents while encouraging local investments and manufacturing. The Automotive Component Manufacturers Association of India (ACMA), a group representing 850 manufacturers, indicated that the PLI scheme will aid India's automotive value chain making it an attractive alternative source for high-end auto components.

From manufacturing to driving a car, there is a whole new set of people and jobs, and therefore,skills related with customer service will come into focus. EVs require more investment in R & D atthis stage to enhance the battery range and make them last longer as well as lighter in weight; all these lead to an increase in the manufacturing costs. Materials like lithium, cobalt, manganese, and nickel are not readily available because they are restricted to a certain geographical location due to which their cost varies from region to region.

Business Opportunities

The result extracted through the first concept web reveals that stakeholders are optimistic about reducing the *hindrance to the adoption of EV*. However, this is dependent on the standardisation of batteries, which requires high capital investment. Stakeholders identify that there is huge potential for the industry to grow provided *sufficient charging infrastructure* across India can be developed.

The second concept web (Figure 7) indicates that India is capable of producing greener energyby securing supplies of rare earth materials, even if the supplies of lithium and neodymium arecontrolled by China. The stakeholders suggest portable inverters as an alternative solution to address the lack of charging infrastructure.

The rest of the concept webs (Figures 8 – 10) reflect the stakeholders' views on various opportunities for the EV market in India. The analysis reveals that they are upbeat and would like to proceed with strategies to participate and profit from the business potential of EVs, as depicted in the following cases. Experts opine that, if the batteries can be standardised with high capital investment, the hindrance to adoption of EV can be reduced to a great extent. Further, evidence shows that the rapid *charging EV* battery was launched as organisations likeAmaron invested a sizeable sum of money, INR 370 million, towards research & developmentof the EV industry. The industry is experiencing huge *expansion*, facilitated by the Governmentof Delhi, which would make nearly 1000 EV charging points *available* to the public shortly. The other state governments including the Government of Telangana have taken initiatives, such as manufacturing 600 new electric vehicles along with charging stations to make India anEV-driven country. Evidence shows that the other states in India have also been participating in this journey. For example, Ather Energy Pvt. Ltd. is going to set up a second manufacturingplant in Hosur, Tamil Nadu, which will have an *annual production capacity* of 280,000 electricscooters. India has been experiencing such initiatives both at the state as well as the central government levels. Yet another such initiative emerged from stakeholders' views. We find thatCoal India Ltd. (CIL) has been instructed by the government to adopt diversification strategiesand produce *more* of *electric vehicles* and to take care of *charging stations* in the country. EVstakeholders are very positive towards such initiatives launched by the Government of India asthis would cause a *huge demand* for EVs in the country.

The concepts webs reveal that there are lots of start-ups who have joined the industry. Oxy Neuron India Pvt. Ltd. in Noida is one such firm which manufactures *portable* inverters whichare claimed to be 94 percent more efficient than the conventional ones. Further, these invertersare compatible with solar panels and can be used for charging EVs. This drew the attention ofTesla India who placed *bulk orders* for these *portable* inverters.

The stakeholders are excited as the Government of Karnataka will acquire 1,500 electric busesover the next three years which will ply in Bengaluru. They welcome this news as there is a constant rise in fuel prices in India. These electric buses need to be charged after every 120 kilometres travelled, which takes 45 minutes for completion. The media claims that Hyundai Motor India Ltd. is going to invest INR 40 billion towards the research & development of electric batteries over the next 7 years. Finally, the EV industry is truly in the trajectory of growth, as the Government of India has approved the Faster Adoption & Manufacturing of Electric Vehicles (FAME II) scheme for implementation, which also provides for high-powerelectric charging points for haul trucks. ABB will include the Ability eMine FastCharge in its portfolio from 2022; it is currently in the pilot phase. This is a fully automated solution designed for the harsh environment in mines. Ability eMine FastCharge can be installed anywhere and can charge any electric truck up to 600KW, the highest power available in the market today, and a suitable level of charge can be achieved within 15 minutes.

Issues and Challenges

Despite a lot of advancements in electric vehicles, many hurdles still remain. One such hurdlethat many owners must face is the warranty period of the battery. Often, this warranty is less than that of the rest of the vehicle parts. Another major hurdle that remains is the lack of charging stations. This limits the use of electric vehicle to mainly cities, and to shorter distances. Until charging stations become widespread, the use of electric vehicles will remain severely limited.

Figure 11 reveals that the stakeholders are concerned with the *EV* energy management *systems*in *India*. EV *charging* requires a parking slot and in India, not every vehicle has a dedicated parking slot; even in large residential complexes, many cars are parked in uncovered open areas. This makes the installation of mass charging stations difficult, except in a few petrol bunks. This poses one of the biggest problems for the EV industry in India. The second majorproblem identified is the lack of *service* options. As the technicians from informal service networks are not exposed to the relatively new EV technology, getting their vehicles serviced would be a challenge to EV users. It is in this regard that the manufacturers make the followingcomment, "*In the absence of an efficient service network, most fleet companies would delay EV adoption.*"

As EV adoption goes up, the demand for minerals for production and for generating power will also increase. There are certain obstacles, including geopolitical risk, capital pressures, and ESG (Environmental, Social & Governance) issues, which may restrict the supply of these minerals, and as a result, the growth and development of the EV industry may be hindered. Therefore, it is a serious concern for automakers and original equipment manufacturers (AutoOEMs) to mitigate risk related to future supply chains.

The concept web in Figure 7, indicates the reasons for the low adoption of EVs in India. It points out that the current ESG system with respect to EVs is redundant. One of the key challenges is with regard to the setting up of EV charging stations. One of the experts opined that this is a classic chicken and egg problem; in their own words, *"People don't buy EVs as the charging infrastructure isn't there and charging infra isn't an attractive business model as there aren't enough EVs on the road!"*

Further, range anxiety has created a major hindrance to the growth of EV industry. It is worth noting the observations of manufacturers that the lack of standardization has created problems with the infrastructure of EV charging stations. One such problem is with regard to the charging connectors. Different charger connector types exist, the most common ones being the CCS / CCS Type 2, Bharat AC-001/Bharat DC-001, CHAdeMO, GB/T, and Tesla Chargers. The EV connector type is provided on the car and on the EV charger as well. Currently, all standards are being adopted, and this creates a problem of supply of EV charging stations. Most cars support the CCS/CCS Type 2 charging connector standard; yet some brands follow GBT or Bharat AC/DC 001 standards.

The concept link depicted in Figure 8 demonstrates that the insignificant resale value of EVs prevents consumers from buying these vehicles. It has been rightly observed by the corporates that there are concerns regarding battery life. EVs depreciate more than ICE vehicles making its *resale value lower*.

Another issue is with regard to power infrastructure upgradation. Most residential users need to determine their sanctioned load, spare capacity, and the power intake requirements of the EV charger that would require additional load. Residential complexes and other buildings need to look at installation of common use charging stations with suitable power backup.

Vehicle service is another issue considering that the EV service network is yet to reach a substantial level. In the absence of an efficient service network, most fleet companies would delay the adoption of EVs. Presently over 80 percent of charging is "captive" – being done at the vehicle owners' homes or residences; with the balance required for road trips and cross city travel requiring top ups at different locations.

EV batteries take a longer time to charge. The typical two-wheeler electric vehicle has a 2-3 Kwh battery, while a four-wheeler battery would range from 30 to 45 kwh. As battery technology evolves, these batteries will increase in size, and also become more efficient. A Level 1 charger would take over 15 hours to charge a four-wheeler. Hence, L2 Smart chargers are the need of the hour at homes, offices, and retail locations – these would charge any typical four-wheeler in five to seven hours. DC Fast chargers have always been in the news because they can charge a four-wheeler up to 80 percent in 30 minutes – but these chargers are very expensive to buy and require a power source between 100 and 400 kW. The case for using DC Fast Charging is for inter-city travel and should be deployed at inter-city outlets. It would require the deployment of a large number – say two to three times the number of EVs on the road at different locations, to make it a fully functional infrastructure, so that

EVs become a mainstay of transportation. Public charging will play as critical a role in this transition as a local supply chain.

Another important factor is the supply chain. While the domestic manufacturing capabilities can produce anything from pins to power trains, the access to battery cells and rare earths is going to be a great challenge and constraint, which could majorly affect the supply chain of EVs.

Implications

The review and analysis of the views about the successful adoption of EVs in India, reveals that various stakeholders are required to take immediate action to address the various issues inthe early and quick adoption of EVs by consumers. Government agencies as well as various bodies of the automobile sector are required to ensure conducive and facilitative support that should be extended to various players such as technology and product development organizations, raw materials suppliers, EV manufacturers, distributors etc. The role of MSME's in this regard cannot be ignored and the government should support these sectors by providing the required amenities and tax concessions and upgrading the policies for encouraging the use of EVs. The government and the other players should emphasize the availability of crucial materials for the development of the battery, the main component of EVs by adopting the latest technologies which will ensure faster chargeable batteries with improved performance at an affordable cost. The government as well as private players are required to establish the infrastructure for charging, powering, and installing the required number of charging stations across the vast stretch of the country.

Limitations and Future Research

In this study, the current status and the future actions envisaged by various stakeholders of theEV market were analysed to decipher the issues and challenges in the adoption of EVs, considering that the market is still in a nascent stage. The manufacturer's perspectives for transforming the existing supply chain and infrastructure to cater to the switch from fuel-basedICE to electric vehicles were elucidated. Looking at the existing infrastructure and the ambitious goal of attaining 100 percent EVs on the road, a lot of ground needs to be covered, which has been discussed in this paper. Taking cues from this paper, further research may lookinto the development of a predictive model for attaining 100 percent adoption of EVs in the two- / four-wheeler segment considering the effect of certain influencing factors such as improvement in battery technology/performance, charging infrastructure, government supportand policies etc.

Conclusion

For faster adoption and smoother transition from ICE-based vehicles to EVs, it can be concluded that certain aspects need immediate attention and implementation. Along with improvements in battery technology, the facilitation of faster charging with higher reach, and sufficient charging infrastructure across the road networks is necessary for the adoption of EVs.For Indian consumers, the purchase price and ownership cost of EVs should be similar to thoseof ICE-based vehicles for faster adoption. Lack of standardisation of batteries and chargers, coupled with high capital investments for setting up of charging stations are the hindrances tothe speedy adoption of EVs. Research suggests that a short driving range is also a major barrier,while the lack of infrastructure for charging and long charging durations affect the demand forEVs, especially considering the erratic power supply across most of the country. EV batteries require lithium and neodymium; the supply of both is heavily controlled by China. This posesconsiderable supply chain issues in the EV industry. India should secure supplies of rare earthminerals in order to pursue greener energies. Some of the minerals required for EVs run the risk of shortages due to geopolitical issues rather than limited availability. Additionally, the disposal of used batteries is one of the greatest concerns for the environment and requires clarity. Land filling would lead to the leaking of toxic chemicals into the soil. The true turning point, though, will be manufacturing EV car batteries indigenously, so prices can drop. Currently, the battery accounts for about half the cost of the vehicle. The government aims to have about 4,500 EV charging stations across India by 2024, up from the current 1,800. However, India will need about 100 times that many — at least 0.4 million charging stations — to match the stated target of 2 million EVs on the roads by 2026.

There are various issues and challenges that must be addressed with regard to the deploymentand adoption of EVs, however, the various stakeholders are upbeat about combating these challenges especially considering the existing business opportunity. The EV industry is still ina nascent stage in India but developing at a rapid pace. Even with the current challenges, electric vehicles have considerable potential to reduce the carbon footprint and provide a cost-effective transportation system.

References

Andwari, A. M., Pesiridis, A., Rajoo, S., Martinez-Botas, R., & Esfahanian, V.(2017). A review of Battery Electric Vehicle technology and readiness levels. *Renewable and Sustainable Energy Reviews*, *78*, 414-430.

Archak, N., Ghose, A., & Ipeirotis, P. G. (2011). Deriving the pricing power of product features by mining consumer reviews. *Management science*, *57*(8), 1485-1509.

Bhalla, P., Ali, I. S., & Nazneen, A. (2018). A study of consumer perception andpurchase intention of electric vehicles. *European Journal of Scientific Research*, *149*(4), 362-368.

Carley, S., Krause, R. M., Lane, B. W., & Graham, J. D. (2013). Intent to purchase aplug-in electric vehicle: A survey of early impressions in large US cites. *Transportation Research Part D: Transport and Environment*, *18*, 39-45.

Gode, P., Bieker, G., & Bandivadekar, A. (2021). Battery capacity needed to powerelectric vehicles in India from 2020 to 2035. *Int. Council on Clean Transport*, 1-16.

Gujarathi, P. K., Shah, V. A., & Lokhande, M. M. (2018). Electric vehicles in India:Market analysis with consumer perspective, policies and issues. *Journal of Green Engineering*, *8*(1), 17-36.

Filla, P., & Klingebiel, K. (2014). Risk profiles for the pre-series logistics inautomotive ramp-up processes. *Procedia CIRP*, *20*, 44-49.

Hackbarth, A., & Madlener, R. (2013). Consumer preferences for alternative fuel vehicles: A discrete choice analysis. *Transportation Research Part D: Transport andEnvironment*, *25*, 5-17.

Hidrue, M. K., Parsons, G. R., Kempton, W., & Gardner, M. P. (2011). Willingness topay for electric vehicles and their attributes. *Resource and energy economics*, *33*(3), 686-705.

International Energy Agency. (2021). Global EV Outlook 2021. https://iea.blob.core.windows.net/assets/ed5f4484-f556-4110-8c5c-4ede8bcba637/GlobalEVOutlook2021.pdf

Jin, L., & Slowik, P. (2017). Literature review of electric vehicle consumer awarenessand outreach activities. *International Council on Clean Transportation. Available frominternet: https://www. theicct. org/sites/default/files/publications/Consumer-EV-Awareness_ICCT_Working-Paper_23032017_vF. pdf.*

Kesari, J. P., Sharma, Y., & Goel, C. (2019). Opportunities and scope for electricvehicles in India. *International Journal of Mechanical Engineering*, *6*(5), 1-8.

Kumar, P., & Dash, K. (2013). Potential need for electric vehicles, charging stationinfrastructure and its challenges for the indian market. *Advance in Electronic and Electric Engineering*, *3*(4), 471-476.

Kumar, R., & Padmanaban, S. (2019). Electric vehicles for India: overview andchallenges. *IEEE India Informatics*, *14*, 139.

Kumar, R. R., & Alok, K. (2020). Adoption of electric vehicle: A literature reviewand prospects for sustainability. *Journal of Cleaner Production*, *253*, 119911.

Liu, C. Y., Wang, H., Tang, J., Chang, C. T., & Liu, Z. (2021). Optimal recovery model in a used batteries closed-loop supply chain considering uncertain residual capacity. *Transportation Research Part E: Logistics and Transportation Review*, *156*,102516.

MarketsandMarkets. (2022). Electric Vehicle Market by Component, Vehicle Type, Vehicle Class, Propulsion (BEV, PHEV, FCEV), Vehicle Drive Type (FWD, RWD, AWD), Vehicle Top Speed (<125 mph, >125 mph), Charging Point Type, Vehicle Connectivity, End Use, Region - Global Forecast 2030. https://www.marketsandmarkets.com/Market-Reports/electric-vehicle-market-   209371461.html?gclid=Cj0KCQjwlK-WBhDjARIsAO2sErT_4iXL_31nqNJs9k27vBBGpu_Rm9uZcD10I3tuKmG1KKIDv 23EaZcaAtYMEALw_wcB

Masurali, A., & Surya, P. (2018). Perception and awareness level of potential customers towards electric cars. *International Journal for Research in AppliedScience & Engineering Technology, 6*(3), 359-362.

Melliger, M. A., van Vliet, O. P., & Liimatainen, H. (2018). Anxiety vs reality–Sufficiency of battery electric vehicle range in Switzerland and Finland. *Transportation Research Part D: Transport and Environment, 65*, 101-115.

Mossali, E., Picone, N., Gentilini, L., Rodriguez, O., Pérez, J. M., & Colledani, M.(2020). Lithium-ion batteries towards circular economy: A literature review of opportunities and issues of recycling treatments. *Journal of environmental management, 264*, 110500.

Pang, B., & Lee, L. (2008). Opinion mining and sentiment analysis. *Foundations andTrends® in information retrieval, 2*(1–2), 1-135.

Schuitema, G., Anable, J., Skippon, S., & Kinnear, N. (2013). The role of instrumental, hedonic and symbolic attributes in the intention to adopt electricvehicles. *Transportation Research Part A: Policy and Practice, 48*, 39-49.

Speirs, J., Contestabile, M., Houari, Y., & Gross, R. (2014). The future of lithiumavailability for electric vehicle batteries. *Renewable and Sustainable Energy Reviews, 35*, 183-193.

Trinko, D., Porter, E., Dunckley, J., Bradley, T., & Coburn, T. (2021). Combining AdHoc Text Mining and Descriptive Analytics to Investigate Public EV Charging Pricesin the United States. *Energies, 14*(17), 5240.

Wolfram, P., & Lutsey, N. (2016). Electric vehicles: Literature review of technologycosts and carbon emissions. *The International Council on Clean Transportation: Washington, DC, USA*, 1-23.

World Economic Forum. (2019). EV-Ready India Part 1: Value Chain Analysis of State EV Policies. https://www3.weforum.org/docs/WEF_EV_Ready_India.pdf

CHAPTER 9

VALUE CREATION FOR VENTURE CAPITAL-BACKED FIRMS BY AVOIDING THE LIKELIHOOD OF MORAL HAZARDS

Vandana Panwar[1], Christopher Erickson[2], Alan Tupicoff[3]

Introduction

In India, venture capital financing is a significant and growing form of financial intermediation. Under SEBI regulations, venture capital firms are categorized as "alternative investment fund" (AIF) defined as an AIF that invest primarily in unlisted securities of start-ups and early-stage venture capital undertakings (Venture Capital in India, 2021). Between 2012 and 2020, VC funding increased at annual rate of 15.7% from $3.1 billion to $10.0 billion. VC funding then jumped in one year from $10.0 billion to $38.4 billion in 2021 (Bain & Company, 2022). Venture capital firms (VC firms) engage in value creation by providing privately held "tech" firms with equity, debt, or hybrid forms of financing, typically also providing managerial expertise and advice. In the process of value creation, VC firms play a disproportionate rule in economic growth by promoting the commercialization of new technologies.

To understand value creation by VC firms requires and understanding of the specialized role played by VC firms. That is, why is there a specialized set of firms that focus on financing the technology sector? After all, tech firms could fund their operations in the same way that moretraditional firms do, by a combination of commercial banks, investment banks, private investors, and stock and bond IPOs (Amit, 1998). If must be then, that VC firm creates value in a way that is different from other sources of funding. In seeking to understand venture capital finance, it therefore is important to ask what exactly is the niche filled by venture capital firms. We argue that VC firms create value by specializing in deals that involve new technologies for which technical knowledge and engineering skill are an important element in making financial decisions along with more traditional financial factors.

Asymmetric information is a prevalent feature of the financial system. Indeed, much of the structural of the financial system is structured so as to mitigate effects of asymmetric information (Einay& Finkelstein 2018, Rowell & Connelly 2012, Wolferen, Inbar, & Zeelenberg 2014, Hossain & Chowdhury 2015). There are two major manifestations of informational asymmetry. One manifestation, referred to as adverse selection, occurs when one party to a transaction knows relevant information that is not known to the other party. An example relevantto venture capital involves an entrepreneur who develops a new product. The entrepreneur may have a better information about potential of the product than do investors. The entrepreneur may have an incentive to overstate the likelihood of successful their product, thereby, misleading investors into funding a profitable project.

[1] Prof Dr Vandana Panwar, Associate Professor-PGDM-Rural Management (Emerging Economies), Prin. L. N. Welingkar Institute of Management Development and Research (WeSchool), Mumbai (India). E-mail: vandana.panwar@welingkar.org
[2] Prof Dr. Christopher Erickson, Garrey E. and Katherine T. Carruthers Professor of Economic Development, New Mexico State University, USA. E-mail: chererick@nmsu.edu
[3] Alan Tupicoff, Founding President–Australia & New Zealand Institute of Sustainable Management (ANZISM), Exec Director - ATsolve Pty Ltd (Australia). E-mail: alan@atsolve.com.au

The existence of adverse selection will cause investment investors to become wary of funding projects. In the extreme, the market could even break down (Stiglitz & Weiss, 1981), making it impossible. VC firms create value for potential investors by using their expertise to distinguish between technology projects with higher potential for success from those with lower potential. VC firms create value for entrepreneurs by funding higher potential projects when otherwise adverse selection might have prevented the entrepreneur from raising capital. By contrast, traditional intermediaries are limited in their ability to create value in the start-up space because they lack the specialized knowledge needed of tech start-up.

The other type of informational asymmetry, referred to as moral hazard, is a situation in which one party to a transaction cannot observe actions taken by the other. For example, an investor may not be able to observe entrepreneurial effort. Assessing moral hazards in entrepreneurial ventures is a significant scientific and practical challenge, as it is more difficult to observe and limit moral hazards than other flaws. A moral hazard can arise when the success of a new business, for example, is strongly reliant on the entrepreneur's effort in operating the business. the entrepreneur has an incentive to disguise their actions (Keuschnigg & Nielsen2004). When expending effort imposes costs on the entrepreneur, entrepreneurs can avoid making the effort, work less efficiently than expected, or take a higher financial risk after receiving external financing, thereby reducing the likelihood of success for their business andexposing lenders to losses (Hyytinen & Vaananen 2006, Ejrnes&Hochguertel 2013). Recognizing that the potential for moral hazard investors may be reluctant to find technology. As a result of moral hazards, the optimal level of external investments in the establishment and development of new businesses gets reduced.

Here again, the VC firm adds value by using specialized of technology-based firms to create value. VC firms will structure deals to minimize the moral hazard thereby increasing the chance of success. This creates value for investors by increasing expected returns to entrepreneurial projects. This creates value for the entrepreneurs by increasing funding available to them. In what follows, we will focus on value creations by VC firms in managing moral hazard.

The primary goal of this article is to investigate the impact of moral hazards on the process of new companies' formation and development in India. This study provides a conceptual framework that identifies the factors that influence the likelihood of avoiding moral hazards, thereby leading to entrepreneurial profits for the VCs and value creation for the venture capital-backed firms.

Background & Related Reference Literature

Several researchers mention the venture capital as a viable source of financing development (Junjuan & Zheng-Qun, 2020; Ifeanyi & Obianuju 2016; Sagari & Guidotti 1991a; Zider 1998). Since venture capital is based on equity rather than debt financing, it is expected to promote growth and development while preserving order and stability. Some of the important studies has been summarised in a table focusing on the important aspects of venture capital financing over the years in table 1.

In the presence of asymmetric information and conflicts of interest between the 'buyers' and the 'sellers in the market (Akerlof 1970), the theory of capital market imperfections predicts that some firms will be unable to obtain external finance at the cost of funds set in centralised securities markets. In these cases, the structure of venture capital is well suited to address the problems of informational asymmetry and agency costs that are most pronounced in high-tech industries and young firms

(Sahlman 1990, 1994a). A major issue with the design of venture capital contracts is therefore moral hazard and adverse selection.

Table 1: Sample of related literature and background

S.No.	Author (year)	Aspects focused on
1	Junjuan & Zheng-Qun, 2020; Ifeanyi & Obianuju 2016 Sagari & Guidotti 1991a Zider 1998	-viable source of financing development -venture capital can significantly improve the technology innovation, profitability, and growth abilityof SMEs. -enterprise growth theory
2	Akerlof 1970	-Asymmetric informtion and conflicts of interestbetween buyers and sellers. -Theory of capital market imperfections
3	Sahlman 1990,Sahlman 1994a	-Structure & design of venture capital
4	Amit 1998	-Asymmetric information as hidden action -Difference between adverse selection nad moralhazard.
5	Mattesini 1993	adverse selection
6	Stiglitz and Weiss (1981)Myers & Majluf (1984)	informational asymmetry and capital marketimperfections
7	Gibbons 1992	-Moral Hazard -game with imperfect information, in which themovement of the other player is not observed
8	Townsend ,1979	Moral hazard in Debt contract
9	Williamson 1986	-Moral hazard in Debt contract -in a debt contract, the borrower's return function isconvex in the project's return, while the lender's function is concave
10	Rozalska-Lilo (2021)	-Value creation in venture capital -VC attracts startups by providing support post-investment. VC platforms, how Value is added, making differetiation through focus, nurturing and skills.
11	Dieffenbacher, S.F. (2022, June 12)	Value Creation Definition, Model, Principles,Importance & Steps
12	Michele E.McHale (2017).	'-Private equity integration & value creation - how to get the most from the investmet after the dealis closed. a rigorous assessment of the business's corestrengths, the best opportunities for increasing its value, and areas of synergy with the rest of the firm's portfolio
13	Sudhir Sethi (2011)	Emerging Markets Private Equity Review

Amit (1998) refers to asymmetric information as "hidden information affecting economic behaviour throughout economic history". When commodities of varied quality are exchanged, adverse selection occurs because one side of the market can observe the quality of the goods while the other side can only guess at its distribution (Mattesini 1993). In this situation, low- quality goods tend to dominate the market, i.e., low-quality goods drive out high-quality ones. The works of Stiglitz and Weiss (1981) and Myers & Majluf (1984) establish the framework for analyzing the connections between informational asymmetry and capital market imperfections.

Moral hazards have a multifaceted impact on the entrepreneurial process. It arises between two parties when one party can affect the quality of the good or service exchanged, while the other party cannot monitor it perfectly. This type of informational asymmetry is described by Amit (1998) as a 'hidden action', in which one party to a transaction is unable to observe relevant actions taken by the other (or at last cannot legally verify these actions). The difference between adverse selection and moral hazard is that, in the former, the informed party knows only the quality of the goods (or service) exchanged but cannot alter it; in the latter, the quality of the goods or service provided can be influenced by the party who is aware.

In terms of game theory, Moral Hazard can be modelled as a game with imperfect information, in which the movement of the other player is not observed (Gibbons 1992). Moral hazard in debt contracts is well documented in many writings, including Townsend (1979, Williamson 1986), among others. Stiglitz and Weiss build their formal analysis on the result derived by Rothschild and Stiglitz (1970) namely that as the variance of a random variable rises, the expected value of any convex function of it also rises. An inverse relationship holds for concave functions. They show that, in a debt contract, the borrower's return function is convex inthe project's return, while the lender's function is concave. As a result, the borrower's expected return increases as the project becomes riskier, i.e., as the project's return variance increases, the lender's decreases. Moral hazard problems, therefore, are inherent in debt contracts.

Given the conflict of interest between the lender and the borrower, as the former raisesthe interest rate, the borrower will have stronger incentives to choose riskier actions. The reason is that higher interest rates make bankruptcy more likely, while other things are held constant. Bychoosing riskier actions, both, extremely high and extremely low returns will be more likely. Since below a certain level of returns the borrower defaults, thus increasing the likelihood of extremely high returns means higher expected returns for the borrower. It is therefore understood that, higher interest rates cause borrowers to choose riskier actions, but this means that expected returns for the lender might decrease, hence, the lender cannot raise the interest rate indefinitely; beyond a certain level, as higher interest causes lower expected returns for the lender. If this critical level is below the market-clearing level, then demand for credit will exceed supply, and rationing is obtained as an equilibrium solution.

As competition among various funds has increased, the venture capital (VC) environment has changed significantly in recent years (Rozalska, 2021). The latest buzzword in the global venture capital ecosystem is venture creation for portfolio companies. A trend is emerging in which VCs attract potential startups by demonstrating how much post-investment support they can provide.

The process of transforming work and resources into something that satisfies other people's needs is known as value creation. In today's environment, intangible assets like brands, ideas, people, and innovation are what create value. The foundation of every prosperous firm is value creation. Therefore, value creation is viewed as a better management tool than merely financial metrics of corporate performance when used extensively. Every firm should be driven by the desire to create value (Dieffenbacher, S. F. 2022)

The goal of every transaction is to create value. Venture capital businesses may ensure they start delivering value from day one in a number of ways (Michele E.M 2017). The majority of businesses create a strong business case for their purchase, which frequently entails conducting in-depth market research. The decisions that affect value creation range from choosing a location for operations to deciding which businesses to close or sell to determining whether the correct items are being offered. Due to conflicting agendas, they search for synergiesthroughout the business.

VCs put in more effort for their startup companies in the early stages by adding significant value. They can extract more value from their portfolio and liquidate it faster by assisting their existing deals. They also attract new startups due to their reputation as committed, hands-on investors who deliver exceptional value. Seth (2017) focuses on early-stage investments in technology and technology-enabled businesses, he describes how venture capitalists can collaborate with local business owners to offer considerable value to Indian enterprises.

It has always been the responsibility of venture capitalists to support businesses, but this has typically been done on an individual, uncoordinated basis by fund partners. To achieve scale, the current trend is to build a process around these added services (fundraising, marketing and business development functions, graphic design, user experience and user interface professionals, financial, legal, HR specialists, mental and emotional support), measure activities at the fund level, and make data-driven improvements. This is where the concept of "value" comes into play and their role is to add an additional set of hands to work on mission-critical parts of the business.

Some of the value-add investors/companies/accelerators that have accepted the value creation model rather than a traditional venture capital firm includes Andreessen Horowitz, Aleph VC, Glilot fund, F2 Capital. Thus, VCs are reinventing themselves by providing differentiated services to their companies based on what they believe are needed or what their startups most want at their stage, industry, and business model.

Venture Capital Investment Framework

The most important operation of the Venture Capital Firms (VCFs) is the examination of proposed enterprises. Since VCs typically invest in small businesses with direct involvement from them, and because such businesses are brand new with no record of accomplishment, venture appraisal cannot be subjected to a high level of quantitative research (Poindexter, 1976). This is supported by venture appraisal experiences in industrialized countries such as the United States (Poindexter, 1976, Tyebjee & Bruno, 1984, MacMillan, Seigal & Narsimha, 1985). While Sahlman (1990), Malik (2019), Gompers et al. (2021), Fried and Hisrich (1994) and Pratch (2005) have researched the venture capital investment process, different frameworks used by VCFs for investing capital, and the value of a venture capitalist after an investment is made.

According to Tyebjee and Bruno (1984), the venture capital investment activity is a six- step process which includes:

(1) deal origination, i.e., identifying a potential firm;

(2) screening or reviewing proposals, particularly in technology, product, and scope of the market;

(3) evaluation or due diligence, i.e., assessment of the business plan (risk and return);

(4) deal structuring, i.e., negotiating and mutually establishing VC agreement;

(5) post-investment activities or providing value-added activities; and

(6) exit from the venture.

Figure 1. Investment decision process

Investment decision process

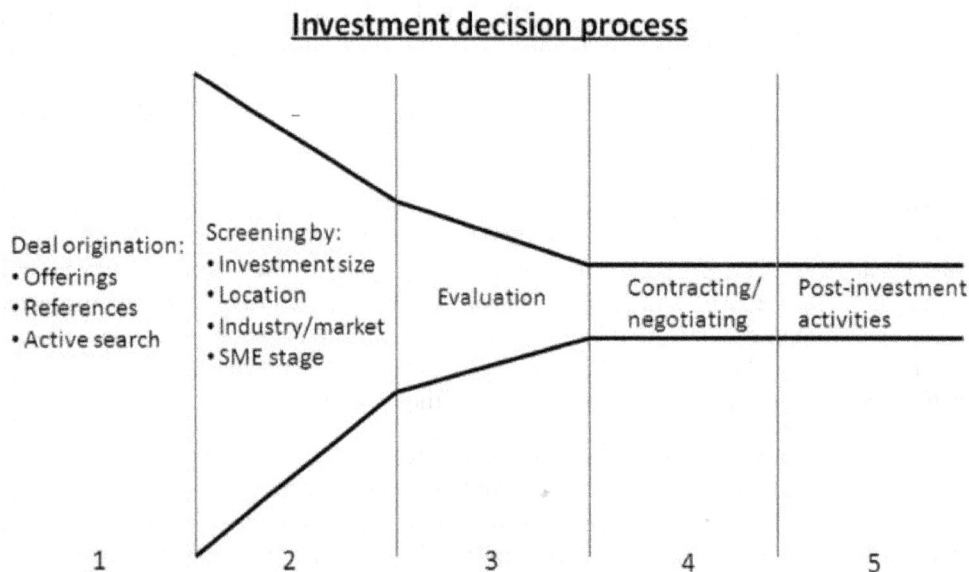

| Deal origination:
• Offerings
• References
• Active search | Screening by:
• Investment size
• Location
• Industry/market
• SME stage | Evaluation | Contracting/
negotiating | Post-investment
activities |

1   2   3   4   5

Source: Author's Own

The screening criteria used by VCs vary depending upon the nature of the industry, geographic location, stage of development, and size of the investment. According to a few research studies, while VCs differentiate investment criteria with diverse purposes, the core categories include entrepreneur's traits, product, competitive strategies, market size, and growth. The main variation, is how criteria are weighted differently.

When entrepreneurs are no longer sole owners of a company, they may engage in post- investment opportunism, providing a "moral hazard" issue for the venture capitalists (Dobrev & Barnett, 2005). Lower degrees of psychological (Guth & MacMillan 1986) and formal ownership (Barney et al., 1996) increase the likelihood that founders prioritize individual self-interest over the interests of their venture (and the VCs) and start behaving as 'agents' (e.g., Wasserman, 2006). This could, for example, lead to 'window dressing' activities, which would skew the venture's success. Entrepreneurs may also redirect firm capital and effort to self-serving activitiesthat are not readily visible to the investors (Bergemann and Hege, 1998).

Thus, the literature indicates that the VCs monitor various aspects of the company's management team, the market, the product or service, and the financial problems that emerge during the post-investment tenure (Riquelme, 1992, Muzyka, 1996 Zacharakis, 2000). Each of these aspects can be further broken down into more specific problems. Some of these have been explained as follows:

Ethical entrepreneurial practices: To a certain extent, moral hazard necessitates honesty, which is a moral value virtue. Individuals engage in moral hazard due to lack of these values. Moral hazard also contributes to corruption because people want to maximize their profit from activities that cost them nothing.

Previous research has placed a high value on the management team (Poindexter, 1976, Bruno & Tyebjee, 1986, Robinson, 1987, Wells, 1974). It is an important factor related to deal acceptance and is also a reason for moral hazard. The management's personality and skill, as wellas the product, market, and financial potential, are all equally important. VCs prefer to invest in teams who have prior industry experience and can draw on a diverse educational background in terms of engineering and management ability (Goslin, 1986, Dixon, 1991, Franke et al., 2008, Amit (1998).

Individual experience does not, however always imply better behaviour or dependability (Shepherd, Zacharakis & Baron, 2003). This could be due to an under-sampling of failure (Denrell, 2003), which leads to increased confidence based on decisions that proved to be correct or successful rather than from a broader range of deals. Issues of moral hazards occur when the entrepreneur's work is not readily visible. When he/she does not put in the required level of effort or select jobs that optimize the investor's return (Rayo, 2007).

While the existing literature recognizes team quality to be an important element in the evaluation process, there is evidence that VCs frequently replace members of the management team and/or the founders before and after an investment is made (Bruton, Fried & Hisrich, 2000).

Product irregularities: According to a previous study, VCs evaluate a venture's product offering based on characteristics such as innovativeness, competitive advantage, product exclusive protection, and the level of need a potential client has for the offering (Wells, 1974). The value of the product varies with the various stages of the venture. At the seed stage, the product is the concept; during the 1st round, it is the proof of concept, functional specification, and product plan. Similarly, during the 2nd round, it may refer to the functional demo or next- generation product plan. In the 3rd round, successful trials, product installation, demonstrable capabilities on the next product, etc., are some of the stages where irregularities may appear.

Operational inefficiencies: In terms of the venture's target market, prior research indicates that VCs prefer market opportunities of significant size, high growth rates, and timing, as these market characteristics provide the conditions for strong revenue growth and high levels of value creation (Tyebjee & Bruno, 1981). As a result of the risk profile of investments, there is a strong emphasis on the size of the investment. It is also important to understand the market depth and the ability to expand to adjacent markets.

The company's growth can be organic, opportunistic, or inorganic. Organic growth is thenatural expansion of all markets. Higher prices and new products that generate incremental top- line returns are examples of opportunistic growth. Inorganic growth is expansion through acquisitions. To make the targeted growth rates more feasible, VCs typically target high-growth industries with similar growth trajectories in end markets.

Timing the market is a difficult needle to thread. It appears to work best when there is an inflection point of mass adoption or a pull market.

Financial impropriety: It is believed that the reason individuals participate in moral hazard is lack of sufficient income or resources to control future costs or cost overrun on budget. The reason people conceal information from a VC is to try and maximize on benefits gained because they have little installed in them to mitigate the future effects of their current activities. Cornelli and Yosha (1997) looked at the problem of an entrepreneur misrepresenting short-term outcomes for 'window-dressing' goals.

One of the major reasons why individuals are engaged in moral hazards is because of the benefits realized from the transfer of risks. The individual will act carelessly in situations where full personal care is required to have full knowledge that the VC or someone else will bear the pain of the risks, he or she indulges in.

The existing literature emphasizes the importance of criteria such as the expected rate of return and the expected risk associated with the venture's financial potential (Poindexter, 1976, MacMillan et al., 1985). In exchange for funding, VCs typically expect a "'10 in 5' or a tenfold increase in investment value over a five-year time horizon, equating to a 58 percent annual compound interest (Zider, 1998). Venture capitalists invest in stages to keep the project under control. They can have better control over the potential moral hazards by monitoring and creating threatening termination. Another challenging problem is to determine when to release funds for continued development and when to abandon a project (Bergemann & Hege, 1998).

Conceptual Framework and Propositions

Based on the above literature review and the VC framework, this study proposes an organizing framework to understand the value creation process for VCs. The primary goal is to determine and investigate the likelihood of avoiding moral hazards. The following conceptual framework will provide us with more managerial relevant implications that can help venture capitalists and entrepreneurs to have a healthy relationship for value creation (Figure 2).

In the given conceptual framework, there are factors and sub-factors, all of which lead to avoiding moral hazard. When you avoid moral hazard, it results in higher entrepreneurial profits which in turn lead to value creation for VCs. But we also propose a moderating variable or a moderating factor which is a business environment. This business environment factor moderates the relationship between avoiding moral hazard and higher entrepreneurial profit. This framework, can be influenced by a number of factors and sub-factors, including but not limited to:

Entrepreneur-related Factors

The entrepreneur-related factors have four sub-factors that may lead to moral hazard. These include

- ethical entrepreneurial practices (non-compliance),

- irregularities with the product,

- operational inefficiencies, and

- financial impropriety.

Ethical Entrepreneurial practices refer to qualifications, work, and industrial experience, as well as the promoters' age and generation, which are all key features that aid VCs in establishing a plant/project based on their core product knowledge. A management team having managerial skills, as well as technical and industrial knowledge, is beneficial in dealing with the obstacles that arise during the operation and while handling risk. Family ties also have a key role in mitigating moral hazards. However, if the entrepreneur's personality is incapable of putting in tremendous effort, his/her reputation in the market, evaluating and reacting to risk effectively, articulating the idea and working attentively, and being aligned with the VC's aims, may result in moral hazard activities.

Figure 2. Conceptual Framework

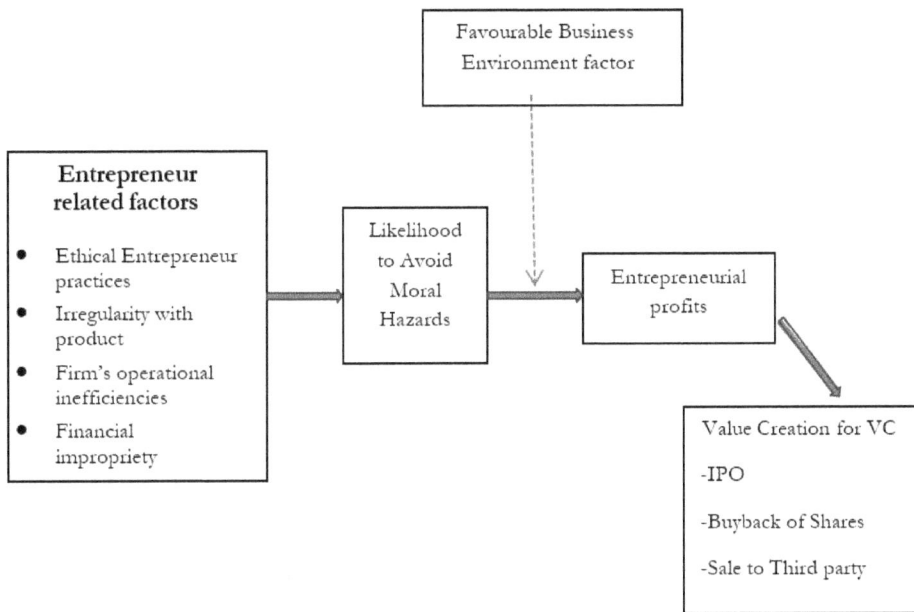

Source: Author's own.

Concerning the above conceptual framework, the author presents the first proposition:

Proposition 1(a): Higher ethical entrepreneurial practices will lead to a higher likelihood of avoiding moral hazards.

Irregularities with product or service might lead to moral hazard if the product does not enjoy or cannot demonstrate market acceptance, or if it cannot be considered as confirming to latest technology.

Proposition 1(b): Higher irregularities with the promised product will lead to a lower likelihood of avoiding moral hazards.

Operational inefficiencies are also responsible for moral hazards if the target market does not enjoy a significant growth rate, entrepreneurs are not familiar with the industry, there is a lot of threat of competition, or if there is an inability to create a new market.

Proposition 1 (c): Higher operational inefficiencies will lead to a lower likelihood of avoiding moral hazards.

Financial impropriety like excellent rate of return or 10 times returns on investment within 5–10 years, where no further investment is expected, and the venture could be easily liquidated, i.e., exit through IPO or purchase by the third party, etc., are some of the elements that will help a VC to mitigate the problems of moral hazards.

145

Personality and experience concerns, in general, dominate financial factors, which are viewed as more significant than product or operational criteria for mitigating the problems of moral hazards.

Proposition 1(d): Higher financial impropriety will lead to a lower likelihood of avoiding moral hazard.

Higher Entrepreneurial Profits

Once the above factors are taken care of, it results in higher entrepreneurial profits. The higher the entrepreneurial profits, the higher will be the value creation for VCs. The rising competition in the investment industry, as well as the amount of money invested in early-stage businesses compels VCs to work harder for their firms. There are two ways in which they add enormous value to their start-ups.

First, by assisting their current deals, they can extract more value from their portfolio and sell it faster. They sell by going public/Initial public offering or selling of shares to third party or repurchase of shares by investee company or promoters.

Second, their reputation as passionate, hands-on investors who provide exceptionalvalue can help them attract new firms.

Taking care of investor-related factors will help in avoiding moral hazards, which in turn will increase entrepreneurial profits and lead to value creation. VCs have always tried to assist businesses, but this has typically been done on an individual, ad hoc basis by the fund's partners. However, to achieve scalability, the current trend is to build a process around these extra services, measure activity at the fund level, and make data-driven modifications. This is whenthe 'value creation' function comes into play.

Proposition 2: The higher likelihood of avoiding moral hazard will lead to higherentrepreneurial profits.

Value Creation for VC

Value creation for VC can be through IPO, selling of shares to third party or repurchase of sharesby investee company or promoters.

Proposition 3: Higher entrepreneurial profits will lead to more value creation opportunities forthe venture capitalist, compared to lower entrepreneurial profit.

Moderator

In our proposed framework, we would like to put forth that business environment factors moderate the effect of avoiding moral hazards on higher entrepreneurial profits. These factors can be broadly classified into market conditions, policy changes, technological changes, and others as well as, the effect of avoiding moral hazards changes due to the business factors such as taxes, government policies etc. The relationship between the above factors, however will remain the same.

Proposition 4: Favourable business environment will lead to a higher likelihood of avoiding moral hazard and positively influence the relationship between entrepreneurial profits comparedto the unfavourable business environment factors.

Table 2: Description of Factors and Relationships with Moral Hazard

Proposition No.	Factors	Description according to the study	Exemplary components	Proposed Relationship with Moral Hazard	Rational for the proposed relationship	Exemplar studies (Author, Yr.)
P1a	Ethical Entrepreneur practices	An entrepreneur who does not share a company's values damages the reputation or culture of the firm.	-Corporate governance -Employment practices -Stakeholder relations -Accounting practices -Issues of product -Corporate responsibility	Direct	Higher ethical entrepreneurial practices will lead to a higher likelihood of avoiding moral hazards.	Tyebjee & Bruno (1984) MacMillan et al. (1985) MacMillan et al. (1987) Robinson (1987) Hall & Hofer (1993) Wells (1974) Poindexter (1976) Timmons et al. (1987)
P1b	Irregularity with product	This variable refers to not delivering the product as promised during the Proposal.	-Low quality -Poor quality of raw material -Delayed launch	Inverse	Higher irregularities with the promised product will lead to a lower likelihood of avoiding morak hazards.	Tyebjee & Bruno (1984) MacMillan et al. (1985) MacMillan et al. (1987) Hall & Hofer (1993) Wells (1974) Timmons et al. (1987)
P1c	Firm's operational inefficiencies	Refers to ineffective marketing professional team, inadequate professionalism	-Poor business development efforts -Insufficient distribution effects -Ineffective advertisements	Inverse	Higher operational inefficiencies will lead to a lower likelihood of avoiding moral hazards.	Tyebjee & Bruno (1984) MacMillan et al. (1985) MacMillan et al. (1987) Robinson (1987) Hall & Hofer (1993) Wells (1974) Timmons et al. (1987)
P1d	Financial impropriety	Refers to the ineffective professional finance team, lack of attention paid by promoters	-Cost overrun -Liquidity crunch -Showing a rosy picture -Careless purchase	Inverse	Higher financial impropriety will lead to a lower likelihood of avoiding moral hazard.	Tyebjee & Bruno (1984), MacMillan et al. (1985) MacMillan et al. (1987) Robinson (1987) Hall & Hofer (1993) Wells (1974) Poindexter (1976) Timmons et al. (1987)
P2	Entrepreneurial profits	Refers to the compensation for the entrepreneur's expertise and efforts	-Increase in Cash flow -Substantial growth -Increase in Rate of Return -Lower risk -Fame	Direct	The higher likelihood of avoiding moral hazard will lead to higher entrepreneurial profits.	Poindexter (1976) Robinson (1987) Timmons et al. (1987)
P3	Value creation for VC	Refers to value created for investors, employees, customers, and the economy	-Through Going Pubic/Initial Public Offering -Selling shares to the third party -Re-purchase of shares by the	Direct	Higher entrepreneurial profits will lead to more value creation opportunities for the venture	Poindexter (1976) Timmons et al. (1987)

			investee company/ promoters		capitalist, compared to lower entrepreneurial profit.	
P4	Favourable Business Environment factor	Sudden unexpected changes in the business environment	Tax exemption, instability of central government, changes in government policies.	Direct	Favourable business environment will lead to a higher likelihood of avoiding moral hazard and positively influence the relationship between entrepreneurial profits compared to the unfavourable business environment factors.	Wells (1974) Poindexter (1976) MacMillan et al. (1985) Robinson (1987) Timmons et al. (1987) Hall & Hofer (1993)

Source: Author's own.

The factors and relationships with moral hazard, discussed in conceptual framework in this section are summarized in the above table for creating mental map and comprehension at a glance.

Discussion and Managerial Implications

One of the most important developments in entrepreneurship has been the growth of venture capital over the past few decades. In India, venture capital-funded companies are on the rise after the introduction of economic reforms. Venture investors play an active role in the administration of the firm. Venture capitalists help the promoter in various ways to nurture companies, by providing a network, recruiting key management employees and building a team, developing financial systems, advising on company law and other legal matters, helping co-investment and arranging working capital facilities from bankers, providing marketing links and contacts, sharing business perspective, helping in long-term strategic thinking and planning, helping to create an entrepreneurial climate and devising incentive systems to promote long-term work, and providing support and confidence during bad times (Mishra & Zachary, 1987).

The present study proposes the framework to understand the value creation process for venture capitalists. Venture capitalists want to cash out their gains in five to ten years after the initial investment. They play a positive role in directing the company towards exit routes. The goal of a real venture capitalist is to sell his/her investment at a big profit, although most venture funds in India strive to make a profit while also achieving their development goals. Public sector venture funds invariably have some developmental objectives, and they would also like to disinvest their holdings at an adequate return to recycle their funds.

Venture capitalists target 10x+ returns on their initial investments. The disinvestment options available to venture capitalists in developed countries are the promoter's buy-back, IPOs,sale to other VCFs, in OTC sale, management buyouts, etc.

In India, a venture may exit in one of the following ways: IPOs, acquisition by another company, purchase of the venture capitalist's shares by the promoter, or purchase of a venture capitalist's stock by a third party. The secondary, over the counter (OTC) market which specializes in the trading of shares of SMEs, plays a critical role in exit through IPOs and acquisitions. Some of the potential options are:

Promoter's Buy-out: The most popular disinvestment route in India is the promoter's buy- back. This approach is well-suited to Indian conditions because it preserves the promoter's ownership and control. The obvious limitation, however, is that in most cases the market value ofthe shares of the venture firm would have appreciated so much after some years that the promoter would not be able to afford to buy them back. In India, the promoters are invariably given the first option to buy back the equity of their enterprises.

Initial Public Offers (IPO): The benefits of divestment via the public issue route are, improved marketability and liquidity, better prospects for capital gains and widely known status of the ventures as well as market control through public share participation. In the Indian context, this option has some restrictions. Because the first-generation entrepreneurs are unknown in the capital markets, promoting the public offering would be difficult and costly. Furthermore, if the entrepreneur's business is viewed as an unappealing investment proposal by investors, problems are bound to arise. Also, Indian investors' focus on short-term earnings and dividends may make the market price unappealing. Yet another difficulty in India until recently was that the Controller of Capital Issues (CCI) guidelines for determining the premium on shares considered the book value and the cumulative average EPS since the new issue's launch. This formula failed to give due weight to the expected stream of earnings of the venture firm. Thus, the formula would underestimate the premium. The Capital Issues Control Act of 1947, as wellas the office of the Controller of Capital Issues, have been repealed by the government. Existing businesses can now set their own premiums on their shares. Because of the inefficiencies of the secondary market in a country like India, the initial public offering for disinvestment of VCF's holdings can result in substantial transaction costs. Furthermore, due to the higher listing requirements of the stock exchanges, this option has become significantly less viable for small businesses. In February 1989, the Government of India raised the minimum capital for listing on the stock exchanges from Rs 10 million to Rs 30 million, and the minimum public offer was Rs 6million to Rs 18 million.

Sale on the OTC Market: An active secondary market provides the necessary impetus to the success of venture capital. VCFs should be able to sell their holdings, and investors should be able to trade shares conveniently and freely. In June 1992, India's OTC Exchange was created. Under the Securities Contracts (Regulations) Act 1989, the Indian government sanctioned the establishment of the Exchange. It has been promoted jointly by UIT, ICICI, SBI Capital Markets,Canbank Financial Services, GIC, LIC, and IDBI. Since this list of markets (who will decide daily prices and appoint dealers for trading) includes most of the public sector venture financiers,it should pick up fast, and it should be possible for investors to trade in the securities of new small and medium-sized enterprises.

Sale to the third party: This is the most common exit for venture capital investments and is very frequently discussed at the time of investment. A strategic acquirer (although sometimes a private equity fund) purchases the company and will pay with exponential revenue / EBITDA depending on the industry growth, profitability, KPIs, market conditions, and the nature of the acquirer, to name a few. The standard benchmark exit Accounting Rate of Return multiple is 10x.

The other divestment mechanisms such as management buyouts or sales to other venturefunds are not considered to be appropriate by VCFs in India.

The present study has implications for VCs, entrepreneurs, and government policymakers. For the VCs, the role of investors in screening, financing, and overseeing a company is especially important in the dramatic growth of the private equity industry.

The implications of this study are to understand the entrepreneurs seeking venture capital, who are Indian individuals or professionals in a position to play the role of intermediariesbetween venture capital seekers and potential venture capital purveyors.

For the economy, the national and regional policymakers, the effectiveness of venture capital arrangements in reducing agency costs suggests that its scope could be expanded to other high-risk environments, like emerging markets in developing countries. Not only would venture capital be more suitable for financing development, it would also help developing countries avoid financial crises like the world debt crisis that many developing countries currently are suffering. Venture capital, therefore, helps promote growth while maintaining financial stability which is necessary for any successful development plan.

Conclusion and Areas of Future Research

The subject is extremely rich, and numerous areas merit further investigation as research on venture capital in India is in its infancy. The problems encountered are not simple as realistic treatment of the issues in venture capital research will require innovative approaches. The future areas of research can be categorized under the following themes:

- Projects funded by different VCs & their different schemes,

- Investee's Perspective,

- Financial constraints by the companies,

- Strategies for Management of Funds,

- Organizational forms, and Venture Capital Performance,

- Entrepreneurial related practices.

To assist in understanding the issues relating to some of the suggested further research requirements, the following is note:

Projects funded by different VCs & their different schemes: A start-up or emerging company might require funding for various purposes. An entrepreneur must be aware of differentschemes to raise funds as per his requirements. VC lets entrepreneurs convert their knowledge into viable projects, helps new products with modern technology become commercially feasible, etc. One extension of the current research is to study the projects funded by different VCs and their different schemes in India. Bygrave and Timmons (1992) provide policy recommendations for expanding the industry in the US (United States). SagariGuidotti (1991a) explores government policies towards risk capital in different developing countries and points to necessary ingredients for venture capital to grow in such countries.

The venture capital providers in India (other than the commercial banks' efforts) can be divided into the following categories:

    a. Specialized financial institutions and their financing schemes.

    b. State-level institutions promoting funding

    c. Public Sector Banks promoting funding

    d. Private agencies

    e. Overseas venture capital funds

The Industrial Financial Corporations of India (IFCI), the Industrial Development Bank of India (IDBI), and the Industrial Credit and Investment Corporation of India (ICICI) are the three primary Indian organizations involved in high-tech new venture funding. The objectives of the schemes reveal the differences and similarities between the three schemes of IFCI, IDBI, and ICICI.

Funds promoted by state-level institutions include APIDC- Venture Capital Ltd. (A- VCL), Gujarat Venture Finance Ltd. (GVFL). Canara Bank Venture Capital Fund, for example,is a fund promoted by a public sector bank (CVCF). Venture capital funds set up in the private sector include Credit Capital Venture Fund (CCVF), 20th Century Venture Capital Fund (India Investment Fund), Indus Venture Capital Fund (IVCF), and SBI Capital Venture (Capital Fund).

Tourism, hospitals, air transportation, information technology, communication, pharmaceuticals, consumer durables, food processing sector, machinery components, textiles, and other fields with high and assured returns are areas where overseas venture capital fundslook for investment. Firstly, AIG, the global insurance giant, has partnered with IL & SF;

Secondly, George has launched the Indocean Fund; andthirdly, NIKKO Securities has partnered with Walden and San Francis Company to launch a venture capital fund.

Stage-wise investment: The policy of venture capital financing in India is focused on financing the high-risk, high-tech, high-growth, small, and medium-sized enterprises started by new entrepreneurs. Thus, a sizable portion of the venture capital funds is invested in start-ups. With significant developments in 2005–06, there has been an increased focus by many funds on larger and mature deals. The various stages of investment include early stage, growth stage, late- stage, Private Issue of Public Equity (PIPE), Buyouts, Private Equity, and others. Some of the Indian corporates that have made plans to enter the PE business are Aditya Birla Group, Tata Group, etc. Other PE funds that are currently raising funds are Avigo, CX partners, Tano, Lazard, etc.

Investment by Industry: In terms of a sector-wise break-up, Pharma, healthcare, and biotech emerged as the largest sector in 2005. Because the pharmaceutical industry is so fragmented, private equity investors have been interested in it for a long time. The other significant sector is IT (Information Technology) & ITES which retained its status as thefavourite among VC investors. BFSI (Banking Financial Services and Insurance) ranked second in terms of VC investments (in terms of value). Other sectors include the financial sector, followed by telecommunications, Infrastructure (10%), transportation & distribution, and utilities. The past trend of PE investment in India, i.e., diversified across various sectors could beone of the key reasons for global investors looking for attractive opportunities in India.

Investment by geographical areas: Venture capital investments are also influenced by the geographical area or location of the entrepreneur's project. While enterprises in South India garnered a bigger number of investments, their Western Indian counterparts received a much larger portion of the pie in terms of value. According to the IVCA report of February 2020, the most attractive cities for PE investments are Mumbai, Delhi (NCR), Bengaluru, Chennai, Hyderabad, Pune, Ahmedabad, and Kolkata. Further research could also be carried out continent-wise (Asian, American, African, European, Australian). Its scope can also be seen in other areas like River-linking projects (Garland project), port-development (Adani Group in Dahej, Gujarat).

Investee's Perspective: Most of the studies have only been carried out from the perspective of the venture capitalist and the views of the investee company have not been taken into consideration. Future research can be carried out to gain an insight into their viewpoints.

All the above factors when considered would be able to present a better picture of the venture capital management scenario and thus, help in devising better strategies for management of the venture capital funds.

Financial constraints for companies: Finally, it might be insightful to examine the effects of venture capital funding on financial constraints for companies after going public. Such research would help to evaluate the effect of 'initial conditions' on the performance and accessibility to capital markets of venture-backed companies. A related issue that has not been resolved is whether venture capitalist as an intermediary adds value within a portfolio firm.

Strategies for Management of Funds across different Sectors/Industries: The strategies in the previous studies are generalized strategies for the management of the venture capital funds, but do not take into consideration the fact that funds across different industries behave differently because of other factors present. Thus, for proper management of venture capital funds, it becomes imperative to study the several factors affecting funding of varied sectors and how they counter affect the management of venture capital funds.

Organizational forms and Venture Capital Performance: There are several types of venture capital organizations. It is understandable that agency conflicts and their solution in one kind of venture capital firm would not apply fully to other firms. Hence, the ties between venturecapitalists and their primary investors vary depending on the type of company they work in. Therefore, further research can be carried out to study the differences in various kinds of firms and thus, to check how the organizational form is associated with performance.

Entrepreneurial related practices: Venture capitalists are overly particular over which companies they invest in, and each firm has a unique investment profile that includes everything from industry focus to cultural fit. However, there is a consistent, formulaic process for determining a start-up's viability. The team will be subjected to extensive due diligence by venture investors. Strong founding teams are distinguished by their vision, product expertise, business acumen, experience, and cohesion.

Product attributes: The most important aspect of the product is product-market fit, which results from overall business model harmony. The consumption and promotion of a product validates its pricing and value chain. The presence of proprietary technology that is difficult to replicate or patents is another valuable component of a product. Finally, the extent to which the product is required for business continuity is still not fully known.

Operational and Market efficiencies: Because of the market's size, growth, and timing, there is a strong emphasis on the size of the investment. To make the targeted growth rates more feasible, venture capitalists typically target high-growth industries with similar growth trajectories in end markets.

Financial propriety: The company's financial health, as well as its performance on key performance indicators, are critical business components that go hand in hand. With growth as the top-line revenue for the firm, gross margin, contribution, and operating margins are some of the important financial parameters that are always taken into consideration.

Entrepreneurial profits: Venture capitalists are looking for businesses that are fundamentally different from the competition. Because of the high-risk profile, venture capitalists are looking to fund future market leaders in large industries. These can be accomplished through market disruption, market expansion, or both.

Table 3: Future areas of research in terms of what research questions, why and their implications has been tabulated below:

Sr. No	Future Area	Research Question (What)	Why	How (Implications)
1	Projects funded by different VCs & their different schemes	RQ1: Is the knowledge of projects funded by different VCs & their different schemes in India helpful for an entrepreneur to fulfil his funding requirements?	Start-ups require funds for various purpose	VC help entrepreneurs convert their ideas into viable projects.
		RQ2: How do public VCs and private VCs differ in their investment strategies concerning investment appraisal and how do they make investment decisions?		
2	Stage-wise investment	RQ3: How does stage-wise investment differ in their investment strategies concerning investment appraisal and how do they make investment decisions?	Timing is very important. VC financing focuses on the high-risk, high-tech, high-growth, small, and medium-sized enterprises.	Commercial viability and Profitability level varies in Different stages It limits the risks of VCs.
		RQ4:How do stage-wise investments by the Private sector and Public Sector differ?		
3	Investment by Industry	RQ5: How does industry-wise investment differ in their investment strategies concerning investment appraisal and how do they make investment decisions?	Industries differ in growth and productivity	Attracts global investors to invest in India
		RQ6: How does industry-wise investment in the Private sector and Public Sector differ?		

4	Investment by geographical areas	RQ7: How does investment by geographical area differ in their investment strategies concerning investment appraisal and how do they make investment decisions?	VCs investments are influenced by location of the entrepreneur	It affects likelihood of returns and profits
		RQ8: How does investment by geographical area in the Private sector and Public Sector differ?		
5.	Investee's Perspective	RQ9: To what extent is being controlled by the venture capitalist firm acceptable to them?	Will give a better picture of the venture capital management scenario	Will help in devising better strategies for management of the venture capital funds.
		RQ10: What is their perception about the separate roles played by the venture capitalist?		
		RQ11: Do they believe that venture capitalist firms add value to their venture by providing expertise and skills other than financial in nature?		
		RQ12: Do they consider them as their strategic partner or still believe themselves to be providers of only capital?		
6	Financial constraints for companies	RQ13: Do Venture Capitalists add value within the portfolio firm?	VCs help relatively unsophisticated management team with strategy formulation and planning.	VCs help in identifying the investment opportunities and making the most out of it.
		RQ14: Do companies perform better when venture capital is present than when it is absent, all else equal?		
7	Strategies for Management of Funds across different Sectors/Industries	RQ15: Does the evaluation remain the same across all industries or does it differ across high technology or low technology-oriented industries?	Patterns of innovation differ in direction, sources and efforts in economic sectors.	
8	Organizational forms and Venture Capital Performance	RQ16: What are the various kinds of firms and how is organizational form associated with performance?	Agency conflicts and their solution in one kind of venture capital firm are not applicable fully to other firms.	Would be helpful to know how the organizational form is associated with performance.
9.	Entrepreneurial related practices	RQ17: Does a better understanding of business factors affect the relationship in unusual ways?	VCs invest in companies with unique profile, vision, product expertise, business acumen, experience and cohesion.	
		RQ18: Does a company with a strong entrepreneurial team, meet the needs of its customers, to create a viable business model avoiding the likelihood of moral hazards?		
9.1	Product attributes	RQ19: Does a valuable product avoid the likelihood of moral hazards?	Product should be market fit with value chain	Help in identifying the unsuitable product/service to

				meet the customer's expressed needs and preferences.
9.2	Operational and market efficiencies	RQ20: Does a sufficiently large, growing, and permeable market avoid moral hazards?	Size of the investment is important due to market size, growth and timing	Will make the targeted growth rates more feasible.
9.3	Financial Propriety	RQ21: Does the financial health and efficiency of the company avoid the likelihood of moral hazards?	Helps in knowing if the borrower is involved in undesirable activities.	Overcome the problems of cost overrun, liquidity crunch, carelessness etc.
10	Entrepreneurial profits	RQ22: Does a favourable business environment avoid the likelihood of morals hazards and increase entrepreneurial profits?	Examining business environment is beneficial in utilizing the resources needed for the firm.	helps in business in managing these resources and transforming them into products and services.

In conclusion, this study has reviewed the origins and effects of moral hazards in venture capital investing in general, as well as the implications for emerging countries like India. For the development of innovative business ideas, venture capital funding is critical. Moral hazards have been studied using the theory of market imperfection, which discusses asymmetric information and conflicts of interest. As an economic issue, moral hazard has the potential to lead to inefficient resource allocation.

Ethical Entrepreneurial Practices, Product Irregularities, Operational Inefficiencies, and Financial Impropriety have all been discussed in depth, leading to the development of a conceptual framework and propositions for Entrepreneurial factors, Higher Entrepreneurial Profits, VC Value Creation, and the Business Environment as moderating factors. The framework for venture capitalists to understand value creation processes is also presented. The advantages and disadvantages of promoter buy-outs, IPOs, and sales on the over- the-counter market, among other options, have been thoroughly examined, along with their managerial implications.

Future study areas have been organised under ten main headings and numerous sub-heads, providing significant possibility for future research on the topic for a developing country like India.

References

Akerl of, G. (1970). The markets for lemons: Quality uncertainty and the market mechanism. *The Journal of Finance*, 49, 371–402.

Amit, R. J. (1998). Why do venture capital firms exist? Theory and Canadian evidence. *Journal of Business Venturing*, 13, 441–466

Bain & Company (2022), *Indian Venture Capital Report*, 2022, June 23. Available at https://www.bain.com/insights/india-venture-capital-report-2022/

BBansal Deepak, examination of venture capitalists' role in Indian economy, 4D International Journal of Management and science (4DIJMS), vol. 4, issue 3-2014, ISSN No. 2250- 0669.

Barney, J. B., Busenitz, L. W., Fiet, J. O., &Moesel, D. D. (1996, July). New venture teams'assessment of learning assistance from venture capital firms.*Journal of Business Venturing, 11*(4), 257-272.

Bergemann, D., &Hege, U. (1998).Venture capital financing, moral hazard, and learning. *Journalof Banking and Finance*, vol. 22, issue 6-8,703–735.

Bruno, A. V., & Tyebjee, T. T. (1986).The destinies of rejected venture capital deals. *SloanManagement Review, 27*(2), 43–53.

Bruton, G., Fried, V., & Hisrich, R. (2000). CEO dismissal in venture capital-backed firms: Further evidence from an agency perspective. *Entrepreneurship Theory and Practice, 24*(4), 69–77.

Barney, J. B., Busenitz, L. W., Fiet, J. O., & Moesel, D. D. (1996, July). New venture teams'assessment of learning assistance from venture capital firms. *Journal of Business Venturing, 11*(4), 257-272.

Bygrave, W. and J.Timmons (1992). Venture Capital at the Cross Roads.

Cornelli, F., &Yosha, O. (1998). Stage Financing and the Role of Convertible Debt.

Dobrev, S., & Barnett, W. P. (2005).Organizational Roles and Transition toEntrepreneurship.*The Academyof Management Journal*, 1-36.

Dossani, R. and M. Kenney (April 4, 2001). Creating an Environment: Developing VentureCapital in India.

Denrell, J. (2003). Vicarious learning, undersampling of failure, and the myths of management. *Organization Science, 14*(3), 227–243.

Depersio, G. (2021, July 21). What are examples of moral hazard in the business world?*Investopedia*. Available at https://www.investopedia.com/ask/answers/040815/what-are-some-examples-moral-hazard-business-world.asp

Dieffenbacher, S.F. (2022, June 12).Value Creation Definition, Model, Principles, Importance & Steps. https://digitalleadership.com/blog/value-creation/

Dixon, R. (1991). Venture capitalists and the appraisal of investments. *Omega, 19*(5), 333–344.Dossani, R., and M. Kenney (2001, April 4). Creating an Environment: Developing Venture Capital in India.World Development Vol. 30, No. 2, pp. 227–253.

Einay, L., & Finkelstein, A. (2018, August May 3). Moral Hazard in health insurance;What weknow and how we know it. *J Eur Econ Assoc*, 957-982.

Ejrnes, M., &Hochguertel, S. (2013). Is business failure due to lack of effort? Empirical evidencefrom a large administrative sample.*The Economic Journal*, Vol.*123*, Issue 571, 791– 830.

Franke, V., Gruber, M., Harhoff, D., & Henkel, J. (2008). Venture capitalists' evaluations of start-up teams: Trade-offs, knock-cut criteria, and the impact of VC experience. *Entrepreneurship Theory and Practice, 32(3)*, 459–483.

Fried, V. H., &Hisrich, R. D. (1994).Toward a model of venture capital investment making.*Financial Management, 23*(3), 28–37.

Gibbons, R. (1992). Game Theory for Applied Economics.

Guth, W. D., & Macmillan, I. C. (1986).Startegy Implementation Versus Middle Management Self-Interest. *Strategic Management Journal, 7*, 313-327.

Gompers, P., Gornall, W., Kaplan, S. N., &Strebulaev, I. A. (2021, March–April). How venturecapitalists make decisions. *Harvard Business Review*.

Goslin, L. B. (1986). Entrepreneurial qualities considered in venture capital support. Wellesley,MA: Babson College.

Hall, J. and C. W. Hofer (1993)."Venture capitalists' decision criteria in newventureevaluation." *Journal of Business Venturing* 8(1).

Hossain, M. M., &Chowdhury, A. M. (2015, July).MoalHarzard in Banking.*Journal of Banking& Financial Services, 9*(1).

Hyytinen, A., &Vaananen, L. (2006). Where do financial constraints originate from? An empirical analysis of adverse selection and moral hazard in capital markets.*Small Business Economics, 27*, 323–348.

Ifeanyi , N., &Obianuju , C. (2016, June). Venture capital as a source of fund for entrepreneurs.*NG-Journal of Social Development, 5*(3), pp 76-87

IVCA.(2021). India Venture Capital Report 2021. Website: https://www.bain.com/globalassets/ noindex/ 2021/bain_report_ india_venture_capital_20 21.pdf

Junjuan , D., & Zheng-Qun , C. (2020). The impact of venture capital on the growth of small- andmedium-sized enterprises in agriculture. *Journal of Chemistry, Volume 2020* Issue 2020 (31 Dec. 2020), pp.1-8

Keuschnigg, C., & Nielsen, B. (2004).Progressive taxation, moral hazard, and entrepreneurship. *Journal of Public Economic Theory, 6*(3), 471–490.

Khosla, D. (2015, January). Analysis of venture capital funding in India.*Gyan Management,Volume 9, Issue 1 Jan - June 2015, pp 123-131*

Kumar, A (2021). Venture Capital in India, *The Ventue Capital Law Review*, London, 2021, pg.57-68

MacMillan, I. C., Seigal, R., &Narsimha, S. (1985). Criteria used by venture capitalists. *Journalof Business Venturing, 1*(1), 119–129.

MacMillan,I., L. Zeman, and P. Narsimha (1987). ""Criterion Distinguishing Successful from unsuccessful Ventures in the Venture Screening Process"." Journal of Business Venturing **2**: 123-137.

Malik, A. (2019, April 3). Applying a comprehensive framework to venture investing. https://medium.com/ @aimunm83/ applying-a-comprehensive-framework-to-venture- investing-c34b3413ee6e

Mattesini, F. (1993). Financial markets: Asymmetric information and macroeconomic equilibrium. Dartmouth Publishing Co Ltd

Michele E.McHale (2017).Private equity integration & value creation. Available at https://946-cty-601.mktoweb.com/rs/946-CTY-601/images/2017_PEG_Value%20Creation%20Guidebook.pdf

Mishra, C. S., & Zachary, R. K. (1987). Moral hazard, entrepreneurial incentives, and risk mitigation. *The Entrepreneurial Value Creation Theory, Chapter 7.*

Mishra, S. C., & Zachary, R. K. (1987).The Entrepreneurial Value Creation Theory, Chapter10

Muzyka, D.B.(1996).Trade-offs in the investment decisions of European venture capitalists. *Journal of Business Venturing, 11*(4), 273–287.

Myers, S., &Majluf, N. (1984). Corporate financing and investment decisions when firms have information that investors do not have. *Journal of Financial Economics*, 187–221.Volume 13, Issue 2

Poindexter, J. B. (1976). *The efficiency of financial markets: The venture capital case-dissertations.* Institution: New York University, Graduate School of Business.

Pratch, L. (2005). Value-added investing: A framework for early stage venture capital firms. *TheJournal of Private Equity*, 13–29. Vol. 8, No. 3 (Summer 2005), pp. 13-29

Rayo, L. (2007). Relational incentives and moral hazard in teams.*Review of Economic Studies*, 937–963.Vol. 74, No. 3 (Jul., 2007), pp. 937-963

Riquelme, H. R. (1992). Hybrid conjoint analysis: An estimation probe in new venture decisions. *Journal of Business Venturing, 7*(6), 505–518.

Robinson, R. B. (1987). Emerging strategies in the venture capital industry.*Journal of BusinessVenturing, 2*(1), 53–77.

Rothschild, M., &Stiglitz, J. (1970).Increasing risk: I, a definition.*Journal of Economic Theory,2(3)*, 225–243.

Rowell, D., & Connelly, L. B. (2012).A History of the term "Moral hazard".*The Journal of Riskand Insurance, 79*(4), 1051-1075.

Rozalska-Lilo, M (2021), Value Creation in Venture Capital- https://blogs.timesofisrael.com/value-creation-in-venture-capital/

Sagari, S. B., &Guidotti, G. (1991a). *Venture capital: Lessons from the developed world for thedeveloping markets.* International Finance Corporation, Discussion Paper No.13.

Sahlman, W. A. (1990, October). The structure and governance of venture-capitalorganizations. *Journal of Financial Economics, 27*(2). pp. 473-521

Sahlman, W. (1994a, July). Insights from the venture capital model of project governance. *Business Economics*, Vol. 29, Iss. 3. pp.35–37.

Saridakis , G., &Pierrakis, Y. (2017, September). The role of venture capitalists in the regional innovation ecosystem: A comparison of networking patterns between private and publicly backed venture capital funds. *The Journal of Technology Transfer, 44*, 850– 873.

Shepherd, D. A., Zacharakis, A., & Baron, R. (2003). VCs' decision processes: Evidence suggesting more experience may not always be better. *Journal of Business Venturing, 18*(3), 381–401.

Sinha, A. B. (2016). *Growth and development of venture capital financing in India with a specialemphasis on selected sectors.* Available at https://www.icsi.edu/media/portals/86/manorama/Venture%20Capital%20SSIM%20B OOK.pdf

Stiglitz, J., & Weiss, A. (1981).Credit rationing with imperfect information.*American Economic Review, 71*, 393–410.

Seth, Sudhir (2017), Value Creation by Venture Capital Investors: The Experience of IDGVentures India, Emerging Markets Private Equity Review December 2011.https://www.globalprivatecapital.org/app/ uploads/2017/03/Dec_2011 _Value_Creation_by_Vent ure_Capital_Investors.pdf

Timmons, J. A., Muzyka, D.F., Stevenson, H.H., and Bygrave, W.D. (1987). "Opportunity recognition: The core of entrepreneurship." Frontiers Of Entrepreneurship Research: 109–123.

Townsend, R. (1979). Optimal contracts and competitive markets with costly state verification.*Journal of Economic Theory,*Volume 21, Issue 2.pp.265–293.

Tyebjee, T., & Bruno, A. (1981).*Venture capital decision making: Preliminary results from threeempirical studies.*In Frontiers of Entrepreneurship Research 1981 (pp. 281–320).Wellesley, MA:Babson College

Tyebjee, T. T., & Bruno.(1984). A model of venture capitalist investment activity.*Management, 30*(9), 1051–1066.

Wang, S., & Zhou, H. (2002). Staged financing in venture capital: Moral hazard and risk. *Journal of Corporate Finance.*

Wasserman, N. (2006). Stewards, Agents andthe Founder Discount:Executive Compensation inNew Ventures. *Academy of Management Journal*, 1-38.

Wells, W. A. (1974). Venture capital decision-making.unpublished doctoral dissertation,Carnegie-Mellon University.

Williamson, S. (1986). Costly monitoring, financial intermediation, and equilibrium creditrationing. *Journal of Monetary Economics, 18*, 156–179.

Wolferen, J. v., Inbar, Y., &Zeelenberg, M. (2014).Moral hazard in the insuranceindustry.*Netspar Panel Paper*, 1-77.

Zacharakis, A. M. (2000). The potential of actuarial decision models: Can they improve the VCinvestment decision? *Journal of Business Venturing, 15*(4), 323–346.

Zider, B. (1998). How does venture capital work? *Harvard Business Review, 76*(6), 131–139.

CHAPTER 10

APPLYING BEHAVIOURAL ECONOMICS TO BRING IN SOCIAL TRANSFORMATION:
RURAL SHORING FOR STAKEHOLDER WELLBEING

Vikramaditya Kanodia[1] and Rima Ghose Chowdhury[2]

Introduction

> The annals of business are littered with products that failed and companies that went bankrupt because of one key mistake: they failed to account for actual human behaviour.

Nobel Prize winner Curt Nickisch on Rethinking Poverty (and Business)

Corporates have won wars with human behavioural dimensions and their interplay as starting points. Using behavioural economics has helped corporates advance business causes and create win-win situations. This chapter aims to highlight the motivating factors of social research such as stimulation of respondents, sense of participation, growth of knowledge, the quest for progress, and curiosity to understand the cause and effect relationship of various social phenomena. The research aims at finding: How a behaviour change impacted society? How a societal outlook change furthered a business cause? This chapter also attempts to provide a strong case for corporates to explore behaviouraleconomics to further their businesses ethically and inclusively. The premise brings unique value to end consumers in a perceived upliftment of socioeconomic worth.

Human beings have "distinctive cultural (learned) characteristics, histories and responses to their environment" and the term 'socio-cultural' is commonly used in anthropological researchto describe these and the "interactions and processes" that this involves (Garbarino 1983: P1). The IT revolution in India led to rapid social changes in urban areas. Over time, technology andBPO firms tried to move from Tier-1 metros to Tier 2 and 3 cities such as Nashik and Pune nearMumbai, Chandigarh and Noida near New Delhi and Puducherry near Chennai. This was not only due to soaring prices in the metros, but also because infrastructure and work environmentin Tier 2 and 3 cities were improving and reaching levels high enough to provide global support.

It was not easy for far-flung villages in India to benefit from this trend due to various reasons –the key being one of mindset. BPO firms tried to propagate the message that if people rode thisbandwagon, the benefits would be manifold - higher value-added jobs and overall upliftmentin their socioeconomic status. For firms, this was Corporate Social Responsibility (CSR) initiative with a cost optimisation strategy and not just a leak in corporate reserves. The value proposition to all stakeholders was tremendous. While corporates benefited from a low-cost operations centre, customers benefited from lower prices. The most significant impact was onrural employees, who benefited financially, economically, socially, culturally and even personally. Further, this also created a deep influence on

[1] Vikramaditya Kanodia, CEO's Office, Datamatics Global Services Ltd, Knowledge Centre, Street No. 17 MIDC, Andheri (East) Mumbai – 400 093 India. E-mail: vikram.kanodia@datamatics.com
[2] Dr. Rima Ghose Chowdhury, EVP and Chief Human Resources Officer, Datamatics Global Services Ltd, Knowledge Centre, Street No. 17 MIDC, Andheri (East) Mumbai – 400 093 India. E-mail: rima.chowdhury@datamatics.com

the rural social fabric in terms of matrimony, education, skill enhancement, personal development, health and social status.

All of this is evident from DataHalli, a rural BPO centre in Karnataka. While office jobs werenot socially accepted in the rural area initially, appropriate nudges and setting examples encouraged the masses to open up to this option. The aim of this paper is to summarise how social acceptance was brought in and how this, in turn, led people to growth and social progress.

Literature Review

The rural shoring model generates significant value for all stakeholders - businesses, employees, customers and society. However, socio-cultural, economic and governance challenges limit employee participation in rural BPOs. Subtle but powerful nudges may be used to overcome these challenges. The nudges could be powerful by virtue of being embedded into the choice architecture as structural elements. Once put into place, they tirelessly exert influence on behaviour without depending on continued human operation. This distinguishes them from certain behaviour-based influencing strategies, such as role-modelling, which could be intermittent.

Thaler and Sunstein (2008) argue that efforts to influence behaviour should first exhaust liberty-preserving methods before bringing into play more iron-fisted ones - the principle of least coercion. While trying to review the literature, it was noticed that some general studies of culture and corporate social responsibility using Hofstede exist (Silvia and Belen 2013), but an in-depth analysis of different understandings and conceptions of terms such as CSR, as a result of socio-cultural influences is lacking.

Carrol and Kareem (2010) reiterate that obligations of corporates towards society, which extend beyond economic and legal obligations, can be termed as ethical and discretionary or philanthropic. Nudging a whole population is a tough task, but when done effectively, dual objectives can be served.

Berger et al. (2007) examine the integration of community considerations in the operational agenda of organisations, and 'mainstreaming' CSR meant aggressively pursuing viable businessopportunities with a CSR dimension.

Theoretical Background

The Concept of Nudge

The book *Nudge: Improving Decisions About Health, Wealth, and Happiness,* by behaviouraleconomist Richard Thaler and legal scholar Cass Sunstein, published in 2008, explains his concept. It proposes positive reinforcement to influence behaviour and decision-making ofgroups or individuals. Nudging contrasts with other ways to achieve compliance, such as education, legislation or enforcement.

A social proof heuristic refers to the tendency of individuals to look at the behaviour of others to help guide their own behaviour. Studies have found some success in using social proof heuristics to nudge individuals to make healthier lifestyle choices. When an individual'sattention is drawn toward a particular option, they are more likely to choose that option. As anexample, in snack shops at train stations in the Netherlands, consumers purchased more fruit and healthier snack options when the products were relocated next to the payment counter. Similar studies have been undertaken regarding the placement of healthier food options close to checkout counters and its effect on the consuming behaviour of customers. This is now considered an effective and well-accepted nudge.

The 2016 United Nations publication, *Transformations for Sustainable Development: Promoting Environmental Sustainability in Asia and the Pacific*, states that transformation towards sustainable resource use could be achieved by high-level policy action to reform theincentive frameworks that govern resource use and investments. Nudging techniques comein many forms, summarised succinctly in Sunstein's article *Nudging: A Very Short Guide*. These techniques include:

- Setting default rules

- Framing, social proof

- Simplifying procedures

- Increasing ease and convenience of desired behaviours

- Using alerts, disclosures and reminders

- Eliciting implementation intentions or soliciting pre-commitments

Heavy-handed influencing methods can reduce a person's intrinsic motivation to behave in desired ways or even lead to oppositional defiance. Nudges are likely to avoid these adverse effects.

Behavioural economics in transformation

Social norms and other contextual influences have a substantial impact on preferences. People are more likely to conform to the desired behaviour if they see (or believe) others are doing it -particularly others similar to them.

According to Shahram Heshmat, "Behavioural economics attempts to integrate psychologists' understanding of human behaviour into economic analysis." Similarly, Harvard defines Behavioural Economics as "variants of traditional economic assumptions (often with apsychological motivation) to explain and predict behaviour, and to provide policyprescriptions."

Behavioural economics also has close ties to the fields of cognitive and social psychology, which according to the American Psychological Association, "is the study of how individuals affect and are affected by other people and by their social and physical environments". Behavioural economics applies these concepts to the economic decisions that people make, inaddition to the rational thinking model.

A team of behavioural scientists at the Yale School of Management tested how small contextual changes can alter consumer decisions and organised the findings into a novel, unifying framework known as the 4Ps Framework for Behaviour Change. It is an agile strategy for nudging behaviour towards desirable outcomes in specific situations.

The intervention domains of the 4Ps framework are:

- **Process – Making it Easy** (removing barriers to the desired choice)

- **Possibilities – Making it Available** (design the right choice set)

- **Persuasion- Making it Attractive** (work with existing beliefs)

- **Person – Making it Motivating** (tap into active goals)

Underlined by the principles of behavioural economics, psychology and marketing, the Yale 4P Framework restructures the environment and guides consumers towards their goals by minimising the effort, time, and willpower.

Applying Nudge Theory and Behavioural Economics to the Case of DataHalli

In the case of DataHalli, both the nudge theory as well as the core tenets of behavioural economics intertwined with driving social transformation. BPO workers experienced severalnudges around them and found that the decisions that drove the transformation were easy to make, available, attractive and motivating.

More specifically, a handful of workers who acted as natural ambassadors highlighted the benefits of being associated with the rural shoring project and influenced and inspired the restto follow the trend. Further, the choice to engage with the rural shoring model was purely voluntary and followed the principles of least coercion.

DataHalli is a unique application of nudge in social transformation. The exercise paved the way for other corporates to follow such techniques of influencing small groups to drive social transformation through large-scale CSR implementations.

Research methodology

This research primarily used a case study method, with a deep exploration of the socio-culturaland economic environment in DataHalli. Data was collected from different primary and secondary sources, organised, analysed, interpreted and presented in relation to the research topic. The method of data collection was a semi-structured in-person interview and observation.

Interviews were conducted across a random sample of individuals but covered a cross-sectionof stakeholders, including:

-   Current DataHalli employees across multiple roles/ positions (team lead, projectmanager, associate)

-   DataHalli leadership and management

-   Family members of DataHalli employees

-   Villagers who were not employed at DataHalli, but were associated with a DataHalli employee

-   JSW Steel CSR leaders

Through the interviews, we tried to understand individual perspectives on DataHalli's value. The discussions explored how and why people work at DataHalli, how a rural shore BPO job is perceived in society - especially one that employs women, and how women use and value the income from their job. The interviews also explored the evolution of employees moving from vocational/ agricultural livelihoods to professional services jobs from the perspective of personal development, individual liberty, learning of hard and soft skills, and exposure to the world. All stakeholders were encouraged to provide an unbiased and realistic view of how and where they realise and drive value through the rural BPO model.

All interviews were conducted in person and in a comfortable environment, in an office setting as well as out of the office, as was professionally and culturally appropriate. Interviews lasted about 30 to 40 minutes, while some stretched to an hour. Given the societal context of the research subject, the interviews tended to drift between English, Hindi and Kannada (the local language). The interviewers were fluent in English and Hindi, but a translator aided the conversations in Kannada. All analysis was done in English, with particular care given to not lose the essence of the messages regardless of the language in which the interviewee responded.

Observational data collection was carried out both in the office environment and outside. Key behavioural aspects were taken into consideration, such as comfort and proficiency at job, social and professional interactions, individual contribution to team tasks, ability to hold constructive discussions, self-awareness, etiquette, and self-confidence. Further, other socio-cultural observations were made, including how DataHalli workers were treated relative to non-DataHalli employees, their interactions at home and in society – especially with older family members and respected members of the community as well as younger villagers.

Observation sessions were conducted throughout the study and lasted between 30 and 90 minutes, depending on the context and goals. The observation was carried out in a non-intrusive manner to collect accurate data on natural behaviour patterns.

Findings

Rural Stakeholder Well-being at DataHalli

Empowerment and enhancement of quality of life is the key story that finally emerges in the research paper, with a win-win proposition for the corporates. Sometimes, multiple Government reform policies and campaigns turn out to be futile even with due robustness around the intent. But, when behaviour mapping, nudge etc form a part of the transformation strategy, the effectiveness increases manifold. Findings indicated significant value generation for all stakeholders. DataHalli, a rural BPO located in the Bellary District of Karnataka, has an explicit focus on improving the lives of rural women in the area, making it a perfect case study for this paper.

Managed by JSW Steel, within its factory campus at Bellary, DataHalli has given a dignified livelihood to local women. These women, essentially SSLC certified (state secondary schooling in Karnataka), look upon the centre as one of the few viable, local, high-value and respectable work avenues.

At DataHalli, the women are trained on both voice- and non-voice-based BPO, with the majority being on data processing such as health claims processing, invoice processing, data tagging and categorisation. They specialise in areas such as e-retail, banking, healthcare and telecom. These women work on projects from leading IT firms around the country and see DataHalli not only as a great opportunity to learn new skills, display their talent and earn money but also as a great alternative to working as labour or staying unemployed.

The impact on the well-being of rural employees at DataHalli is evident and is at the core of its management philosophy. For corporates in the IT and BPO space, the cost advantage of setting up a rural BPO in Bellary is significant. Initial setup, real estate and some infrastructure costs are lower than setting up a similar operation in a Tier-1 city. While training costs might be slightly higher involving teaching employees how to use computers, converse in English, maintain office etiquette and use project-specific software, running costs are significantly lower. The steel factory where

DataHalli is located in the largest steel manufacturing facility in India. Therefore, the centre enjoys 24/7 uninterrupted power and adequate infrastructure support to sustain daily operations.

Figure 2. Low Cost Advantage: Bellary v/s Mumbai

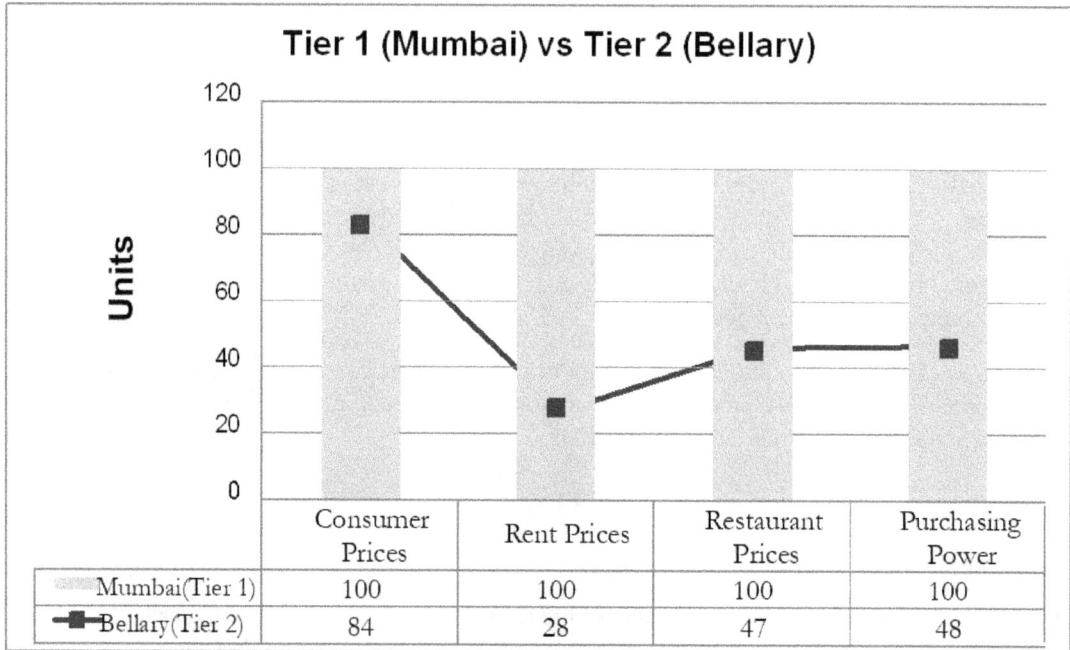

	Consumer Prices	Rent Prices	Restaurant Prices	Purchasing Power
Mumbai(Tier 1)	100	100	100	100
Bellary(Tier 2)	84	28	47	48

Behaviour Mapping

While there is significant value on the table, findings indicated that the decision process to unlock this value by pursuing the correct behaviour path is critical. Some open-minded villagers saw the long-term value associated with DataHalli. They came to the early realisation that other alternatives, such as domestic service or agriculture, would not provide them with the opportunity to effectively apply their education, and they would be limited to low-end tasks and not intellectual ones. The lack of openness and subsequent conversion of the same people to patrons of change can also be explained by behaviour mapping, which reveals that even when some behaviours of some stakeholders do not make sense, there could be entirely rational reasons for their behaviour – perhaps a cognitive bias influences them to act irrationally.

Behaviour mapping is a technique that analyses a behaviour by breaking it into three stages:

- Intention

- Action

- Follow-through (Datta & Mullainathan 2012)

Stage 1: Intention - Did women in rural areas, who were not empowered enough to contribute financially and end the socioeconomic imbalance, really intend to take action or did they say they would but had no real intention of following through?

164

The reason for lack of intent can always be a mental model, which is at odds with the desired behaviour.

Stage 2: Action - If the intent of empowerment was there, did they take action? Did they look for avenues of education and opportunity? Was procrastination the usual enemy or lack of support from the ecosystem? If the intent is there, then the approach to deal with this problem could be different. An attempt could be made to make the desired behaviour the default choice,so it is the path of least resistance.

The first step of employment, which is the contract letter was like a public commitment to demonstrate that the desired behaviour is the norm.

Stage 3: Follow through - Did they initially adopt the right behaviour but fall off? Is the behaviour sporadic at best and thus lacking impact? We all have limits to self-control. In this case, with the paychecks coming in, there was support from the home ecosystem.

Creating the right environment for these behaviour patterns can be achieved by projecting effective social nudges.

Table 1: DataHalli Differentiators

Employment Options in Bellary	Income (INR per month)	Working hours (per day)	Environment	Social Status Impact	Skill Enhancement
DataHalli BPO	8500 - 18000	8	Best (Comfortable Air Conditioned facilities)	High	High (Technical + Inter-personal)
Tailoring	8000	8	Good (But Non Air Conditioned)	Medium	Medium
Farming	4000	12	Poor (Harsh Climatic Conditions)	Low	Low
DomesticWork (in cities)	7000	12	Poor (Have to travel tocities outside the village)	Low	Low

A Success Story as Nudge

Sujata was one of DataHalli's first employees. She moved to the JSW township because her husband was appointed as a supervisor in the adjoining steel plant. Her family was well settled in Hubli before they shifted to the JSW premises. She worked as a kindergarten teacher in a small private school in the town earlier, while her husband worked in a small private firm. Sujata has two sons, who she encouraged to pursue higher education.

Sujata is a team leader at DataHalli, delegating work, checking quality, and solving problems, both technical and personnel. She used cutting-edge text recognition and artificial intelligence- based Intelligent Document Processing (IDP) software to detect and sort information from documents originating around the globe. She was the first person in her family to learn how to use a computer and the first woman in generations to have a formal job. Through her work at DataHalli, Sujata has also impacted how she and other women in her village are perceived.

While in conversation with her, Sujata mentioned that other women in her village joined DataHalli because they saw her change from being a traditional village woman to a more confident, outspoken and modern person. She said several women asked her questions about her work and whether they could join the centre.

What is most striking about Sujata's story is how she has channelised her work to benefit her family. When her children finished high school, Sujata was keen that they pursue higher education. Having been a teacher herself, she understood the value of education and the opportunities that would open up for her children if they obtained degrees. So, she began running the entire household with just her income. She leveraged the budgeting skills she learned as a team leader at DataHalli to manage household expenses to fit within her budget so that her husband's income could be used to fund their children's education.

With this model, she was even granted an education loan by the local bank – a notable achievement given that most rural people do not qualify for bank loans and are generally indebted to informal money lenders. Because of this, both her sons have undergraduate degrees. Her younger son is now working in a private sector firm, while her older son is pursuing an MBA. This was made possible because of the additional income she generated for the family. She said, with tears of gratitude, that DataHalli had helped her empower the next generation.

This is just one of many successful transformational stories at DataHalli, which is visible to stakeholders. In her daily life, Sujata can see how her own story is acting as a nudge to encourage other women to think like her, use her as inspiration and follow the same decision-making path as she did.

Discussion

It is evident that there is a significant economic, financial and social value generated by the rural BPO model. It is also evident that this value can be realised only by increasing and encouraging participation from all stakeholders. Leveraging the principles of behavioural economics is an effective way of driving this participation, which might be hindered by socio- cultural factors. Creating effective social nudges and making participation simple and accessible demonstrate how this value can be unlocked for the well-being of all stakeholders.

Let us understand how DataHalli and other Rural BPOs have and can further leverage these approaches.

Designing a Behavioural Nudge

Richard Thaler and Cass Sunstein define a nudge as "any aspect of the choice architecture that alters people's behaviour in a predictable way without forbidding any options or significantly changing their economic incentives. To count as a mere nudge, the intervention must be easy and cheap to avoid. Nudges are not mandates. Putting fruit at eye level counts as a nudge. Banning junk food does not". Examples such as Sujata act as a behavioural nudge for the community.

Given India's cultural and spiritual heritage, social norms (that play a very important role in shaping behaviour) can drive behavioural change. A key principle of behavioural economics is that while people's behaviour is influenced significantly by social norms, understanding the drivers of these social norms can enable change. In India, where social and religious norms play such a dominant role in influencing behaviour, behavioural economics can provide a valuable instrument for change as it requires continuous effort to dislodge mindsets that have prevailed for decades.

In 2019, Abhijit Banerjee, Esther Duflo and Michael Kremer won the Nobel Prize for their "experimental approach to alleviating global poverty" and, in doing so, brought the power of behavioural economics and sociology into the mainstream. Beyond saving money, behavioural economics affects the way people make decisions, who they love, how they spend time, where they work, and choices they make related to their health. It also helps explain why we have corruption in government, why it is so hard to pull oneself out of poverty, why leaders are not acting with enough urgency to address the climate crisis, and why we have rising inequalities.

Understanding the Factors Creating an Effective Nudge towards Desirable Behaviour at DataHalli

The success of DataHalli comes from its ability to demonstrate the transformation in the lives of its employees. Below are the key nudges that villagers themselves highlighted.

Impact on Financial Health and Debt

In the rural environment, few jobs provide a stable income. Of these, most involve manual labour and long, arduous working hours, often with no holidays. A manual labour job also meansmost workers are paid near minimum wage, which is not enough to sustain the average rural Indian family size of nearly six. Rural BPOs pay significantly more, and this additional incomeis spent on improving the quality of daily life for employed villagers.

Over 50% of households in every village had unpaid debts. With meagre incomes as farmers, people spent most or all of their income on day-to-day living and could not repay their debts. Debt, especially when taken from an informal money lender who charges interest rates of over 30% per annum, causes significant stress in the household. Farmer suicide waves are rampant in India, and its leading cause is indebtedness - their inability to repay their loans and the heavy burden of interest. Though there are no documented cases of a rural BPO worker managing to pay off debts, thereby avoiding suicide, it is clear why the additional financial support is helpful. Rural BPOs allow this employment model to change, shifting villages to a more modern and formal employment regime.

Rural BPO employees are entitled to individual provident fund and protected by employment laws. In contrast, other rural jobs like farming have no guarantee of payment; farmers are usually self-employed, so there is no organisation to maintain their welfare. They are thus free to be exploited. In most cases, they don't even earn a minimum wage. With a formal salary, which transfers directly into a bank account, the workers get the benefit of interest on their savings accounts. Furthermore, with a declared stable income, the workers gain eligibility for bank loans which levy interest rates of around 14% versus 30% charged by informal money lenders. Therefore, loans can be repaid quicker, thus reducing the debt burden and helping avoid the debt trap.

DataHalli's average salary is only a supplement to the total income of the families of the women. According to the manager, this is approximately 30% of the total family income. All of the women employees work with the knowledge that their salary, though not enough to run the entire household, is an extremely important addition to their family wealth. Most women see their contribution to the family corpus as the reason that their family has a respectable share of disposable income. They have seen an average rise of over 25% in disposable income. Interestingly, most of this income is not spent but saved. Savings are also facilitated by DataHalli's policy to provide everything that the women need at the centre, including food and transport, which reduces their need to spend.

Figure 3: DataHalli financial impact

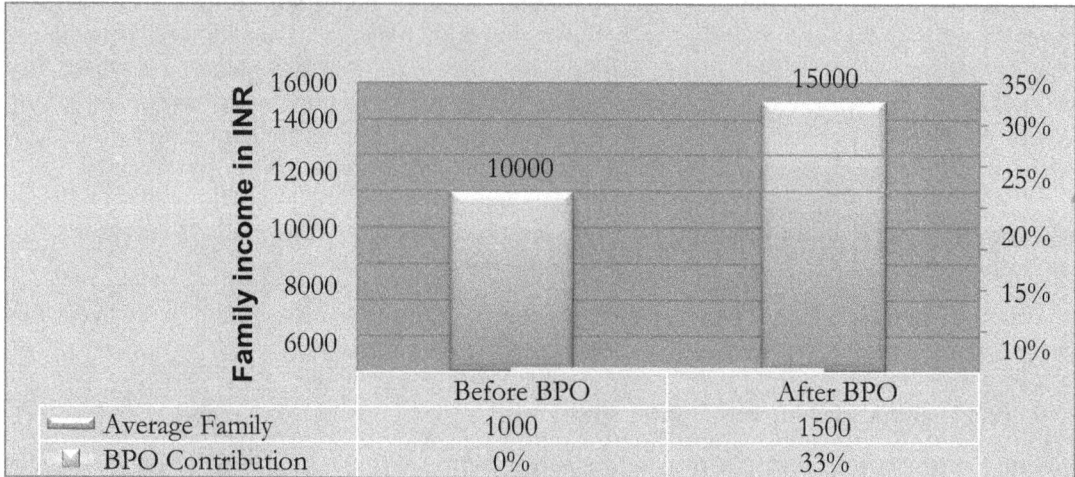

	Before BPO	After BPO
Average Family	1000	1500
BPO Contribution	0%	33%

Impact on Matrimony

Since working in a BPO centre requires no physical work, rural BPOs tend to attract more women and have a female-to-male ratio of around 70:30. Married women, accounting for around 65% of DataHalli's total workforce, tend to save for long-term needs and emergency requirements or the possibility of their marriage failing. In that case, they would have to look after themselves and, most probably, several children as well. Increased finances provide increased security for her and her family.

Unmarried women, on the other hand, unanimously agree that their main purpose of saving is to be able to marry into a good family, as their savings would enable them to pay a higher dowry, consequently improving the probability of finding a better groom and family. The dowry system is still rampant in the rural areas of India, and, therefore, unfortunately, this implication also rules.

Furthermore, having a stable job and comparatively higher education makes the women of DataHalli extremely valued individuals in the marriage market. Their exposure to modern thought also means that they know the importance of education, financial stability and compatibility.

Previously, however, the only condition for the family of a girl to select a boy to marry their daughter was willingness and age. The willingness of rural women to learn and earn also helps postpone their marriages as both women and men prefer to work (at BPOs) rather than start a family. This is also controlling child marriage, which in turn postpones motherhood and positively impacts the health of the women.

Impact on Education and Skill Enhancement

DataHalli ensures that all its workers have a minimum education level of SSLC, secondary education as per the state board of Karnataka, and are at least 18 years of age. With its success as a viable employment option for local women, more people want to meet these criteria so that they can work at DataHalli. Because of this, the villages around DataHalli have seen a growth in average schooling from Grade 4 to Grade 7 over eight years – a phenomenal improvement for the region. This average, however, conceals the fact that female averages have grown even more. Several women at DataHalli are pursuing diploma studies while still working. In fact, further education is so important for the women at DataHalli that most of them choose this job because it is an opportunity to learn. DataHalli also trains its employees in computer skills and the English language.

Beyond academic education, the employees at rural BPOs also learn management skills such as planning and project management, scheduling, prioritisation, crisis management, people and team management, communication and client handling. Parveen, an employee at DataHalli, says that the primary benefit of coming to DataHalli is an improvement in knowledge, management skills and communication skills. Women, in general, seem to place financial benefits secondary to the intangible benefits that they may gain, such as leadership skills.

Rural BPOs generally follow a team-based operation model, where each team is charged with operations for one of their customers. Each team also has a team leader. Here, a few individuals are given the opportunity to learn and exercise their leadership skills. With these skills, team leaders develop patience, teamwork, and, most importantly, confidence. A BPO worker, who preferred to remain anonymous, said her family is more than capable of supporting her completely, yet she chooses to work at the centre because she gains knowledge about systems, businesses, situational action and interacting with clients and colleagues.

Impact on Overall Education Level

A job at the BPO centre gives employees the opportunity to gather funds for formal education that they could possibly never afford. Villagers now value education as they realise that education is the key to progress and growth. Married women are now prioritising education for their children. They realise the value of being educated, and they want to give their children what they could never have.

Extrapolating this trend, we believe this will result in educated offspring who will, in turn, look for partners with equal or higher education. This upward spiral will continue. Consequently, we see that this trend will lead to more educated and successful generations in future. This can already be seen in some cases - 80% of the children of BPO employees had undergraduate degrees, whereas the average education levels in the region were below Grade 10.

Impact on personal development and exposure

Most rural women are underexposed to cities, industries and other such modern establishments. Women working at rural BPOs, however, are constantly using computers and the internet and work largely on non-Indian business processes. This gives them immense exposure to worlds that they could never fathom. Because Rural BPO employees are in constant touch with 'the outside world', they tend to have a more modern outlook, which is reflected in their personalities. With this exposure, they are able to not only understand their work better and become better at their jobs but also manage themselves in metropolitan setups. Some workers develop an entrepreneurial interest and express their desire to start their own BPO centres because this exposure has given them the know-how to manage and run a business.

Rural workers tend to lack confidence and are extremely reserved and insecure. But by working as leaders at a BPO, they gain communication skills and the ability to express themselves, which helps them overcome their insecurities. Several rural BPO employees said their job has taught them to be more outspoken and confident and has given them social skills that they may never have otherwise developed. With enhanced leadership, managerial and communication skills, ability to earn and be respected in society, and treated as equals, rural women gain substantial self-confidence.

Through their exposure, education and a corporate job, the employees build self-esteem and realise their self-worth. They also feel more respected in their villages as people see them going to work and being self-sufficient. Several women said that even their children felt proud to say that their mother knows how to use a computer and that she works in an office. Personally, the women feel proud that they can support the family financially.

Despite the changing social climate, a large population still believes that women should not be permitted to work outside their households. So, women leaving the house itself is a huge step toward a more liberal mindset: essential to modernism and growth.

When interviewed, the father of a girl from the village of Tornagallu working at DataHalli said that he was vehemently against the idea of his daughter going to an alien place, working on machines and returning at night. He said that this meant there was one less person to do household chores and help him on the family farm. On the other hand, another girl's brother said that at first, the family was hesitant to let her work at the BPO centre (not surprisingly for similar reasons to the previous interviewee), but when they saw other girls in the village doing the same, they felt that they should take the risk (third P - Persuasion of Yale's 4P framework). Now, they are extremely happy with the way the girl can communicate with people and support herself.

Several women also said that their spouses and families are now more understanding about their work and often "cook their own food" if the woman is late. This, though seemingly a small step, is a huge leap towards liberal thought and social equality, as it means that men are now acknowledging the value of women in the villages. Women are being treated equally and seen as individual forces rather than being overshadowed by men. Many rural women now want to have a respectable job that gives them an opportunity to grow in all fields – financially, personally, socially and professionally.

Impact on Social Status

A rural BPO creates a wave of social change in the village. With increased financial independence and financial contributions to the family, women BPO workers are being treated as important assets to the family. The women can also read and write English and have computer skills, both of which are viewed as extremely prestigious faculties. BPO workers can take full responsibility for themselves financially and socially. People recognise these qualities, and this changes the perception of BPO workers. They are now seen as advanced, modern, capable and even as role models. Their elevated social status gives them an advantage in marriage, and BPO workers tend to receive more proposals than the average person. Several women working at DataHalli also said that they receive more respect, and other women often ask for counselling on the benefits of a high-value job. In fact, most families who send their daughters to work only do so because they can see the benefit that their neighbour's daughter has gained. BPOs are therefore promoting women's empowerment.

Impact on Health

As in the large cities, rural families are now learning to set aside money for emergencies, which usually tend to be medical. It is often the case that because of a lack of funds, families spend just on basic treatment. These costs recur, and sometimes all efforts are in vain, and family members cannot be saved. The family ends up spending on treatments that eventually have no effect on the patient. With additional funding through an emergency fund, families can avoid these circumstances by being able to buy adequate treatment.

Rural Transformation

Rural India is the foundation stone for progress of urban India and the process of rural transformation is a process of comprehensive societal change whereby rural societies diversify their economies and reduce their reliance on agriculture; become dependent on distant places to trade and to acquire goods, services, and ideas. It is a strategy that tries to obtain an improved productivity, higher socio-economic equality and ambition, and stability in social and economic development. The process of change depends on many factors and dynamics; the challenges and opportunities of rural transformation derive from rural-urban linkages and also community- corporate linkages, as evidenced in the paper.

Implications

Rural BPO centres bring with them opportunities for education, financial empowerment, modernisation, structured industry and, consequently, transformational social change. Encouraging people to make participative choices is a key factor in this transformational success.

Theoretical Implications

The research reflects on how the principles of behavioural economics can create a paradigm shift in people's mindsets and bring about a revolutionary change in the lives of rural BPO employees. The literature review highlights that not much research has been carried out on corporate initiatives that apply aspects of behavioural economics to lead social transformation. Most of the prior research has been undertaken in countries other than India.

This chapter is an attempt to bridge the gap in this area. The qualitative aspects of the study strengthen the premise of corporates playing a major role in taking the nation forward, not only economically but also socially.

Managerial and Economic Implications

Over 55% of the world's IT & BPO outsourcing is based in India. Therefore, a large workforce is required to service this industry. Outsourcing even a small part of this workforce to rural areas would imply redeploying a large number of people from farming and other informal vocations to formal BPO centres. For the remaining farmers, this means that they have more land to cultivate individually, opening up opportunities for larger-scale farming (possibly even the use of large machinery) and a higher income per farmer.

By expanding the hi-tech industry to include the rural areas of India, a rural BPO centre will tap human resources that otherwise would probably have been relegated to low-value labour. This labour can be trained to work with hi-tech instruments and perform higher-value tasks. Training and exposure further encourage higher education levels as people want to enter the industry. Technical training gives people access to technology that the rural population may not be exposed to or not be able to afford for several years. It also gives them access to the internet and expands their world from a small village to the entire globe. By increasing an individual's reach and influence, rural BPOs broaden perceptions and give a whole new paradigm. In the volatile talent market, corporate managers can harness the potential of relatively unexplored talent demographics.

Conclusion and future research

Behavioural economic decision factors and social nudges are effective ways to drive transformation through the rural shoring model. Rural shoring improves the financial state of people and gives them a wider scope of life to explore. It helps society break the mould that rural women find themselves trapped in. Though rural BPOs only provide incremental income, we can see that the nudge they provide towards a transformed society is enabling people to advance at a much faster rate.

Behavioural economic factors that drive individual decisions towards formal employment and education are stimuli for economic prosperity and social transformation. This system creates a platform for whole and inclusive growth through empowerment of women and, consequently, healthy upbringing of their children, therefore, impacting future generations. The real impact of rural BPOs can be seen in the rising rate of education, increasing self-worth and evolving thought processes of the people. These factors are directly driven by the employment of the 4Ps and social nudges.

The current scope of the research was tightly focused and addressed the merits of the rural shoring model for stakeholder well-being. There is potential to expand the scope of this study to cover additional aspects.

One limitation of the current study is that there are few rural BPOs operating on a commercial model (most operate on a training model). Further, the research was centred primarily on DataHalli, which might lead to local biases, especially around the socio-cultural contexts – though the authors took particular care to be vigilant of these biases.

Another limitation is the fact that most interactions and interviews were conducted multi- lingually and often in the local language, which the authors were not fluent in and had to depend on translators for assistance. Addressing these limitations would yield more robust results.

A key expansion would be to test these findings across other rural BPOs. This would entail benchmarking the socio-cultural contexts of other similar operations as well as understanding their operating model, financial model and impact model on society. This was, in fact, part of the scope of this study. The initial secondary research indicates some consistency in results, but they cannot be considered robust as primary responses are low.

Other aspects to study could be the interrelationships between rural infrastructure and business growth. Literature suggests that business growth and middle-class wealth creation act as seeds for governments and administrations to pay more attention and tend to increase funding to these locations. This, in turn, helps businesses grow. Rural BPOs are often the first-scale driven enterprises in rural environments and, hence, are a perfect subject to study this interrelationship. Further, additional studies could explore how rural BPOs stabilise over time and become part of the fundamental fabric of society, gaining independence of the seed BPO itself.

Declaration of conflicting interests

The authors declared no potential conflicts of interest with respect to the research, authorshipand/or publication of this article.

Funding

The authors received no financial support for the research, authorship and/or publication of this article.

Interview Question Guide

DataHalli Impact Interview

The research paper intends to examine the impact of behavioural economics and the subsequent social change amongst the women of DataHalli. Thank you for sparing your valuable time to respond to the questions. The gesture is most appreciated. It is hoped that the results will meaningfully contribute to the body of knowledge on the subject matter. Your need for confidentiality will be respected at all times.

Q1	How long have you been working in the data centre?
Q2	Who inspired you to take up this job?
Q3	Did you face any resistance from family?
Q4	How did you overcome the resistance?
Q5	What is your experience working there?
Q6	How do you interact with your teammates?
Q7	What does your family think about your job now?
Q8	What have been your key learnings from the job?
Q9	Do you sense any change in yourself after you started working here?
Q10	How do you use your income?
Q11	What are your future aspirations?
Q12	Do you have a role model?

References

Berger, IE, Cunningham PH, Drumwright ME (2007) Mainstreaming CorporateSocial Responsibility: Developing Markets for Virtue. California Management Review

Belen, F, Silvia, R (2014). Effect of Stakeholders' pressure on transparency ofSustainability reports. Journal of Business Ethics.

Carrol, A. Kareem, S (2010) The Business Case for Corporate Social Responsibility:A Review of Concepts, Research and Practice. International Journal of ManagementReviews

Chance, Z., Gorlin, M., Dhar, R., (2014). Why Choosing Healthy Foods is Hard, andHow to Help: Presenting the 4Ps Framework for Behaviour Change.

Dhar, R., (2017). Nudging the Consumer: How to Make Desirable Behaviour the Pathof Least Resistance, Insights Association https://www.insightsassociation.org/article/nudging-consumer-how-make-desirable- behaviour-path-least-resistance

Das, G., (2011), Financial Express: Rural BPO DataHalli is on a mission to empowerwomen https://www.financialexpress.com/archive/rural-bpo-dataHalli-is-on-a- mission-to-empower-women/759063/

Grand View Research, Market Analysis Report : Business Process Outsourcing Market Size, Share & Trends Analysis Report By Service (Finance & Accounting,Human Resources, KPO, Procurement & Supply Chain), By End Use, By Region,And Segment Forecasts, 2020 - 2027

HBR, 2019, Economic Development podcast, A Nobel Prize Winner on Rethinking Poverty (and Business) JSW Foundation homepage : https://www.jsw.in/foundation

Sai, P. (2017). A Comperative study of CSR practice in India before and after 2013.Asian Journal of Managemnet Research, 7(3), 242-255.

Samson, Alain 2018, Social Psychology v. Behavioural Economics: 3 KeyDifferences

Schubert, Christian (2015-10-12). "On the Ethics of Public Nudging: Autonomy andAgency". Rochester, NY. *SSRN 2672970*

Simon, Carsta; Tagliabue, Marco (2018). "Feeding the behavioural revolution:Contributions of behaviour analysis to nudging and vice versa". Journal of Behavioural Economics for Policy. 1 (2): 91–97.

Thaler, R. H., & Sunstein, C. R. (2008). Nudge: Improving decisions about health,wealth, and happiness. Yale University Press.

Thite, Russell 2007 : India and Business Process Outsourcing, Researchgate.netpublication

www.ingramcontent.com/pod-product-compliance
Lightning Source LLC
Chambersburg PA
CBHW061816210326
41599CB00034B/7019